POLITICS & ECONOMICS

D.F. PAULAHA, PH.D.

PATRON BOOKS

Copyright © 2008 by Dennis F. Paulaha.

All rights reserved. No portion of this book may be reproduced or transmitted in any form whatsoever or by any means, electronic or mechanical, including printing or photocopy, without permission in writing from the publisher, except for short quotes in critical articles or reviews.

ISBN 978-0-9723619-5-8

First published 2008 by:
Patron Books
E-mail: patronbooks@hotmail.com

"A lot of good arguments are spoiled by some fool who knows what he is talking about."

    Miguel de Unamuno
    Spanish essayist, novelist, poet, playwright, and philosopher.
    September 29, 1864 – December 31, 1936

CONTENTS

INTRODUCTION

I. IDEAS ABOUT MARKET ECONOMIES
1. Market Ideas   15
    1. The Republic by Plato (360 BCE)   16
    2. Adam Smith for free markets   27
    3. Karl Marx for the people   32
    4. Ludwig von Mises for *laissez faire*   34
    5. Paul Samuelson for the middle ground   36
    6. Milton Friedman for the middle ground   39
2. Disagreements and Conditional Forecasts   42
    1. A great danger   42
    2. Forecasts must be conditional   44
    3. Today's critical economic issues   45
    4. Assumptions   47
    5. Conclusion   47
3. Politics & Economics   48
4. The Really Big Idea   50
    1. Enlightenment   50
    2. Truth   50
5. The Notice—A Fictional Story   53

II. INDIVIDUAL MARKETS
1. Believing is Seeing   65
    1. "I wouldn't have seen it if I didn't believe it."   65
    2. Given what Plato believed, what did he see?   67
2. A Line in the Sand   75
    1. The easy questions   75
    2. The difficult questions   76
    3. The role of government   77
    4. Who provides the things we use, buy, or have around?   80
    5. The fuzzy line   82
    6. A line in the sand   86
3. What We Know   91
    1. Economics does not support the *laissez faire* doctrine   94
    2. Economics does not support the communist doctrine   96
    3. Specialization and industrialization create wealth   97
    4. Specialization is the only true argument for free trade   97
    5. Specialization eliminates some independent craftspeople   98
    6. Economic efficiency is not an absolute   99
    7. There is no "inherent good" in a market equilibrium   100

CONTENTS

4. Eight Market Problems   102
    1. The public goods problem   103
    2. The negative externality problem   104
    3. The positive externality problem   107
    4. The common property resources problem   110
    5. The exclusion problem   112
    6. The "bad things" problem   115
    7. The "bad things we buy" problem   116
    8. The market failure problem   118
    9. Conclusion   119
5. Dialogues About Markets   122
    1. The Declaration of Independence   122
    2. The Constitution of the United States   125
    3. The news   126
    4. A few dialogues   128
        (1) Perfect competition   128
        (2) Externalities   129
        (3) Protecting the environment hurts the economy   130
        (4) We can't stop pollution   132
        (5) Government should not provide goods and services that can be provided by the private sector   140
        (6) Government is too big   145
        (7) Government should stop trying to manage natural resources and let the market do it   149
        (8) Price supports help farmers   153
        (9) Price ceilings help consumers   154
        (10) Economic laws   155

III. THE ECONOMY
1. What Do We Want?   158
    1. The best of all possible worlds   159
    2. Weighing the winners against the losers   159
    3. The economic solution   160
    4. Models   160
2. An Economic Story   162
    1. The Questions   162
    2. Economics in the Park   165
    3. Rubber Ducky Economics   168
    4. The Model   172
    5. The Right Amount of Water   175
    6. GDP and Employment   177
    7. GDP and Unemployment   178
    8. GDP and Happiness   179
    9. Consumer Spending   181
    10. Tax Cuts   182
    11. Fiscal Policy   185
    12. Monetary Policy   186
    13. Market Failure - Monopoly   187

14. Positive Externalities   188
15. Negative Externalities   189
16. Common Property Resources   191
17. Public Goods   193
18. Investment Spending   194
19. Government and Markets   195
20. Exports   196
21. Imports   198
22. Outsourcing   200
23. Inflation   201
24. Recession   210
25. The Business Cycle   211
26. The National Debt   212
27. Economic Growth   218
28. The Japanese Economic Miracle   224
29. The Chinese Economic Miracle   225
30. A Little More Free Trade Theory   227
31. The Federal Reserve   231
32. A Few Conclusions   240
3. Summary   242

I READ THE NEWS TODAY OH BOY
1. What You Now Know About Economics   246
2. What You Now Know About Politics & Economics   247
3. I Read the News Today Oh Boy   249
    1. A time to read and write   250

APPENDIX
1. Commonly Used Terms   254
2. A Market Model   256
    1. Economics is the study of decision-making   256
    2. Making decisions   257
    3. Decisions and opportunity cost   258
    4. The purpose and objective of economics   259
    5. Explaining and predicting   260
    6. Judging   261
    7. Market supply and demand   263
    8. The simple logic of supply and demand   263
    9. Other possibilities for supply and demand   266
    10. Reading supply and demand curves   268
    11. A "normal" individual market   269
    12. A change in supply and demand versus a change in the quantity supplied and the quantity demanded   269
    13. Most microeconomic problems are solved using market supply and demand   270
    14. Equilibrium   271
    15. Is the equilibrium stable or unstable?   272
    16. How to solve economic problems   274

CONTENTS

17. Rules of action   278
18. A problem with apples   282
How To Solve Microeconomic Problems—A Worksheet   285

Introduction

"This is a weird book. People are going to be scratching their heads, wondering what to make of it."

"Who are you?"

"Richard Green."

"Who?"

"Richard Green. The guy you made fun of in one of the stories in your book."

"But, you are a fictional character."

"So what? No one likes to be made fun of."

"I didn't make fun of you."

"Yes you did. You had me doing stupid things, based on my political beliefs. And you did not give me a chance to explain."

"Explain what?"

"Explain what I believe."

"I already know what you believe. I made you up."

"So why didn't you finish the job and let me explain?"

"I thought it would be better if the students finished the job."

"But some students will think I am stupid."

"That's okay."

"Maybe for you; not for me."

"It's too late anyway. The book is finished. I expect some students to think you did the right thing and others to disagree with you. That is why I wrote the story. I want students to spend some time thinking about political doctrine before they look at the economics behind the issues that confront them each day. And your story seems like a good way to do it."

"Well, I still think you should change it."

"If I change it, it won't work. I could drop it completely. But if I do that, we would not be having this conversation. So, I guess it is up to you. Do you want to exist or not exist?"

"Okay. But I still think it's a weird book. It is a jumble of normal textbook stuff, dialogues, stories that you wrote, and long quotes from others. It doesn't even look like a textbook."

INTRODUCTION

"I know."

"What do you expect students to get out of your mess?"

"I expect every student to end up with a functional understanding of microeconomic theory, macroeconomic theory, monetary theory and policy, and environmental economics."

"But you don't have any charts or diagrams, and no mathematical or geometrical models. You don't even use much economic jargon."

"None of that is necessary to understand how to use economics in the real world. But I do expect the book to be accompanied by a wide range of supplementary materials."

"No one will know how to use this book in a class."

"Of course they will. Although each instructor knows how he or she wants to conduct classes, I expect a lot of them to first complete the book, bringing in related issues when appropriate, and to devote the remainder of the semester to discussing and writing about current and historical issues taken from local and national newspapers, magazines, television and radio news shows, political talk shows, and topical books."

"Which issues?"

"As many as possible, past and present. I hope they will have students explain the Republican and Democratic positions on each issue; and to then explain the economics of each issue. The objective is for students to come up with functional solutions to real problems."

"That's a lot to do."

"By the time the semester is over, each student should have some knowledge of the historical development and importance of economics, an understanding of the different political stands on virtually all current issues and problems, and the ability to use economics to offer solutions to real-world problems."

"Some people are going to think this is a politically biased book; that you are on one side of the great liberal versus conservative debate."

"It is not. I am writing as an economist. Anyone who sees this book as being either liberal or conservative understands neither politics nor economics. It is, however, political economics."

D.F. Paulaha, Ph.D.

Why study economics?

Because the economy affects our lives.

The following article is an example of how economics and the economy affect you personally. It was in the *St. Paul Pioneer Press* on May 26, 2007.

Men in their 30s lag behind dad's pay
Downturn shown in generational study
BY GREG IP
Wall Street Journal

American men in their 30s today are worse off than their father's generation, a reversal from just a decade ago, when sons generally were better off than their fathers, a new analysis of Census data shows.

The study, the first in a series on economic mobility undertaken by several prominent think tanks. Also says the typical American family's income has lagged far behind productivity growth since 2000, a departure from most of the post World War II period.

The findings suggest "the up escalator that has historically ensured that each generation would do better than the last may not be working very well," says the study, released Friday.

The study was written principally by John Morton of the Pew Charitable Trusts, which is leading the series, called the Economic Mobility Project, and Isabel Sawhill of the Brookings Institution.

In 2004, the median income for a man in his 30s, which is a good predictor of his lifetime earnings, was $35,010, the study says, 12 percent less than for men in their 30s in 1974—their father's generation—adjusted for inflation. Just a decade ago, median income for men in their 30s was $32,901, 5 percent higher than 30 years earlier. The median is the midpoint: half of men earn more, half earn less.

Sawhill said she isn't sure why men's wages have stagnated. "It seems there's been some slowdown in economic growth, it's possible that the movement of women into the labor force has affected male earnings, and it's possible that men are not working as hard as they used to."

The study suggests that absolute mobility—the rate at which an entire generation's financial lot improves relative to previous generations—has declined recently.

Of course, the men who run American companies don't have much to complain about. CEO pay increased to 262 times the average worker's pay in 2005 from 35 times in 1978, according to the report's analysis of Congressional Budget Office statistics. The pay gap between executives and the average worker continues to fuel outrage on Capitol Hill and among corporate shareholders nationwide.

The report also found that between 1947 and 1974, productivity, or output per hour, and median family income, adjusted for inflation, both roughly doubled. Between 1974 and 2005, productivity rose 16 percent while median income fell 2 percent, challenging "the notion that a rising tide will lift all boats," the report says.

This report includes information from the Associated Press.

Questions:

What is happening? What went wrong? It is because of women in the work force? Or immigrants in the work force—legal and illegal? Or the outsourcing of American jobs? Or American corporations moving production to low-wage countries? Or imports? Or the foreign trade deficit? Or the national debt? Or the Federal Reserve's policy of fighting inflation by keeping economic growth low? Or something we have not even thought about? And, what about women's wages?

Or is it a false concern? Is it something that will "automatically" correct itself? If we think it will turn around by itself, what do we see that might cause a change in course?

If it is a real concern, why is it happening? Is it natural? Or is it the result of bad policies?

Most important, if the decline is real, can it be reversed? Should we expect the trend to turn around on its own? Or should we do something? If so, what should we do?

Trying to answer these, and other questions raised by the article, requires an understanding of microeconomic issues, macroeconomic issues, monetary theory and policy, and environmental economics, because real income is affected by market failure, externalities, economy wide events and changes, and monetary policy.

And remember: The decline in incomes reported in the study took place before the escalation of oil prices in the summer of 2008 created an economic downturn, before the Federal Reserve's decision in the summer of 2008 to increase interest rates to fight what it perceived to be an inflation when soaring oil prices raised the Consumer Price Index (the act that triggered the mortgage collapse), before the mortgage collapse in the fall of 2008, before the financial collapse in the winter of 2008-2009, and before it was accepted that the US was in a recession by the spring of 2009.

IDEAS ABOUT MARKET ECONOMIES

1. Market Ideas

The following lengthy passage is from Book II of Plato's *Republic*. It is worth reading, because it shows how much was known about markets more than 2,300 years ago.

We knew how markets work.

We knew about the concept of specialization.

We knew how markets and specialization increase wealth.

We knew about supply and demand.

We knew about the relationship between markets and the State.

We knew how the advantages of markets and specialization could have negative effects on individuals and the State.

In other words, more than 2,300 years ago, Plato did exactly what economists do today: He explained both the wealth-creating power of free markets and the limitations and potential problems of such markets.

In *The Republic*, written in 360 BCE, Plato created a conversation where Socrates examines most of the issues that, even today, remain at the core of modern, free-market economic thought, as well as at the core of communist thought.

Although few would agree with Plato's conclusion that free markets inevitably foster an insatiable greed that leads to territorial expansion and war, or that the specialization that helps create wealth then makes it difficult to win such wars, economists have always been aware of the benefits and potential costs of free markets. As such, it would be possible to use the following passage as the sole "text" for a course by carefully examining each point Plato makes.

1. *The Republic* (360 BCE).

The following is from a translation by Benjamin Jowett.

A State, I said, arises, as I conceive, out of the needs of mankind; no one is self-sufficing, but all of us have many wants. Can any other origin of a State be imagined?
There can be no other.

Then, as we have many wants, and many persons are needed to supply them, one takes a helper for one purpose and another for another; and when these partners and helpers are gathered together in one habitation the body of inhabitants is termed a State.
True, he said.

And they exchange with one another, and one gives, and another receives, under the idea that the exchange will be for their good.
Very true.

Then, I said, let us begin and create in idea a State; and yet the true creator is necessity, who is the mother of our invention.
Of course, he replied.

Now the first and greatest of necessities is food, which is the condition of life and existence.
Certainly.

The second is a dwelling, and the third clothing and the like.
True.

And now let us see how our city will be able to supply this great demand: We may suppose that one man is a husbandman, another a builder, some one else a weaver; shall we add to them a shoemaker, or perhaps some other purveyor to our bodily wants?
Quite right.

The barest notion of a State must include four or five men.

Clearly.

And how will they proceed? Will each bring the result of his labours into a common stock? --the individual husbandman, for example, producing for four, and labouring four times as long and as much as he need in the provision of food with which he supplies others as well as himself; or will he have nothing to do with others and not be at the trouble of producing for them, but provide for himself alone a fourth of the food in a fourth of the time, and in the remaining three-fourths of his time be employed in making a house or a coat or a pair of shoes, having no partnership with others, but supplying himself all his own wants?
Adeimantus thought that he should aim at producing food only and not at producing everything.

Probably, I replied, that would be the better way; and when I hear you say this, I am myself reminded that we are not all alike; there are diversities of natures among us which are adapted to different occupations.
Very true.

And will you have a work better done when the workman has many occupations, or when he has only one?
When he has only one.

Further, there can be no doubt that a work is spoilt when not done at the right time?
No doubt.

For business is not disposed to wait until the doer of the business is at leisure; but the doer must follow up what he is doing, and make the business his first object.
He must.

And if so, we must infer that all things are produced more plentifully and easily and of a better quality when one man does one thing which is natural to him and does it at the right time, and leaves other things.
Undoubtedly.

Then more than four citizens will be required; for the husbandman will not make his own plough or mattock, or other implements of agriculture, if they are to be good for anything. Neither will the builder make his tools--and he too needs many; and in like manner the weaver and shoemaker.
True.

Then carpenters, and smiths, and many other artisans, will be sharers in our little State, which is already beginning to grow?
True.

Yet even if we add neatherds, shepherds, and other herdsmen, in order that our husbandmen may have oxen to plough with, and builders as well as husbandmen may have draught cattle, and curriers and weavers, fleeces and hides--still our State will not be very large.
That is true; yet neither will it be a very small State which contains all these.

Then, again, there is the situation of the city--to find a place where nothing need be imported is well-nigh impossible.
Impossible.

Then there must be another class of citizens who will bring the required supply from another city?
There must.

But if the trader goes empty-handed, having nothing which they require who would supply his need, he will come back empty-handed.
That is certain.

And therefore what they produce at home must be not only enough for themselves, but such both in quantity and quality as to accommodate those from whom their wants are supplied.
Very true.

Then more husbandmen and more artisans will be required?
They will.

Not to mention the importers and exporters, who are called merchants?

Yes.

Then we shall want merchants?
We shall.

And if merchandise is to be carried over the sea, skilful sailors will also be needed, and in considerable numbers?
Yes, in considerable numbers.

Then, again, within the city, how will they exchange their productions? To secure such an exchange was, as you will remember, one of our principal objects when we formed them into a society and constituted a State.
Clearly they will buy and sell.

Then they will need a market-place, and a money-token for purposes of exchange.
Certainly.

Suppose now that a husbandman, or an artisan, brings some production to market, and he comes at a time when there is no one to exchange with him, is he to leave his calling and sit idle in the market-place?
Not at all; he will find people there who, seeing the want, undertake the office of salesmen. In well-ordered States they are commonly those who are the weakest in bodily strength, and therefore of little use for any other purpose; their duty is to be in the market, and to give money in exchange for goods to those who desire to sell and to take money from those who desire to buy.

This want, then, creates a class of retail-traders in our State. Is not 'retailer' the term which is applied to those who sit in the market-place engaged in buying and selling, while those who wander from one city to another are called merchants?
Yes, he said.

And there is another class of servants, who are intellectually hardly on the level of companionship; still they have plenty of bodily strength for labour, which accordingly they sell, and are called, if I do not mistake, hirelings, hire being the name which is given to the price of their labour.

True.

Then hirelings will help to make up our population?
Yes.

And now, Adeimantus, is our State matured and perfected?
I think so.

Where, then, is justice, and where is injustice, and in what part of the State did they spring up?
Probably in the dealings of these citizens with one another. I cannot imagine that they are more likely to be found anywhere else.

I dare say that you are right in your suggestion, I said; we had better think the matter out, and not shrink from the enquiry.

Let us then consider, first of all, what will be their way of life, now that we have thus established them. Will they not produce corn, and wine, and clothes, and shoes, and build houses for themselves? And when they are housed, they will work, in summer, commonly, stripped and barefoot, but in winter substantially clothed and shod. They will feed on barley-meal and flour of wheat, baking and kneading them, making noble cakes and loaves; these they will serve up on a mat of reeds or on clean leaves, themselves reclining the while upon beds strewn with yew or myrtle. And they and their children will feast, drinking of the wine which they have made, wearing garlands on their heads, and hymning the praises of the gods, in happy converse with one another. And they will take care that their families do not exceed their means; having an eye to poverty or war.

Socrates - GLAUCON

But, said Glaucon, interposing, you have not given them a relish to their meal.
True, I replied, I had forgotten; of course they must have a relish-salt, and olives, and cheese, and they will boil roots and herbs such as country people prepare; for a dessert we shall give them figs, and peas, and beans; and they will roast myrtle-berries and acorns at the fire, drinking in moderation. And with such a diet they may be expected to live in peace and health to a good old age, and bequeath a similar life to their children after them.

Yes, Socrates, he said, and if you were providing for a city of pigs, how else would you feed the beasts?

But what would you have, Glaucon? I replied.
Why, he said, you should give them the ordinary conveniences of life. People who are to be comfortable are accustomed to lie on sofas, and dine off tables, and they should have sauces and sweets in the modern style.

Yes, I said, now I understand: the question which you would have me consider is, not only how a State, but how a luxurious State is created; and possibly there is no harm in this, for in such a State we shall be more likely to see how justice and injustice originate. In my opinion the true and healthy constitution of the State is the one which I have described. But if you wish also to see a State at fever heat, I have no objection. For I suspect that many will not be satisfied with the simpler way. They will be for adding sofas, and tables, and other furniture; also dainties, and perfumes, and incense, and courtesans, and cakes, all these not of one sort only, but in every variety; we must go beyond the necessaries of which I was at first speaking, such as houses, and clothes, and shoes: the arts of the painter and the embroiderer will have to be set in motion, and gold and ivory and all sorts of materials must be procured.
True, he said.

Then we must enlarge our borders; for the original healthy State is no longer sufficient. Now will the city have to fill and swell with a multitude of callings which are not required by any natural want; such as the whole tribe of hunters and actors, of whom one large class have to do with forms and colours; another will be the votaries of music--poets and their attendant train of rhapsodists, players, dancers, contractors; also makers of divers kinds of articles, including women's dresses. And we shall want more servants. Will not tutors be also in request, and nurses wet and dry, tirewomen and barbers, as well as confectioners and cooks; and swineherds, too, who were not needed and therefore had no place in the former edition of our State, but are needed now? They must not be forgotten: and there will be animals of many other kinds, if people eat them.
Certainly.

And living in this way we shall have much greater need of physicians than before?

Much greater.

And the country which was enough to support the original inhabitants will be too small now, and not enough?
Quite true.

Then a slice of our neighbours' land will be wanted by us for pasture and tillage, and they will want a slice of ours, if, like ourselves, they exceed the limit of necessity, and give themselves up to the unlimited accumulation of wealth?
That, Socrates, will be inevitable.

And so we shall go to war, Glaucon. Shall we not?
Most certainly, he replied.

Then without determining as yet whether war does good or harm, thus much we may affirm, that now we have discovered war to be derived from causes which are also the causes of almost all the evils in States, private as well as public.
Undoubtedly.

And our State must once more enlarge; and this time there will be nothing short of a whole army, which will have to go out and fight with the invaders for all that we have, as well as for the things and persons whom we were describing above.
Why? he said; are they not capable of defending themselves?

No, I said; not if we were right in the principle which was acknowledged by all of us when we were framing the State: the principle, as you will remember, was that one man cannot practice many arts with success.
Very true, he said.

But is not war an art?
Certainly.

And an art requiring as much attention as shoemaking?
Quite true.

And the shoemaker was not allowed by us to be husbandman, or a weaver, a builder--in order that we might have our shoes well made; but to him and to every other worker was assigned one work for which he was by nature fitted, and at that he was to continue working all his life long and at no other; he was not to let opportunities slip, and then he would become a good workman. Now nothing can be more important than that the work of a soldier should be well done. But is war an art so easily acquired that a man may be a warrior who is also a husbandman, or shoemaker, or other artisan; although no one in the world would be a good dice or draught player who merely took up the game as a recreation, and had not from his earliest years devoted himself to this and nothing else?

No tools will make a man a skilled workman, or master of defence, nor be of any use to him who has not learned how to handle them, and has never bestowed any attention upon them. How then will he who takes up a shield or other implement of war become a good fighter all in a day, whether with heavy-armed or any other kind of troops?

Yes, he said, the tools which would teach men their own use would be beyond price.

And the higher the duties of the guardian, I said, the more time, and skill, and art, and application will be needed by him?
No doubt, he replied.

Will he not also require natural aptitude for his calling?
Certainly.

Then it will be our duty to select, if we can, natures which are fitted for the task of guarding the city?
It will.

And the selection will be no easy matter, I said; but we must be brave and do our best.
We must.

Is not the noble youth very like a well-bred dog in respect of guarding and watching?
What do you mean?

I mean that both of them ought to be quick to see, and swift to overtake the enemy when they see him; and strong too if, when they have caught him, they have to fight with him.

All these qualities, he replied, will certainly be required by them. And your guardian must be brave if he is to fight well?
Certainly.

And is he likely to be brave who has no spirit, whether horse or dog or any other animal? Have you never observed how invincible and unconquerable is spirit and how the presence of it makes the soul of any creature to be absolutely fearless and indomitable?
I have.

Then now we have a clear notion of the bodily qualities which are required in the guardian.
True.

And also of the mental ones; his soul is to be full of spirit?
Yes.

But are not these spirited natures apt to be savage with one another, and with everybody else?
A difficulty by no means easy to overcome, he replied.

Whereas, I said, they ought to be dangerous to their enemies, and gentle to their friends; if not, they will destroy themselves without waiting for their enemies to destroy them.
True, he said.

What is to be done then? I said; how shall we find a gentle nature which has also a great spirit, for the one is the contradiction of the other?
True.

He will not be a good guardian who is wanting in either of these two qualities; and yet the combination of them appears to be impossible; and hence we must infer that to be a good guardian is impossible.

I am afraid that what you say is true, he replied.

Here feeling perplexed I began to think over what had preceded. My friend, I said, no wonder that we are in a perplexity; for we have lost sight of the image which we had before us.
What do you mean? he said.

I mean to say that there do exist natures gifted with those opposite qualities.
And where do you find them?

Many animals, I replied, furnish examples of them; our friend the dog is a very good one: you know that well-bred dogs are perfectly gentle to their familiars and acquaintances, and the reverse to strangers.
Yes, I know.

Then there is nothing impossible or out of the order of nature in our finding a guardian who has a similar combination of qualities?
Certainly not.

Would not he who is fitted to be a guardian, besides the spirited nature, need to have the qualities of a philosopher?
I do not apprehend your meaning.

The trait of which I am speaking, I replied, may be also seen in the dog, and is remarkable in the animal.
What trait?

Why, a dog, whenever he sees a stranger, is angry; when an acquaintance, he welcomes him, although the one has never done him any harm, nor the other any good. Did this never strike you as curious?
The matter never struck me before; but I quite recognize the truth of your remark.

And surely this instinct of the dog is very charming; your dog is a true philosopher.
Why?

Why, because he distinguishes the face of a friend and of an enemy only by the criterion of knowing and not knowing. And must not an animal be a lover of learning who determines what he likes and dislikes by the test of knowledge and ignorance?

Most assuredly.

And is not the love of learning the love of wisdom, which is philosophy?

Plato's winners and losers.

If the above passage from *The Republic* were to be used as the basis for a class, the first question would be: Is it difficult to understand how markets work? The answer is, no.

Regardless of how much effort goes into normal Principles books to explain the interaction of supply and demand, it is relatively easy to explain and predict what happens to the equilibrium price and quantity in a market if there is a change in some variable that affects either supply or demand.

The second question, which is more import and which should be asked of all economic ideas, is: Who wins and who loses if the idea becomes reality?

In Plato's case, the answer, using either reason or the ability to look back at history, is clear: The winners in Plato's small, pre-industrialized world were those already in power.

Plato made it clear that the greedy, self-interested people could not be trusted with either political power or market power. It was an idea that dominated virtually all societies for another 2,000 years. Until the Industrial Revolution in the 1700s, power was maintained in the hands of an aristocracy that shared wealth mainly with the monopolies and cartels it supported and protected.

How were they protected? By restricting foreign trade; by preventing the free movement of capital and labor; by not allowing "unfair competition" to hurt the profits of the merchants, farmers and manufacturers who supported those in power.

2. Adam Smith for free markets.

As proof that there are more than enough ideas in the above passage to use it as the basis for a course, Adam Smith turned it into a two volume, five-book treatise that is still considered to be the foundation of free-market economics (although the term "economics" was not in use in 1776).

In *An Inquiry Into the Nature and Causes of the Wealth of Nations*, published in March of 1776, Adam Smith expanded on Plato's, and others', descriptions of specialization and of how markets work, but his conclusions were different. Instead of agreeing with Plato's negative picture of what to expect from free markets, meaning that unbridled greed would lead to exploitation and war, Smith's conclusion was that self interest and greed would lead to stable markets and increase the wealth of the nation. As such, *The Wealth of Nations* is normally referred to as the first comprehensive "defense" of free markets.

Although *The Wealth of Nations* fills five books, Smith's major arguments can be understood by looking at three famous passages, possibly the three most famous economic passages of all time.

The first is Smith's example of how the specialization of labor in a pin factory increases wealth. In *The Republic*, Plato's specialization leads not only to wealth, but also to wars that cannot be won. *In The Wealth of Nations*, Smith shows how specialization increases the wealth of the nation.

> "To take an example, therefore, from a very trifling manufacture; but one in which the division of labour has been very often taken notice of, the trade of the pin-maker; a workman not educated to this business (which the division of labour has rendered a distinct trade), nor acquainted with the use of the machinery employed in it (to the invention of which the same division of labour has probably given occasion), could scarce, perhaps, with his utmost industry, make one pin in a day, and certainly could not make twenty. But in the way in which this business is now carried on, not only the whole work is a peculiar trade, but it is divided into a number of branches, of which the greater part are likewise peculiar trades. One man draws out the wire, another straights it, a third cuts it, a fourth points it, a fifth grinds it at the top for receiving the head; to make the head requires two or three distinct operations; to put it on, is a peculiar business, to whiten the

pins is another; it is even a trade by itself to put them into the paper; and the important business of making a pin is, in this manner, divided into about eighteen distinct operations, which, in some manufactories, are all performed by distinct hands, though in others the same man will sometimes perform two or three of them. I have seen a small manufactory of this kind where ten men only were employed, and where some of them consequently performed two or three distinct operations. But though they were very poor, and therefore but indifferently accommodated with the necessary machinery, they could, when they exerted themselves, make among them about twelve pounds of pins in a day. There are in a pound upwards of four thousand pins of a middling size. Those ten persons, therefore, could make among them upwards of forty-eight thousand pins in a day. Each person, therefore, making a tenth part of forty-eight thousand pins, might be considered as making four thousand eight hundred pins in a day. But if they had all wrought separately and independently, and without any of them having been educated to this peculiar business, they certainly could not each of them have made twenty, perhaps not one pin in a day; that is, certainly, not the two hundred and fortieth, perhaps not the four thousand eight hundredth part of what they are at present capable of performing, in consequence of a proper division and combination of their different operations."[1]

The above passage is at the very beginning of *The Wealth of Nations*. It is the first of many real-world examples Smith uses to make his free-market argument. It can also be used to explain the benefits of free trade.

After leaving no doubt that specialization creates wealth, Smith turns to explaining how self-interest or greed is good, turning Plato's negative into a positive.

Plato's conclusion was that self-interest and greed among the people would lead to chaos and war.

Smith's conclusion was that it would create stable markets, promote the public interest, and increase the wealth of the nation. There is, however, in Smith's pin factory example, one observation that is often ignored. It is that while the factory was turning out thousands of pins, presumably making its

---

[1] *An Inquiry Into the Nature and Causes of the Wealth of Nations*; Adam Smith. 1776.

owners wealthy, the workers "were very poor."

The second key passage from *The Wealth of Nations* is Smith's description of the "invisible hand" of supply and demand.

Although it is a rewrite of Plato's observation that individuals act in their own interest, but with a catchy title, it again turns Plato's negative into a positive.

In this wonderful paragraph, Smith explains how individual producers acting "for their own gain" end up promoting the public interest. These few lines, by themselves, may be the single best argument for free markets ever published.

> "Every individual endeavors to employ his capital so that its produce may be of greatest value. He generally neither intends to promote the public interest, nor knows how much he is promoting it. He intends only his own security, only his own gain. And he is in this led by an invisible hand to promote an end which was no part of his intention. By pursuing his own interest, he frequently promotes that of society more effectually than when he really intends to promote it."[2]

The third key passage expands the invisible hand idea to show not only how the self-interest of producers promotes the interests of society, but also how the self-interest—not the benevolence—of buyers and sellers serves the public interest. In other words, the public interest is served well by free-market greed:

> "Whoever offers to another a bargain of any kind, proposes to do this. Give me what I want, and you shall have this which you want, is the meaning of every such offer; and it is in this manner that we obtain from one another the far greater part of those good offices which we stand in need of. It is not from the benevolence of the butcher, the brewer, or the baker that we expect our dinner, but from their regard to their own self-interest."[3]

The butcher-baker paragraph is a clear description of how the self-interest of buyers and sellers makes markets work. And its conclusion, which is that

---

[2] *An Inquiry Into the Nature and Causes of the Wealth of Nations*; Adam Smith. 1776.
[3] *An Inquiry Into the Nature and Causes of the Wealth of Nations*; Adam Smith. 1776.

such self-interest leads to stable markets while increasing the nation's wealth, remains at the center of free-market economic teaching.[4]

Adam Smith's winners and losers.

Whom did Adam Smith's ideas help or hurt?

Again, using reason and historical hindsight, the answer is clear: The New Industrialists were big winners. Independent artisans and independent makers of pins were not. Neither were those who belonged to England's old, landed aristocracy.

To the New Industrialists, who, in 1776, were in the process of wrenching power from the old, landed aristocracy and the old cartels and trade unions, nothing could be better than a *laissez faire*[5] policy that would keep all markets free of government interference or support (and, therefore, free for them to monopolize). To promote the idea, they falsely claimed that such policies were supported by the arguments in Adam Smith's book. Politically, it was a smart campaign, because while Adam Smith was famous, few people actually read *The Wealth of Nations*.

One simple example explains how the interaction of Smith's economic ideas and public policy determines who wins and who loses. After *The Wealth of Nations* became a famous book, the emerging industrialists argued, using the laissez faire idea, that the British government should eliminate its tariffs on imported grains that were protecting British agriculture, meaning the landed aristocracy, from what the landed aristocracy called the unfair competition of cheap, imported grains. It was a successful political campaign, and when the tariffs were dropped, the expected happened: British agriculture declined, because it could not compete with foreign produce, and there was a mass migration of serfs, who were no longer needed by the landed aristocracy, into the cities where they became the cheap labor the New Industrialists wanted for their factories.

---

[4] The invisible-hand paragraph and butcher-baker paragraph helped lay the foundation for free market economics. Of course, few ideas are totally original. Smith owed a debt to Bernard Mandeville, another Scottish intellectual, who in his 1714 analogy between humanity and bees, *Enquiry Into The Origin Of Moral Virtue, Or The Fable Of The Bees*, predated Smith in asserting that the actions of individuals not on following the conventional wisdom, but on self interest; and, of course, to Plato who, in *The Republic*, presented the same idea 2,000 years earlier.

[5] A 19th century French synonym for a strict free market economy.

Was the elimination of tariffs a "neutral" act aimed at creating free markets, or was it a policy intended to help one identifiable group at the expense of another? In other words, were the industrialists just lucky?[6]

Obviously, luck had little to do with it. Any impartial observer would have been able to identify who would win and who would lose before the tariffs were eliminated. Which raises another question: Why did the landed aristocracy allow the government to drop the tariffs? The only reasonable answer is not that they were stupid, but that they did not have the power to stop it, meaning they did not have the power to stop the government from switching sides—from switching its support from the old aristocracy to the new industrialists.

More important, regardless of what some continue to argue, Smith's paragraph does not apply to everything of importance in the real world or justify a total laissez faire stance regarding the role of government.

The baker may give you bread in return for money, or for something else of value, but no one can give you clean air or national defense or laws or courts just because you are willing and able to pay for them. No one can give you these, and many other crucial things, because private markets for such things either do not exist or are far from efficient.

Aside from the self-interest, or greed-is-good, arguments in *The Wealth of Nations*, there was another free-market issue that led to untold turmoil. It was the belief, held by Adam Smith and virtually all other early economists, that while free markets would increase the wealth of the nation, the vast majority of people would continue to live in abject poverty, like the workers in the pin factory. In other words, the rich would get richer, while the people would remain poor.

It was that conclusion, which many economists spent a lot of time explaining and defending, that caused economics to be called "the dismal science."

---

[6] Like Bob Dylan in *Idiot Wind*: "They say I shot a man named Gray, and took his wife to Italy, She inherited a million bucks, and when she died it came to me. I can't help it if I'm lucky."

3. Karl Marx for the people.

Not surprisingly, there were some who were not totally sold on the idea that people should be happy to live in poverty while working to help the wealthy become even wealthier.

One who was not happy with the idea that free markets would make the rich richer while keeping the people poor was Karl Marx. If the predicted, everlasting poverty had been a minority view, Marx might not have had an audience. But in the mid-1800s, there were a lot of poor people; and because those in power, including mainstream economists, claimed that those people would have to remain poor in order for capitalism to work, it was inevitable that someone would complain.

Marx, who was in many ways a mainstream economist, did what other mainstream economists did: He came up with his own explanation of why capitalism would keep people living in poverty. The difference was that Marx concluded that people would not be content to live under such dismal circumstances forever, and that there would eventually be a revolution where the proletariat would overthrow the bourgeoisie.

Marx's explanation of why it was inevitable that capitalism would lead to the exploitation of workers was based on one of Adam Smith's ideas—an idea that David Ricardo reworked years later—that was intended to explain the inherent value in things. Early economists spent a lot of time trying to figure out how to determine the inherent value in things. It was time not well spent.

In *The Wealth of Nation*, Smith presented what is called the diamond-water-paradox, which is: Why are diamonds, which are useless baubles, so expensive, while water, which is necessary for life, so cheap? This paradox interested economists for years, a fact that is not particularly good advertising for economists. The answer, of course is that prices are determined by supply and demand, not by some false notion of "inherent value"; even if there were such a thing as inherent value, in order to understand what is happening, or is expected to happen in markets, it is only necessary to understand prices.

Unfortunately, before the heated inherent-value debate cooled off, Smith came up with a bad idea called the labor theory of value, which was that the inherent value of a thing is equal to the quantity of labor it takes to make it.

It was a not-very-smart theory, but it was exactly what Marx needed as the centerpiece for his exploitation argument. What Marx concluded was simple. If the value of something is equal to the labor it takes to make it, then that thing cannot be sold for more than its labor value. But, in order to make things, producers need capital as well as labor, and capital, like labor, must also be paid. And therein lies the rub. If the price of something is limited to its labor value, then the only way to get money to pay capital is to take it out of the wages of workers. That, according to Marx, is the exploitation that cannot be avoided under capitalism. It cannot be avoided, because there is nothing capitalists can do about it. Like it, or not, they have to exploit workers in order to pay for the capital they need. Therefore, as capitalism matures, the exploited workers will eventually rise up and overthrow the bourgeoisie (the old trade class turned into industrialists).

Although mainstream economists had dismissed the labor theory of value and given up on the idea of inherent value, the communist idea—that government control and production is better than free markets—took hold around the world. Even though Marx's economic analysis was terrible, there were still a lot of poor people. And whether or not Marx's economic ideas made sense, there were people who were willing to use revolution as a path to a change in power. The communist revolutions, however, did not take place in countries suffering from mature capitalism, but in countries ruled by dictatorships or monarchies. And they did not give power to the people. They gave power to the leaders of the revolutions.

Karl Marx's winners and losers.

Marx's manifesto[7] led to revolutions carried out in the name of the people, but which, in truth, created new dictatorships with their own methods of exploitation.

Even so, some of Marx's recommendations, especially progressive taxes, a central bank, unions, equality of opportunity, and public education worked their way into all Western democracies, including the United States, without violent revolutions. In some European countries, Socialism, a more democratic and more free-market form of communism, became dominant. In all others, as well as in the United States, economies became "mixed," meaning that they combined both free markets and government production and interference.

On a theoretical, and even on a practical, level, almost everyone wiould agree with some of Marx's objectives.

---

[7] *The Communist Manifesto* by Karl Mark and Frederick Engels; 1848.

But, because communist revolutions replaced one dictatorship with another, it is not surprising that the rise of communism spurred an ongoing intellectual backlash against government interference and a new drive to prove the value of unfettered free markets—markets totally untouched by government production or regulation.

4. Ludwig von Mises for *laissez faire*.

There is no particular reason to choose Ludwig von Mises as a spokesman for laissez faire politics, other than that he is still considered by many to be a key figure in the intellectual justification of conservative policies.

Von Mises, who wrote during the 1930s and 1940s, devoted his life to exposing the evils of communism and promoting the laissez faire philosophy.

Here is how Ludwig von Mises elevates the laissez faire idea to the level of a religion while painting all government interference as the devil's work:

> "Whatever freedom individuals can enjoy within the framework of social cooperation is conditional upon the concord of private gain and public weal. Within the orbit in which the individual, in pursuing his own wellbeing, advances also—or at least does not impair—the wellbeing of his fellow men, people going their own ways jeopardize neither the preservation of society nor the concerns of other people. A realm of freedom and individual initiative emerges, a realm in which man is allowed to choose and to act of his own accord. This sphere of freedom, by the socialists and interventionists contemptuously dubbed 'economic freedom,' is alone what makes any of those conditions possible that are commonly called freedoms within a system of social cooperation under the division of labor. It is the market economy or capitalism with its political corollary (The Marxians would have to say: with its 'superstructure'), representative government."[8]

Mises also wrote his own version of Plato's self-interest and Adam Smith's "invisible hand" passages, in which he, again, casts government as the enemy of individual freedom.

---

[8] *Human Action*, Ludwig von Mises; 1949.

"Those who contend that there is a conflict between the acquisitiveness of various individuals or between the acquisitiveness of individuals on the one hand and the commonweal on the other, cannot avoid advocating the suppression of the individuals' right to choose and to act. They must substitute the supremacy of a central board of production management for the discretion of the citizens. In their scheme of the good society there is no room left for private initiative. The authority issues orders and everybody is forced to obey."[9]

This is a case of misrepresenting the "enemy" in an attempt to win an argument, because it falsely implies that all government actions are communist acts intended to suppress individual freedom. It also implies that only Mises and his friends care about individual freedom.[10]

In other words, even in those cases where government interference is used to correct the misuse of resources caused by some form of market failure, according to Mises, it is still an act of communist suppression.

President Theodore Roosevelt took the opposite view when he broke up John. D. Rockefeller's oil trust, J. P. Morgan's railroad trust, and James B. Duke's tobacco trust. Although those actions, along with government suits against forty-three other trusts and monopolies, earned him the nickname, "the trust buster," Roosevelt said he did not want to bust big business, but to regulate it for the good of society, an objective that most people, other than those who accept the von Mises doctrine, agree with.

Most important, instead of defining a free market to be a market free of market failure, von Mises defined a free market to be a market with no government interference. By doing so, he dismissed the need to correct the price distortions caused by market failure, imperfect markets, and the lack of markets. The result is a doctrine that claims a limited use for government—mainly the protection of private property rights—a government function with which all economists agree.

---

[9] *Human Action*, Ludwig von Mises; 1949. Chapter 27.
[10] I was once on the faculty of a college where the person who taught Principles of Economics was totally incompetent. The students thought he was brilliant. When I asked them why they thought he was so smart, they said it was because they could not understand anything he said.

Ludwig von Mises' winners and losers.

The von Mises redefinition of free markets does not support free markets or individual freedom as much as it supports policies that hand markets over to those who can exploit them with monopoly power or who can profit from the lack of real markets. Even so, the von Mises claim that any and all government actions that affect markets is communist or socialist intervention is a knife-edged fallacy that is still used to call anyone who promotes the legitimate economic role of government a communist or socialist.

In terms of economic knowledge, Ludwig von Mises is in the same ballpark as Karl Marx. Neither one understood economics very well. Each had a political objective that he tried to promote by using the little economics he did understand. Each was comfortable redefining economic terms and principles to suit his needs. And each created a doctrine that amassed a large number of followers. As such, neither can be dismissed, because their followers continue to wield considerable political power, even today.

Von Mises, and the current followers of the "government is evil" doctrine, may be correct in criticizing communism. In fact, they may not go far enough to explain the economic inefficiency of communism. But, to argue that any regulatory action or production undertaken by a democratically elected government is an act of communist suppression is not only pointless and dysfunctional, it is dangerous—just as dangerous as the dogma of Marxists.

5. Paul Samuelson for the middle ground.

Some continue to believe that Adam Smith's invisible hand and butcher-baker passages blindly support the extreme free-market doctrine of Ludwig von Mises. Others believe that Smith's prediction of people living in abject poverty, including those in his pin factory, along with the labor theory of value, support Marx's communist agenda.

Mainstream economists, both liberal and conservative, are in the middle, meaning that they understand both the benefits of free markets and the need for government interference.

In particular, both conservative and liberal economists understand that the invisible hand doctrine applies only when markets are perfectly competitive.

Here is how Nobel Prize winning economist Paul Samuelson explained it in the best-selling principles textbook of all time:

> "One of the major results in all economics is that the allocation of resources by competitive markets is efficient. This important result assumes that all markets are perfectly competitive. It further assumes that there are no external effects like pollution and says nothing about the fairness of the distribution of income in competitive markets."[11]

In other words, while some claim that *The Wealth of Nations* is an unqualified defense of markets without any government intervention, real economists, including Adam Smith, know that "the invisible-hand doctrine" applies only when markets are perfectly competitive, which is seldom the case in the real world, either because of imperfect competition (monopoly), imperfect markets (public goods), or a lack of markets (for things such as common property resources, environmental quality, or the external benefits of things such as education and health care).

Here are two of Smith's passages from Book 7 of *The Wealth of Nations*:

> "A monopoly granted either to an individual or to a trading company has the same effect as a secret in trade or manufactures. The monopolists, by keeping the market constantly under-stocked, by never fully supplying the effectual demand, sell their commodities much above the natural price, and raise their emoluments, whether they consist in wages or profit, greatly above their natural rate."

> "The price of monopoly is upon every occasion the highest which can be got. The natural price, or the price of free competition, on the contrary, is the lowest which can be taken, not upon every occasion indeed, but for any considerable time altogether. The one is upon every occasion the highest which can be squeezed out of the buyers, or which, it is supposed, they will consent to give: The other is the lowest which the sellers can commonly afford to take, and at the same time continue their business."[12]

---

[11] *Economics* by Paul Samuelson and William Nordhouse. 1995
[12] *An Inquiry Into the Nature and Causes of the Wealth of Nations*, Adam Smith; 1776. Mises; 1949.

Paul Samuelson's winners and losers.

From the end of World War II, mainstream economists believed that the nation's wealth could be maximized only with help from government. The Great Depression was a good, if unpleasant, learning experience.

One of the main lessons was that it is a mistake to assume market economies will automatically generate acceptable levels of growth and employment. Although the idea of using government interference to increase the level of economic activity was, for many years, considered to be a "liberal" idea, today, it is embraced by both sides of the political spectrum.

The first time the government ever attempted to use changes in taxes and spending to intentionally fix a slow economy was the Kennedy tax cut of 1964.

Although the Kennedy tax cut was widely criticized by Republicans, especially conservative Republicans, it was only a few years later that President Richard Nixon declared, "We are all Keynesians now," meaning that Republicans now believed in using the same tax and spending policies recommended during the Great Depression by the "liberal" British economist, John Maynard Keynes.

President Ronald Reagan used tax cuts, tax increases, and discretionary government spending in an attempt to improve the economy.

And President George W. Bush, hoping to bring the economy out of a recession, implemented his own tax cuts.

So it seems Nixon was correct: All politicians *are* now Keynesians, although the thinkers who confuse Keynes with Marx will never want to be called Keynesians.

The second great lesson, which was actually there from the beginning, is Adam Smith's warning that there is no guarantee that individual markets, left to operate on their own, will meet the conditions of economic efficiency. According to Smith, both monopolists and trades will conspire against the public good.[13]

What truly changed after the Great Depression, however, was the

---

[13] People of the same trade seldom meet together, even for merriment and diversion, but the conversation ends in conspiracy against the public, or in some contrivance to raise prices. It is impossible indeed to prevent such meetings, by any law which either could be executed, or would be consistent with liberty and justice. But though the law cannot hinder people of the same trade from sometimes assembling together, it ought to do nothing to facilitate such assemblies; much less to render them necessary. *An Inquire Into the Nature and Causes of the Wealth of Nations*, Adam Smith; 1776.

recognition by most economists that the government's role in the economy should be more active than it had been in the past. As a result, a large part of economists' time is now spent trying to understand the causes of market failures, including monopoly, and how to correct those failures for the good of the nation's wealth. That belief, however, is not shared equally by everyone, which is why there are still political arguments that divide the left and the right when it comes to government regulation of or interference in individual markets.

6. Milton Friedman for the middle ground.

It is not only Democratic economists who understand the need to correct market failures. Even conservative economists, such as Nobel Prize winning Milton Friedman, do not support the extreme laissez faire view of Ludwig von Mises.

Here is how Friedman explains the role of government in a market economy where the ultimate objective is the "…freedom of the individual, or more realistically the family."

> "In such a free private enterprise exchange economy, government's primary role is to preserve the rules of the game by enforcing contracts, preventing coercion, and keeping markets free. Beyond this, there are only three major grounds on which government intervention is to be justified. One is natural monopoly or similar market imperfection which makes effective competition (and therefore thoroughly voluntary exchange) impossible. A second is the existence of substantial neighborhood effects, i.e., the action of one individual imposes significant costs on other individuals for which it is not feasible to make him compensate them or yields significant gains to them for which it is not feasible to make them compensate him, circumstances that again make voluntary exchange impossible. The third derives from an ambiguity in the ultimate objective rather than from the difficulty of achieving it by voluntary exchange, namely, paternalistic concern for children and other irresponsible individuals."

Contrary to the strict laissez faire argument, Friedman does not say that government intervention is always wrong and never justified. Although he wants to support the conservative idea that government should play a minor role in a free-market society, which is why he identifies "only" three grounds that justify government intervention in a free private enterprise economy, the truth is that Friedman's definition of the role of government is virtually the same as Samuelson's.

The idea that government is to "preserve the rules of the game by enforcing contracts, preventing coercion, and keeping markets free," is at the core of all free societies, because if government fails in this task, there can be no business, no markets, and no individual freedom. This is not a minor task.

Then there are Friedman's three additional grounds for government interference or regulation.

The first is to regulate monopoly.

Friedman, along with all other free-market economists, understands that monopolies and other market imperfections destroy economic efficiency and reduce the wealth of the nation by disrupting the price system, and that one legitimate role of government is to correct such market failures.

The second is to regulate neighborhood effects.

Friedman's "neighborhood effects" are the same as Samuelson's "externalities." And Friedman offers the standard economic solution for negative externalities (*costs* imposed on other individuals by polluters, for example, for which it is not feasible for them to pay damages), public education (significant *gains* to others for which it is not feasible to collect payment), and the production of public goods (goods and services the private market cannot provide, such as national defense.)

The third is the paternalistic concern for children and other irresponsible individuals.

Even someone as conservative as Milton Friedman does not, as an economist, believe that those who cannot take care of themselves should be turned out into the streets. In fact, it was Milton Friedman who devised the "negative income tax" idea that remains the best, although not yet adopted, welfare program. It does not abandon welfare payments; it eliminates the government bureaucracy involved in handing out the money and introduces incentive into a truly dismal program. Both Richard Nixon and George McGovern tried unsuccessfully to implement Friedman's plan, but each was stopped by conservatives who were unable or unwilling to understand the free-market underpinnings of the plan.

Most important, Friedman, like Samuelson, uses the economic model of perfect competition as the standard against which to measure price distortions.

As such, he knows that price distortions are caused not only by government, but also by market failure. Therefore, Friedman argues that the role of government is to correct the price distortions caused by monopoly and by what he calls *neighborhood* effects in "…a society that takes freedom of the individual, or more realistically the family, as its ultimate objective."

Milton Friedman's winners and losers.

The difference between Friedman and von Mises, the two "conservatives" in this section, is that while von Mises claims that individual freedom is hurt by any and all government interference, Friedman believes that individual freedom can exist only if there is government interference in imperfect markets.

As such, the winners in Friedman's markets are the people and the nation. The potential losers are those who benefit from a strict laissez faire policy—the monopolists and others who should be regulated to prevent their exercising power over imperfect or nonexistent markets.

In the end, Milton Friedman, like Adam Smith and Paul Samuelson, is focused on the real wealth of the nation.

2. Disagreements and Conditional Forecasts

"Only when we realize that there is no eternal, unchanging truth or absolute truth can we arouse in ourselves a sense of intellectual responsibility."

Hu Shih, LaJeunesse Nouvelle, 1919

1. A great danger.

One of the dangers we face in dealing rationally with some of the most critical issues of our time is the constant focus on disagreements among economists.

Pushing the idea that economists do not agree on anything creates the mistaken belief that there is no body of economic theory. In effect, it leads people to believe that no one knows anything and that one opinion is as valid as another.

Surgeons disagree, but if you need an operation you will probably want to choose a surgeon, not a carpenter who read a book on home health remedies.

Carpenters disagree on what the best house would look like, but if you are building a home you will probably chose a carpenter, not a surgeon whose hobby is woodworking.

And economists disagree on the impacts of policies intended to make the world better. But if you are faced with a serious economic problem, you should probably talk to trained economists, not a lawyer who read a few books written by self-taught economists.

No one would walk into a health club and expect to be the physical equal of someone who has been training for many years. But many Americans are not willing to accept the fact that a similar effort is required to develop the ability to deal with problems that are addressed by each intellectual discipline.

We live in a society that seems to have a need for simple truths, where a growing number of Americans seems unwilling to spend the effort required to master intellectual achievements that lead to further questions instead of absolute truths.

Harry Truman once said, "If all the economists in the world were laid end to end, they still wouldn't reach a conclusion."

It is an old joke, but still funny—to economists.

Unfortunately, what began as an inside joke is now a justification for ignorance. Anyone who does not want to take the time to study economic theory can pretend that his or her opinion is the equal of anyone else's, because economists do not agree anyway.

The fact is, economists do agree on almost everything when it involves basic economic theory. The disagreements are the inevitable result of trying to solve real-world problems.

It is commonly believed that although there is general agreement among physical scientists, every social scientist has his or her own view of how the world works. But there is a well developed, cohesive, and widely agreed upon body of theory for every social science, just as there is for every physical science. In each case, however, trying to apply "laboratory" theories to the real world raises innumerable complications.

One of the simplest physics experiments involves a feather and a penny in a vacuum tube. When you turn the tube upside down, the feather and the penny drop to the bottom together—at the same speed. By using a simple equation, anyone can calculate the time it will take them to fall.

Will all physicists, therefore, agree on the time it will take a feather and a penny dropped out of a 10th story window to hit the ground? Not a chance. No matter how exact the formula is, it is only precise for an object in a vacuum. In an environment with air resistance and wind, a penny will obviously fall faster than a feather. But if both are dropped out of a 10th story window, the feather could actually hit the ground first—if, for example, the penny is blown into an open window or onto a ledge. Even if both fall all the way to the street, no physicist would claim to know exactly how long each would take. Ask 100 physicists and you will get 100 different estimates for the feather and 100 for the penny.

Is physics, therefore, useless? Or is anyone's guess as valid as that of a physicist? Hardly. It is possible that someone standing on the corner might make a lucky guess that turns out to be more accurate than all the educated estimates from the 100 physicists. But if you are going to bet your life savings on which forecast will be the most accurate, you would not seriously consider the guess from the guy on the corner, even if you knew he had won such a contest in the past.

Economic issues are no different.

Economists agree on all sorts of "vacuum tube" theories. What they cannot agree on is exactly what will happen when those theories are used in a real world full of ledges and open windows.

For example, the Reagan tax cut was based on the theory that if you give the rich some more pennies to spend, some of those pennies will eventually trickle down to the not so rich. Although some economists agreed with the theory, the questions were: How long will it take? Will any pennies actually trickle all the way down? Or will they get stuck along the way? In other words, even if you agree with the theory, you might question its outcome in the real world.

Some people argue that the Reagan tax cut helped the rich at the expense of the poor. Others say that everyone won. There are even disagreements about the numbers. The Urban Institute says that, from 1977 to 1986, incomes in the bottom quintile *increased* by 28% while the incomes in the top quintile increased by only 11%. However, according to the House Ways and Means Committee, from 1979 to 1987 (not exactly the same years), family incomes for the bottom fifth, adjusted for inflation, *declined* by 6.1% while the wealthiest fifth increased by 11.1%.

Can we determine which numbers are correct? Of course. More important, however, is another question: Do you know which numbers Republicans like to use and which Democrats prefer? The answer to that question is, as they say, a no-brainer.

2. Forecasts must be conditional.

Any responsible forecast must, therefore, be conditional. It must specify the exact assumptions used to drive it.

One reason for being specific about assumptions is to let others see what is behind the forecast. Then they can decide for themselves whether or not it is logical. The other reason for conditional forecasts is honesty. By stating his or her assumptions, no one is able to take credit for an accurate forecast made for the wrong reasons.

A careful listing of assumptions also offers some protection. If a forecast misses the mark, others will be able to see it was because the assumptions did not hold, not because the logic was bad.

3. Today's critical economic issues.

Americans can be proud of the fact that in terms of total production, the United States is currently the world's wealthiest nation. Our past success is undeniable. But we must also keep an eye on the future.

Although the economy is growing, real wages could be in a long-term decline, the average American has little job security, and we can no longer simply assume that America's standard of living will increase in the future.

We spend more money per person on health care than any other industrialized nation, but we do not have the best medical care; out of 22 industrialized countries, the U.S. ranks 18th in infant mortality.

We sold off the last remaining stand of virgin American forests in Oregon and Washington to foreign lumber mills; and, for just two dollars each, we sold off 500 year-old trees in Alaska.

We cannot eat fish from many of our rivers, lakes, and streams.

Our ocean beaches are littered with dangerous garbage.

We are slopping oil in our oceans, from Alaska to Rhode Island to Delaware to Texas.

We have no idea what to do with our nuclear waste.

We are struggling to remain competitive with foreign producers while our trade deficit mounts.

We are already the world's largest debtor nation, and our foreign debt continues to escalate.

Our educational achievements are dismal when compared to other developed nations.

Our position as the world economic leader is being threatened on a number of fronts.

Personal saving, which helps finance productive investment, continues to decline.

The growing government debt is putting the future economy at risk.

Meanwhile, the Federal Reserve has, for many years, intentionally slowed economic growth to fight an inflation that cannot logically be blamed on either fast growth or it high oil prices.[14]

As a nation, we have been focusing our attention and fears on economic distortions, such as inflation and recession, while assuming that the basic,

---

[14] The disturbing thing about this list is that it was compiled in 1989.

underlying economy is doing fine. But it is not doing fine. The potential disasters of inflation and recession cannot be ignored, but neither can the long-term health of the U.S. economy.

If the U.S. is to reach its true potential, we must make wise economic decisions. But the ability to make such decisions is seriously hampered by two popular myths: that economists never agree and that economic forecasts are of little value because they are conditional.

Most of today's important economic issues can be traced to the fact that we are not willing to accept or live within real constraints.

Although the refusal to be limited by existing constraints may be the driving force behind the advancement of civilization, it can also turn achievement into disaster.

We should never be satisfied with what we have today. We should never accept the status quo as the end of our quest.

But we must always be aware of the consequences of our actions.

We live in a world of limited resources. Therefore, every action requires a tradeoff or imposes costs on ourselves or someone else.

Part of the increase in our measured national wealth comes from the government living beyond its means. Government spending is one part of measured Gross Domestic Product. Therefore, the higher the level of government spending, the higher GDP is. But the mounting debt used to finance that spending has yet to be accounted for.

Another part of our increasing national wealth has come at the expense of the environment. By treating the environment as a free good or a free dumping ground, we reduced our costs of both production and consumption. But the environment is critical to our wellbeing. It is part of the production process as well as a valuable part of our lives, and we have not yet begun to add up the damages.

Even so, individual living standards seem to have stopped their "automatic" rise. And the Federal Reserve is proud of itself for being able to slow economic growth as it "fights the good fight" against inflation while ignoring the danger of recession.

4. Assumptions.

This book is based on the following assumptions:

1) We live in a world with limited resources.

2) In a world with limited resources, every action requires tradeoffs and creates costs.

3) When such costs are not represented in the market, economic theory cannot justify the existing "free market" solution as being "best" for society.

4) Bureaucratic solutions based primarily on political self-interest seldom offer the best solution for society.

5) Those who claim that economic theory justifies or defends the status quo, implying that the "free market" gave us what exists today, are wrong. In economic terms, our world is a far cry from the textbook definition of a free market.

6) Major economic improvements can be made by forcing everyone to be responsible for his or her actions, which is what a true free market would do

7) We should not give up on free market economics just because we have problems.

8) We can make the world better only if we approach our goals rationally.

5. Conclusion

In the pursuit of wise policies, there are no absolute truths. There is only rational thought versus prejudice, self-interest, and laziness. Although some may prefer easy answers, the purpose of economics is to find real solutions.

3. Politics & Economics

Economics is about big ideas, about which there are often huge, sometimes violent, disagreements. Some people love capitalism. Some love communism. Economics is also about little ideas, about which we also disagree. Some want to own a lot of things. Some do not.

Here is what Albert Einstein wrote in 1931:

"To inquire after the meaning or object of one's own existence or that of all creatures has always seemed to me absurd from an objective point of view. And yet everybody has certain ideals which determine the direction of his endeavors and his judgments. In this sense I have never looked upon ease and happiness as ends in themselves—this ethical basis I call the ideal of a pigsty. The ideals which have lighted my way, and time after time have given me new courage to face life cheerfully, have been Kindness, Beauty, and Truth. Without the sense of kinship with men of like mind, without the occupation with the objective world, the eternally unattainable in the field of art and scientific endeavors, life would have seemed to me empty. The trite objects of human efforts—possessions, outward success, luxury—have always seemed to me contemptible."
Albert Einstein
Living Philosophies, 1931. p. 3

Is it possible for someone to follow Einstein's beliefs while living in a "free-market" economy where almost everyone seems focused on producing and consuming the "trite" things that Einstein considered contemptible? Of course.

That is what free markets do—they generate all sorts of diversity. That is why Albert Einstein and Malcolm Forbes were able to live in the same state, if not on the same kind of estate. However, it is not necessary to share either Einstein's or Forbes' views, or even Superman's belief in truth, justice, and the

American way, to know that big ideas are just as important to our lives as the little ideas over which we think we have more control.

Understanding the big ideas may or may not require us to consider the ideals of Kindness and Beauty, but it is with absolute certainty we can say there is no possibility of reaching meaningful conclusions if we ignore Truth. And that is what economics is about: searching for the truth in ideas that can add to the wellbeing of individuals and society as a whole.

As such, the economic solution to problems is often different from political solutions, and because there is a wide split between the political doctrines of the left and the right, economics is always at odds with someone. In theory, economics is non-political; it is based not on the doctrine or dogma of either the left or the right, but on reason, logic, and evidence. As such, a particular economic conclusion may appeal to either the left or the right, which is why politicians from both sides of the aisle will, off and on, use economic arguments to support their political objectives. And that is the crux of the problem. Politicians have political objectives. Economists have an economic objective, which is to maximize the wellbeing or welfare of the nation while also supporting the health and happiness of individuals.

The question is: Do economists always have answers?

The answer is: Not always, but most of the time.

Unfortunately, while it should make sense to at least consult economists before making policy decisions that affect millions of people, economic policies and programs are carried out not by economists, but by politicians and the Federal Reserve Bank, which means that economic policies in the real world are affected by and conducted by non-economists and special interests.

Therefore, although this book is politically neutral, meaning that it should irritate both Democrats and Republicans, because each Party has its own special interests to serve, it does not even pretend to avoid the reality that economics is tied to politics.

4. The Really Big Idea

1. Enlightenment

More than two centuries ago, Immanuel Kant argued that individual enlightenment comes from questioning what is happening. He believed that individuals must both follow the rules and question the rules. He argued that to be enlightened—to use reason—individuals must overcome four self-imposed blocks: laziness, prejudice, cowardice, and allowing others to do their thinking for them. As such, an enlightened individual would find it difficult to accept the idea that we should act before thinking or that we should be less interested in big ideas than in small, personal ideas. This book may not help anyone overcome his or her laziness, prejudice, or cowardice, but it might help some overcome the block of letting others do their thinking for them.

As Bob Dylan said,

> Don't follow leaders
> Watch the parkin' meters[15]

2. Truth.

There is one economic truth. It is that while free markets can create great wealth, unregulated markets are not always the best way to allocate resources, or to provide a sufficient quantity or quality of goods and services to society, or to maximize the wealth or wellbeing of society.

Ignorance of this truth is responsible for many of the worst political and economic decisions made since the publication of Adam Smith's *An Inquiry Into The Nature And Causes Of The Wealth Of Nations* in 1776, the same year in

---

[15] Subterranean Homesick Blues; Bob Dylan. 1965.

which the first volume of Gibbons' *The Decline and Fall of the Roman Empire* appeared, and also the same year in which the American colonies declared independence from England.

Looking back, it seems easy to see how these events were interrelated. In 1776, Adam Smith used reason and logic to establish forever the theoretical beauty of the free market. He also declared that the great weakness of free markets is that those with the power to exploit markets are free to do so—and will do so. As such, "free" is a double-edged adjective that can cut in opposite directions when it is used to describe a market.

In 1776, Gibbons concluded that Rome began to decline after power was dissipated throughout the Empire.

On July 4, 1776, American colonists declared independence from England.[16] Eleven years later, in 1788, following Adam Smith's economic thesis and Gibbons' argument, Americans ratified a Constitution based on the belief that a successful nation requires both the protection of individual rights and a strong central government, a belief that had to be defended less than 80 years later when America fought its Civil War.

Of course, the true genius of the founding fathers, as well as of Abraham Lincoln, was the recognition and understanding of the limitations of democracy. That is why, when we pledge allegiance to the flag, we do not pledge allegiance to the democracy for which it stands, nor to the representative democracy for which it stands, but to the *republic* for which it stands.

In a true democracy, fifty percent plus one of the people can do whatever they decide to do to the other fifty percent minus one of the people. In a republic, individuals are granted unalienable rights—individual rights that are not subject to a vote—things such as life, liberty, and the pursuit of happiness.

However, there has always been opposition to the principle of a strong union. Intellectual and political arguments over the balance of power between federal and state government, and between government and individual rights, have been part of the American experiment from the time the founding fathers sat down to write the Constitution.

The fictional story that follows has, as its hero, someone who fails to understand that political ideologies are intellectual ideas, which, if used to guide real actions, can lead individuals and governments to do unintelligent things. In the story, an individual who puts political doctrine ahead of reason makes some

---

[16] The first shot in the Revolutionary War was fired fourteen months earlier, on April 19, 1775 at Lexington and Concord.

regrettable decisions. In the real world, politicians and governments caught up in political dogma also make regrettable decisions.

5. The Notice—A Fictional Story

I.
The City of River Flats
OFFICE OF THE MAYOR
City Hall

OFFICIAL NOTICE TO MR. RICHARD GREEN

The City of River Flats, after careful consideration of the written correspondence and verbal demands received from Richard Green during the past three years, and with due regards for Mr. Green's claims that his rights are being violated by the welfare-state tax and spending policies of local government, hereby grants Richard Green total absolution from all local taxes, both city and county. As of the first day of the month following the delivery of this NOTICE, Richard Green will be permanently removed from the local tax role. By freeing Richard Green from the responsibility of paying any and all property taxes, Richard Green will be given the freedom to spend his own money any way he chooses, thereby bringing to life one of his basic and often repeated principles, which is that he can spend his money better than government can.

In return for being allowed to live his life free of all local government interference, Richard Green will meet one simple condition:

By virtue of not having to pay exploitive property taxes, Richard Green will refrain from the use of all city and county services.

In particular, Richard Green will, beginning on the first day of the month following the delivery of this NOTICE meet the conditions listed below:

Richard Green will remove his children from the public schools, which should be no burden, because he has continually claimed that private schools in our city cost only $3,500 per student per year whereas the public schools are spending $12,000 per student per year.

Richard Green will refrain from the use of all city and county water and sewer services. To guarantee compliance, such services will be disconnected on the aforementioned day.

Richard Green will refrain from using all roads maintained by the city or county.

Richard Green will refrain from using all public sidewalks and will not set foot on any public property.

Richard Green will have his electricity, natural gas, and telephone lines disconnected, because those services were connected to his house only because government gave utility companies the right to run their lines through other people's private property.

Richard Green will receive no police or fire protection.

Richard Green will not be allowed to use the county court system to make claims against anyone.

Richard Green will not be allowed to hire any employee who was educated in the local public schools or who would use city or county maintained roads to come to work.

Richard Green will not be allowed to receive any mail delivered by anyone or any service that would use city or county maintained roads to make such deliveries.

If Richard Green wants to leave his house, he will

have to make private-market arrangements that will allow him, presumably for a fee, to trespass on others' private property.

If Richard Green trespasses on private property without having a free-market agreement to do so, the owner of such property is given the right to do whatever he or she chooses to do to Richard Green, with no legal repercussions, because Richard Green is not protected by any local laws or any city or county law-enforcement agency.

Finally, to abide by Richard Green's often-repeated proclamation that the only legitimate role of government is to protect private property, the City of River Flats will protect the ownership of his property, the fee for such protection to be determined in negotiations with the City prior to the aforementioned date. If an agreement cannot be reached that is satisfactory to both parties, such property rights will, on the aforementioned date, become a matter for the free market to determine, without the use of any legal or contractual arrangements supported by local government. In other words, the ownership of Richard Green's house will then fall to the toughest or, as they used to say, the fastest gun in the West.

The city and county cannot help Richard Green with his unfair state and federal taxes and services, but we are doing all that is within our power to end the ongoing persecution of Richard Green by local government's abusive tax and spending policies.

In conclusion, should Richard Green desire to rejoin the corrupt society of River Flats, he can do so by delivering to the city a petition containing the names of more than fifty-percent of the eligible voters in the county. It goes without saying that none of the above-described conditions can be broken in the collection of such names or in the delivery of

```
such petition.
   Because this is a legal NOTICE issued by the City
of River Flats, any violation will call for the
immediate arrest and imprisonment of Richard Green,
without recourse to the court system from which
Richard Green is barred.
```

II

"This can't be happening," Richard said. "How could everything have gone so wrong? It seemed so simple when I started."

Richard Green was sitting alone, trapped inside his three-bedroom rambler on the outskirts of a small mid-western town, with virtually no way out. Until yesterday, he had shared this house with a wife and two middle-school children. Richard, who was in his forties, wore a tan hunting jacket, attended church each Sunday, drove a pick-up truck with a rifle hung across the back window, and believed strongly in the first and fourth amendments to the United States Constitution. "How could there be no exit?" he wondered aloud. The answer, of course, was in the truth.

You must know, then, that Richard, whenever he was not working, devoted himself to reading books on economics and government, especially those steeped in free-market philosophy, with such energy that he put his studies ahead of his marriage, his children, and his opportunity to earn money. He was so committed that he chose to drive a twenty-year old, two-wheel drive Chevrolet pick-up truck so that he would have the money to buy as many of these books as he could find. His library was impressive. But of all the books it contained, the ones he liked the most were the novels of Ayn Rand—*Atlas Shrugged* and *The Fountainhead*—and the economic philosophies of Ludwig Von Mises, the famous Austrian economist from the 1920's. Richard also copied bits and pieces of wisdom from many sources. One of his favorite sources was The Objectivist Center, created by followers of Ms. Rand's philosophy. One of its editorials contained the following, which he liked to show to anyone unfamiliar with the ideas to which he had become so dedicated:

> "Rand is best known as a logical yet passionate advocate of individual
> liberty and laissez-faire capitalism who stands out from others because
> she was principally a novelist. In *Atlas* her heroes were businessmen

and -women, productive individuals whose achievements were responsible for the country's prosperity. This is in stark contrast to the usual portrayal of business executives as villains in books, movies, TV shows, sermons and political pronouncements. Rand didn't simply explain her perspective; her stories showed us her characters' love for their work; it was exciting to read about how they strove with zeal, using their minds, independent judgment, integrity and strength to produce railroads, oil wells and steel mills.

Rand's plots taught economic lessons better than do most college textbooks, showing exactly how one government regulation after another can punish productive individuals and destroy a country. Even more important, in her novels and her non-fiction works she developed a philosophy - Objectivism - that provided a moral defense of free markets.

These are the ideas that drove Richard.

Because of the knowledge Richard had gained from his reading, knowledge that not everyone had been fortunate enough to acquire, he had many heated arguments with shopkeepers, teachers, businessmen, and government officials in his little town. He also had many intellectual arguments with like-minded Objectivists over which past or current hero had done the most to promote the philosophy of the independent thinker and businessman struggling patriotically against the destructive force of government regulation. One of his friends claimed, "No one has done more than Rush Limbaugh to promote and defend the philosophy of individual freedom." Another argued, "Bill O'Reilly has done even more than the admittedly great Limbaugh." Still another always said, "Ronald Reagan, America's greatest president, summed up everything with the simple statement that, 'Government cannot solve our problems; government is the problem.'" Richard's choice was always Ayn Rand herself, arguing that she showed everyone the way. He liked to remind his friends of the joint survey conducted by the Library of Congress and the Book of the Month Club that concluded *Atlas Shrugged* is the "second most influential book for Americans today" after the *Bible*. "That 1957 novel," Richard liked to repeat, "is the most influential and controversial work of the 20th Century. And, as the reviewers said,

"Ayn Rand's magnum opus is a philosophical thriller, the story of a society's slow collapse as the men of ability go on strike against the creed that treats them as sacrificial animals. From the blast furnaces of a steel mill to the drawing rooms of high society, from the classrooms of philosophers to the decks of a pirate ship, Ayn Rand portrays the role of reason in Man's life."

Richard would have given everything to be one of Ayn Rand's heroes.

Thus was Richard brought to the decision that moved his life toward its manifest destiny. Standing in front of the bathroom mirror on a Saturday morning three years earlier, he repeated the famous line by John Galt, the hero of *Atlas Shrugged*: "I swear by my life and my love of it that I will never live for the sake of another man, nor ask another man to live for mine." On his previous birthday, Richard's wife, who enjoyed literary novels, had bought him a fountain pen—a beautiful Parker Duofold made in the 1920s—that she had found in an antique store. The night before he stared at his future in the bathroom mirror, he had placed the pen, a bottle of sapphire blue Parker ink, and a three-ring binder filled with wide-lined paper on the desk in the basement that he used as his study.

In short, he hit upon the notion that it was correct and essential, not only for his own honor, but for the sake of his country, that he should make a writer of himself, using his Parker Duofold to right the wrongs of government intervention while exposing himself to the attacks of communists and socialists.

He knew that if he had had the opportunity, he could have been a great architect, like Howard Roark in Ayn Rand's *The Fountainhead*, but he also believed that the pen is mightier than the sword. He thought about the impact he could make by writing the truth, although he knew he was not yet ready to write the great books, such as Newt Gingrich's *Contract With America*. That would come later. He would begin by writing letters to the editor of the local newspaper. And so, pulled by the anticipation of protecting the world from the tyranny of government interference, he set out to put his plan into action.

III

The first thing Richard did, after turning away from the bathroom mirror, was to sit at his desk and write down what he liked to call "The Five Commandments Of The Free Market," beginning with Ronald's Reagan's famous truth:

1. Government cannot solve the problem; government is the problem.
2. Individual freedom and government intervention is a zero sum game; you cannot have more of one without having less of the other.
3. Government cannot create wealth.
4. Government cannot create quality of life.
5. People can spend their money better than government can.

The second thing Richard did was to copy down the "To Do" list from *The Communist Manifesto*, so that he would have a constant reminder of what he said were "the many faces of evil that it is now my job to combat." He wrote down, from what he liked to call the most immoral book ever written, what Marx and Engels described, in 1848, as the objectives of the Communist Party:

1. Abolition of property in land and application of all rents of land to public purposes.
2. A heavy progressive or graduated income tax.
3. Abolition of all right of inheritance.
4. Confiscation of the property of all emigrants and rebels.
5. Centralization of credit in the hands of the State, by means of a national bank with State capital and an exclusive monopoly.
6. Centralization of the means of communication and transport in the hands of the State.
7. Extension of factories and instruments of production owned by the State; the bringing into cultivation of waste-lands, and the improvement of the soil generally in accordance with a common plan.
8. Equal liability of all to labour. Establishment of industrial armies, especially for agriculture.
9. Combination of agriculture with manufacturing industries; gradual abolition of the distinction between town and country, by a more equable distribution of the population over the country.

10. Free education for all children in public schools. Abolition of children's factory labour in its present form. Combination of education with industrial production, &c., &c.

In place of the old bourgeois society, with its classes and class antagonisms, we shall have an association, in which the free development of each is the condition for the free development of all.

I'm not sure what that last paragraph means, Richard thought, b*ut I know that Marx's ten-point Communist Party platform reads like the platform for the Democratic Party, or the current Republican Party, for that matter. They're the same now, anyway. The destruction of property rights, progressive taxes, central banks, unions, equality, public education. We're living in a communist state run by a single Party with two branches—Democrats and Republicans.*

Richard posted his two lists on the wall over his desk. He carefully put his weapons away and drove his Chevy to one of the local coffee shops where he went to read the papers every morning.

In the past, when Richard read the news, his blood boiled and he got into arguments with almost anyone. Last week, after reading that the local school board had accepted a new middle-school class intended to introduce students to the realities of high school, he had confronted the high-school girl working in the coffee shop.

"Did you need to be introduced to high school?" he demanded.

"I'm already in high school," she said.

"I know," he said. "Did you need a course in middle school telling you what to expect when you started high school?"

"No," she said. "Why?"

"Well, the local communist school board thinks we should pay taxes so that someone can get paid to run a course that tells kids what high school is like," he said. "No wonder our taxes are so high. And if that's what they think education is, no wonder our test scores are slipping. I bet you could tell all sorts of stories about what they're doing in our overpriced public schools."

"I'm not sure," the sixteen-year old, blonde, high school girl said. "But I better wait on the other customers."

"That's what I mean," he said. "Kids don't know anything any more."

Today was different. Today, Richard had a mission. He was looking for his first adventure. He was looking through the papers to find his first socialist idea to slay.

That is when Richard Green began writing letters to the local newspaper, the local school board, and all the town officials, from the mayor to the City Clerk. Three years later, the city decided to send its NOTICE to Richard Green.

NOTE: We have been told that this little piece of fiction does not sit well with political conservatives, some of whom have called it an attack on the principles of free markets. They say this is not what they mean when they argue that they can spend their money better than government can. Regardless of which side of the political debate you are on, there is a time in every person's life when he or she should have an opportunity to examine his or her beliefs under the bright light of knowledge.

Before going on, each student should write a short, or lengthy, paper that supports either Richard Green or the Town of River Flats.

If you think you are a conservative, explain how the story distorts what conservatives do mean. If you think you are a liberal, explain why the story correctly exposes the fallacy of the "People can spend their money better than government can" doctrine.

INDIVIDUAL MARKETS

1. Believing is Seeing

1. "I wouldn't have seen it if I didn't believe it."

One of the most astute observations ever made is Yogi Berra's statement, "I wouldn't have seen it if I didn't believe it."

We see what we believe.

If we believe something to be true, we see all sorts of evidence to support that "fact." If we believe something to be false, we see all sorts of evidence to support *that* fact.

If you believe that environmental regulations hurt the economy, you will see more than enough evidence, whether it is quotes from intellectuals or "statistical proof," to claim that environmental regulations do, in fact, hurt the economy.

If you do not believe that environmental regulations hurt the economy, you will see more than enough evidence, whether it is quotes from intellectuals or "statistical proof," to claim that environmental regulations do not, in fact, hurt the economy.

The question is: If two people have the same information and knowledge, how can they reach absolutely opposing conclusions? Because, as Yogi Berra pointed out, we see what we believe.

The bigger question is: Why do we believe what we believe? In many cases, it is not because of facts or truth; it is because we form beliefs that fit our own selfish interests or prejudices.

If you are a Republican, why are you a Republican?

If you are a Democrat, why are you a Democrat?

The principles at the core of this book are logic and common sense. Therefore, anyone who does not like any or all of the conclusions it presents should show why they are illogical or do not make sense, either because of what we know about the real world or because the argument used to reach a particular conclusion is fallacious. That is what education is about.

Or, as Alfred North Whitehead, the British mathematician and philosopher, more eloquently wrote in 1918, "Education is the acquisition of the art of the utilization of knowledge." Whitehead believed that education should be functional; that education means acquiring not just knowledge, but the ability to use that knowledge. Of course, a century later, Whitehead's ideas still remain outside the goals of most educational institutions.

As such, if someone's sole reason for disagreeing with conclusions based on knowledge and facts is that the conclusions contradict the political dogma he or she believes in, and he or she is unwilling to set that dogma aside in order to look at the world rationally, that is his or her free choice.

Why did we include such a long passage from *The Republic* when the common wisdom is that Plato's contribution to modern, free-market economics is negligible, either because he lived in and wrote about a small, pre-industrialized world or because some consider him to be a "communist?"

The answer is that the passage from *The Republic* "proves" the substance of Yogi Berra's wisdom. It lets us examine how Plato, and then later economic writers using virtually the same descriptions of specialization and markets, reached different conclusions as each saw what he or she believed.

In his 2007 book, *The Curtain*, Czech writer Milan Kundera writes this about the Spanish writer Cervantes, who, when he wrote *Don Quixote*, gave the world its first true novel: "It is by tearing through the curtain of pre-interpretation that Cervantes set the new art going; his destructive act echoes and extends to every novel worthy of the name; it is the identifying sign of the art of the novel."[17]

Whether it is Yogi Berra saying, " I wouldn't have seen it if I didn't believe it," or Milan Kundera writing about "…tearing through the curtain of pre-interpretation…" it is necessary to, if not destroy, at least pull the curtain back on our pre-interpretations or beliefs in order to discover how to go forward, not just with novels, but with politics and economics.

---

[17] *The Curtain, An Essay In Seven Parts*, Milan Kundera. Translated by Linda Asher. Harper Collins.

2. Given what Plato believed, what did he see?

What did Plato believe, and what did he see?

Plato did not trust giving political power to the people; in fact, he thought that government officials should earn a barely sustainable living so that no one would seek public office for its monetary rewards. His idea was that if politicians had to live in virtual poverty, only those with great ideals and a great sense of public service would enter into such a profession.[18]

Plato lived in a slave State, where slaves were held in low regard; and he believed that merchants were pretty much on the same level as slaves.

Plato was an isolationist who believed in the class society that existed and the need to keep political power in the hands of those who knew how to dispense Justice.

Plato believed that regular people were too greedy and too easily tricked, so that, if given a chance, they would let their greed destroy the orderly and relatively equal income society in which he believed.

Given such beliefs, it is easy to look at *The Republic* as Plato's opportunity to see what he believed. In *The Republic*, Plato uses a dialogue with himself to see how his beliefs are supported by logic. Of course, there is not always a lot of logic involved when you are debating or examining an issue with yourself, because you can have one character say whatever you want and then have another character agree that it must be so. Therefore, it is up to the reader to decide which descriptions or conclusions might be accepted and which should be rejected. As a rule, Plato's descriptions of markets are good; but some of his major conclusions are seen as little more than the result of manipulating his dialogues so that the reader will also see what he believes.

Regardless of the weakness of some of Plato's conclusions, it is worth looking more closely at the previous passage to see how much of current economic thinking is covered in a few pages from *The Republic*, beginning with his concept of a State.

A State, I said, arises, as I conceive, out of the needs of mankind; no one is self-sufficing, but all of us have many wants.

This is a simple, functional description of a State, based not on dogma or doctrine, but on the idea that the State serves a purpose, which is to help meet the needs of mankind. It is an idea that, in many cases, has been replaced with

---

[18] This is an idea that might be worth discussing.

self-serving dogma.

Many persons are needed to supply our wants. When they gather together, we term it a State.

Plato's interaction of markets and the State is, again, a functional marriage, not a way to impose values on others.

And they exchange with one another, and one gives, and another receives, under the idea that the exchange will be for their good.

This sentence is the precursor to all subsequent "insights" into how markets work, especially the idea that individuals and companies buy and sell things to benefit themselves. Although Adam Smith is often given credit for explaining how independent actions based on self-interest add to the common good, Plato covered the concept fully as he explained how the greedy actions of individuals end up providing necessities for others. Plato's necessities are food, dwelling, and clothing.

And now let us see how our city will be able to supply this great demand: We may suppose that one man is a husbandman, another a builder, some one else a weaver; shall we add to them a shoemaker, or perhaps some other purveyor to our bodily wants?

The beginning of Plato's answer is the recognition of how the interaction of supply and demand brings wants to markets.

And how will they proceed? Will each bring the result of his labours into a common stock? --the individual husbandman, for example, producing for four, and labouring four times as long and as much as he need in the provision of food with which he supplies others as well as himself; or will he have nothing to do with others and not be at the trouble of producing for them, but provide for himself alone a fourth of the food in a fourth of the time, and in the remaining three-fourths of his time be employed in making a house or a coat or a pair of shoes, having no partnership with others, but supplying himself all his own wants?

Should we be self-sufficient, or should we specialize? That is the question. Plato's answer is:

Adeimantus thought that he should aim at producing food only and not at producing everything.

Why? Because, according to Plato,

...we are not all alike; there are diversities of natures among us which are adapted to different occupations.

Adam Smith, writing 2,000 years later, at the beginning of the Industrial

Revolution, realized that Plato's idea of specialization applied not only to individual professions, based on the fact that different people have different skills or aptitudes, but that individuals working in factories can specialize, with each performing a single part of the production process, as they did in his pin factory.

The result of the specialization described by Smith, and all later economists, is exactly the same as that described by Plato.

And will you have a work better done when the workman has many occupations, or when he has only one?

When he has only one.

The combination of specialization and supply and demand based on self-interest leads to more stuff for the nation, although Plato seems to see more of the stuff going to the workers while Smith sees the workers remaining very poor.

So far, the only difference between current economic thought and Plato's discussion is that today's economic textbooks claim that we do not "need" anything. More precisely, they argue that we do not need any particular thing, because there are always substitutes. Plato says we need food. Current textbooks say that we do not buy *food*; we buy individual food items, because there is no way to buy *food* or *meat* or *vegetables*; there is only a way to buy a particular cut of beef, or chicken, or pork, or a type or brand of carrots or whatever. The difference is partly semantics and partly real. We do need food, as Plato says, but we do not need Cheerios, because there are numerous substitutes for Cheerios. That is the semantic part. The real part is that we do, in fact, need food. The difference is the difference between supply and demand, and the difference between having an income that is sufficient to let us choose what we are willing and able to buy, given all the choices, and not having such an income. The modern idea that we do not need any particular thing applies to the demand facing a seller, because there are always substitutes to whatever it is the seller is selling. However, regardless of how many word games someone wants to play, he or she does, in fact, need food. And it a logical error to assume that everyone has the income to buy what he or she "needs." Although that may seem to be an obvious, but not particularly important fact, it is crucial to understanding what markets actually do and do not do in the real world.

The next two pages of Plato's dialogue have yet to be matched in current textbooks. Textbooks, in their desire to focus on the theoretical aspects of economics, ignore the true beauty and functionality of markets. In just a few paragraphs, beginning with his descriptions of specialization and supply and demand, Plato describes the creation of an entire economy. After recognizing that specialization causes a disconnect between producers and buyers, he shows how that disconnect is solved by the creation of wholesalers and retailers and many other professions or crafts. Less than two pages later, we have an entire economy.

...we must infer that all things are produced more plentifully and easily and of a better quality when one man does one thing which is natural to him and does it at the right time, and leaves other things.

Then more than four citizens will be required; for the husbandman will not make his own plough or mattock, or other implements of agriculture, if they are to be good for anything. Neither will the builder make his tools--and he too needs many; and in like manner the weaver and shoemaker.

Then carpenters, and smiths, and many other artisans, will be sharers in our little State, which is already beginning to grow?

Yet even if we add neatherds, shepherds, and other herdsmen, in order that our husbandmen may have oxen to plough with, and builders as well as husbandmen may have draught cattle, and curriers and weavers, fleeces and hides--still our State will not be very large.

Then, again, there is the situation of the city--to find a place where nothing need be imported is well-nigh impossible.

Then there must be another class of citizens who will bring the required supply from another city?

But if the trader goes empty-handed, having nothing which they require who would supply his need, he will come back empty-handed.

And therefore what they produce at home must be not only enough for themselves, but such both in quantity and quality as to accommodate those from whom their wants are supplied.

Then more husbandmen and more artisans will be required?

Not to mention the importers and exporters, who are called merchants?

Then we shall want merchants?

And if merchandise is to be carried over the sea, skilful sailors will also be needed, and in considerable numbers?

Then, again, within the city, how will they exchange their productions? To secure such an exchange was, as you will remember, one of our principal objects when we formed them into a society and constituted a State.

Clearly they will buy and sell.

Then they will need a market-place, and a money-token for purposes of exchange.

Suppose now that a husbandman, or an artisan, brings some production to market, and he comes at a time when there is no one to exchange with him, is he to leave his calling and sit idle in the market-place?

Not at all; he will find people there who, seeing the want, undertake the office of salesmen. In well-ordered States they are commonly those who are the weakest in bodily strength, and therefore of little use for any other purpose; their duty is to be in the market, and to give money in exchange for goods to those who desire to sell and to take money from those who desire to buy.

This want, then, creates a class of retail-traders in our State. Is not 'retailer' the term which is applied to those who sit in the market-place engaged in buying and selling, while those who wander from one city to another are called merchants?

And on and on.

It is all here, which is why this lengthy passage has been repeated from its earlier place in this book.

Given the implied availability of resources, such as land, labor, and capital, Plato moves from individual specialization, which allows people to create things that can be traded for other things in order to get what each needs, and even more than what is needed, to the creation of supply and demand based on self-interest. Then it all unfolds beautifully as numerous markets and jobs and professions emerge in the orderly creation of a complete economy.

There is no better description of how specialization successfully fulfills society's basic needs, and of how the drive to fulfill those needs leads to the development of markets, jobs, and professions that generate an efficient use of society's resources and to the installation of a government that helps it all work for the benefit of those involved.

Why would someone, such as a retailer, buy shoes from a specialized shoemaker? To make a profit by reselling the shoes for more than he paid for them. Does the shoemaker lose by selling his shoes at less than the retail price? No. The shoemaker, given the opportunity to sell his shoes to a "middleman," can concentrate on making shoes without being interrupted by the need to market and sell what he produces. Therefore, the shoemaker is made wealthier by the retailer who buys and holds (as inventories) his shoes until someone comes along who is willing and able to buy them.

What about the eventual buyer of the shoes? He or she also benefits from the existence of the specialized shoemaker and the retailer, because he or she can not only purchase shoes instead of making them, the shoes can be purchased at a time that is convenient, instead of having to arrange a meeting with the shoemaker.

Why does each person choose to do what he or she does? To benefit himself or herself.

Who gains? Everyone, including the State as a whole.

Plato even included money in his economy. Why? Because money is the key to truly efficient markets. Without money, markets require barter, which means that anyone who wants a particular thing has to find someone else who has that thing and who is willing to trade that thing for something else. Of course, if the person who is willing to trade the thing that is wanted does not want anything the other person is willing to trade to get that thing, then it is necessary to find out what that person does want and to then find a way to trade with someone else who has that thing and then go back to make the desired trade. Sometimes, that might be accomplished in one step. Sometimes, it might take numerous intermediate trades before getting back to the original trade. All of which is a great waste of resources, compared to using money to buy and sell things. In other words, the reality of barter is as confusing and time consuming as explaining how it works.

Not only did Plato understand the importance of money, he called it "money-token," meaning that he understood money in its modern form, as opposed to money made from precious metals or money with some form of precious-metal backing. Although some continue to believe that money is "good" only if it is made from or backed by precious metals, the truth is that whether money is "fiat money," meaning that there is nothing of value behind it, or backed by precious metals, its real value is always dependent on the monetary authority that creates or controls it—whether that is a government, a central bank, or an individual bank, each of which has been the case, at one time or another, in the U.S.

So far, so good. Not only good, but as good as it gets.

And then Plato turns his attention to seeing what he believes. What he believes is that his carefully described market economy can not sustain itself, a view shared by some who followed, such as Karl Marx, and opposed by others, such as Adam Smith and most modern economists. Here, after summarizing the working of his basic-needs market economy, is where Plato begins to set up his dire predictions.

But if you wish also to see a State at fever heat, I have no objection. For I suspect that many will not be satisfied with the simpler way. They will be for adding sofas, and tables, and other furniture; also dainties, and perfumes, and incense, and courtesans, and cakes, all these not of one sort only, but in every variety; we must go beyond the necessaries of which I was at first speaking, such as houses, and clothes, and shoes: the arts of the painter and the embroiderer will have to be set in motion, and gold and ivory and all sorts of materials must be procured.

A couple thousand years later, as markets were growing in importance, Adam Smith took Plato's explanation of a market economy, added a number of real-world examples, such as a pin factory, and tackled two crucial questions raised by Plato's conclusion: Will a market economy based on the self-interest of its members be stable, or will it collapse under the weight of unbridled greed? Will such greed increase or decrease the nation's wealth over time? Smith's conclusions were: The self-interest behind the forces of supply and demand causes markets to be inherently stable. Greed increases the wealth of the nation.

It was those conclusions, which seemed to contradict Plato's dark ending, that caused *The Wealth of Nations* to be called the first defense of free markets.

However, Plato already understood exactly how the self-interest or greed that generates supply and demand in individual markets creates stable markets, and how that same self-interest increases the wealth of the nation. Therefore, Smith did not add much to Plato's description of how specialization and markets create wealth, jobs, professions, and a lot of stuff. The greed that gives us stable markets is not the greed that concerned Plato. The greed that concerned Plato is the greed that concerned a number of later economists, such as Thorsten Veblen, who, in his 1899 book, *The Theory of the Leisure Class*, gave us the descriptive, and intentionally negative, term *conspicuous consumption*. It is also the greed that Einstein referred to in the quote at the beginning of this book.

As such, a legitimate question for discussion is: Did Adam Smith, who was not stupid, conclude that his free-market economy would be different from Plato's by assuming away the wealth that led to Plato's conclusions? In other words, how important was it to Adam Smith to assume that the vast majority of people would continue to live in abject poverty? Because, if it is assumed that the people will remain poor, without accumulating *art and gold and ivory and all sorts of materials*, would that not negate the following prediction that comes from Plato's previous conclusion about all the things people will want to acquire?

Then we must enlarge our borders; for the original healthy State is no longer sufficient. Now will the city have to fill and swell with a multitude of callings which are not required by any natural want; such as the whole tribe of hunters and actors, of whom one large class have to do with forms and colours; another will be the votaries of music--poets and their attendant train of rhapsodists, players, dancers, contractors; also makers of diverse kinds of articles, including women's dresses. And we shall want more servants. Will not tutors be also in request, and nurses wet and dry, tirewomen and barbers, as well as confectioners and cooks; and swineherds, too, who were not needed and therefore had no place in the former edition of our State, but are needed now? They must not be forgotten: and there will be animals of many other kinds, if people eat them.

And living in this way we shall have much greater need of physicians than before?

And the country which was enough to support the original inhabitants will be too small now, and not enough?

Then a slice of our neighbours' land will be wanted by us for pasture and tillage, and they will want a slice of ours, if, like ourselves, they exceed the limit of necessity, and give themselves up to the unlimited accumulation of wealth?

And so we shall go to war, Glaucon. Shall we not?

Most certainly, he replied.

And so, what began with great promise ends badly.

At least it ends badly as far as Plato is concerned.

2. A Line in the Sand

Looking back, with the proverbial 20/20 hindsight, should we conclude that Plato's belief in a bad end to free markets was an absurd, unjustified prediction, or that Plato understood, better than Adam Smith did 2,000 years later, where uncontrolled greed, coupled with growing wealth, might lead society?

What is the current view of Plato's *unlimited accumulation of wealth*?

Or of Thorsten Veblen's *conspicuous consumption*?

Or of Albert Einstein's *trite objects of human efforts—possessions, outward success, luxury*—that, to Einstein, seemed contemptible?

Or of Karl Marx's call for government production and distribution to replace virtually all private markets?

Or of Ludwig von Mises' belief that whatever happens in his version of free markets is best, both for individuals and the nation?

Or of Paul Samuelson and Milton Friedman arguing that there is a functional difference between laissez faire and perfect competition, and that the nation may benefit if government corrects the misallocation of resources caused by market failures and externalities?

These are some of the issues or questions that must be addressed by any society that wants to call itself "free."

1. The easy questions.

Understanding how markets work is not nearly as difficult as understanding their limitations. In most cases, it is also not as important. We have known how markets work for more than 2,300 years, but we still argue over the big-issue results. And we continue to do unwise things by failing to use what we know. We are good at explaining and predicting the results of changes in individual markets. We are not as good at explaining and predicting the overall implications of allowing political doctrine to direct economic decisions and policies.

In an hour or two, virtually anyone can learn how to use the concepts of supply and demand to explain and predict how virtually any change will affect the equilibrium price and quantity in virtually any market. It is not a difficult task, especially when, in most cases, the answer requires only the ability to determine the direction of change of price and quantity, not exact values.

If, for example, a freeze destroys a large part of the Florida orange crop, what will happen to the equilibrium price and quantity of oranges in the market? If your answer is that you think the quantity will decrease and the price will increase, you just saved yourself the hour or two someone might use to show you how to draw all sorts of supply and demand diagrams.

You do not need a diagram to answer the above question. Or to answer a related question: What happens to the equilibrium price and quantity of apples if a Florida freeze causes the quantity of oranges to decrease and the price of oranges to increase? If oranges and apples are *substitute products* for many people, then a higher price of oranges will cause some people to substitute some apples for some oranges, meaning they will buy more apples and fewer oranges, which, given the supply of apples, will cause the equilibrium quantity and price of apples to increase.

Questions about products that are used together, things economists call *complimentary products*, are just as easy to answer. If the price of gasoline increases, what happens to the equilibrium price and quantity of tires? If higher gas prices cause some people to drive less, their tires will last longer (in time, not miles). Therefore, the demand for tires will decrease, causing the quantity and price of tires to fall.

These are the kinds of questions economists, and even non-economists, are good at answering.

2. The difficult questions.

The questions that are difficult to answer are not about stable markets or equilibrium prices and quantities, but about what society thinks is good or bad about the observed or predicted equilibrium in a particular market and in the economy as a whole.

That is what Plato addressed. After describing what was good about a free market economy, he then turned to what was bad, which was his belief that unbridled greed would bring it all down in wars that, because of the same specialization that created so much wealth, cannot be won. Whether or not you agree with Plato's view that free markets will not work, because wealth and greed will eventually lead to aggression and, most likely, disaster, it is necessary to understand the importance of asking questions about what is good and what is bad.

That is why Adam Smith and other 18th and 19th century economists were concerned about the *value* of a thing. Smith had no trouble observing that diamonds cost more than water, or that changes affecting the supply and/or demand for either would affect its market price. But he wondered if there might not be something else to consider about diamonds versus water, or about needs versus conspicuous consumption. Of course, as later economists pointed out, the solution to the diamond-water paradox is simply to be specific about measurement. A cup of diamonds might sell for more than a cup of water, but it makes no sense to compare the price of a cup of diamonds with the price of a cup of water. The truth is, for any given diamond, there is a quantity of water that sells for more. Unfortunately, when economists dismissed Smith's diamond-water paradox, by explaining the measurement issue and by pointing out that it is price, not value, that matters when trying to understand markets, they also stopped thinking about the big idea of good and bad. In fact, they decided that economics has nothing to say about some ill-defined concept of what is good and what is bad. As such, they decided that economics would, from then on, focus on the ideas of economic efficiency and the wealth of the nation.

3. The role of government.

One of the big-idea political questions that continues to divide people is the role of government in a free society. On one extreme are those who believe that totally free markets (laissez faire) are best. On the other extreme are those who believe that free markets lead to bad results and that government should control virtually everything (communists). In the middle are those who believe that individuals, the overall economy, and society are best served by free markets complemented by government control, production, and regulation.

Therefore, the previous discussion is not intended to be either a "short history" of economic thought or a digested philosophy of economics. Its purpose is to show that throughout history, people who are not stupid have had conflicting views regarding free markets and government interference. It is not economics with a political bias. It is political economics.

Although the politics of economics is clear to some, for others, economic knowledge is happily replaced by political dogma. As such, whether it is Plato thinking that the people cannot be trusted with free markets or Ludwig von Mises arguing that government cannot be trusted at all, economic ideas have too often been co-opted to serve one political faction or another.

For many years, the ongoing political debate in democracies (or democratic republics) has been between those who believe government is evil and those who believe government is good. A rational person can easily find examples of each—examples of government being very bad and examples of government being very good, as well as examples of free markets being very good and very bad. A truly rational person would use such examples, along with all available knowledge, to look for ways to eliminate the bad and encourage the good.

A not-so-rational person, especially someone who puts political doctrine ahead of knowledge, will use even one or two examples of bad government to justify throwing in with the Mises laissez faire dogma or one or two examples of bad private markets to justify throwing in with Marx's communist doctrine.

Whatever the Age of Enlightenment may have accomplished, it seems we are still bogged down by laziness, prejudice, cowardice, and allowing others to do our thinking for us. Regardless of what Kant wrote more than two hundred years ago, we continue to let dogma, not reason, control our government and our economy.

One way to bring reason to the liberal versus conservative political squabble is to replace dogma with economic logic. We can do that by carefully examining the political versus the economic view of who should provide goods and services—private markets or government—and how little or how much government regulation is good for individuals and the economy as a whole.

On the following page is a short list of things someone said he uses or buys or deals with every day. Some are things he said he might like to have around, even if he doesn't use them himself. Some are things he said he does not like, or thinks are bad for individuals or society (such as heroin), but which exist anyway.

He said he spent about a minute making the list, thinking about what he sees or uses or thinks about after waking up in the morning.

A LINE IN THE SAND

THINGS WE USE, BUY, OR HAVE AROUND

Dux Bed
Cotton sheets
Ralph Lauren down comforter
Blankets
Sony clock radio
News on Public Radio
National defense
Air to breathe
Safe tap water
Hot water
City sewer
Pants, Shirt
Gap underwear
Abercrombie and Fitch sweater
Mephisto walking shoes
Bottled water
Stove
Sink
Pots and pans from Target
Bowls
Hot cereal
Whole-wheat toast
Orange juice
Crystal sugar
Silverware
Sidewalk
Roads
Freeway
Books
Parker 51 fountain pen and Parker bottled ink
Retirement program
High school
Drug addict (seen on television)
Health care
Automobile
Air pollution
Stoplights
Stop signs
Road signs
Parking lot
MacBook
Prescription drugs.

4. Who provides the things we use, buy, or have around?

The above list is obviously far from complete. A complete list would be pretty long. To get a feel for how many things you deal with every day, you should make your own list. Take as much time as you want. Use as many pieces of paper as you want.

But, for everything you write down, as well as for the items on our short list, identify who provides it.

If it is provided by private markets, put a P after it.[19]

If it is provided by government, put a G after it.

If it is provided by nature, put an N after it.

Examples of things provided by private markets are the things we buy and sell every day.

Examples of things provided by government are national defense and roads. In most cases we pay for government goods and services with taxes; sometimes we pay an additional "use fee," such as admission to a national park.

Examples of things provided by nature are natural resources, however defined. Air, sun, wind, water, fish, birds, oil, etc. Some are processed and used by consumers or as inputs to production, such as when oil is refined into gasoline or iron ore is processed into steel and then into cars, or gold is processed into coins, or jewelry, or gold bars. Some are used directly, such as the air we breathe.

If you spend any time at all on this project, you will quickly have a very long list.

Although the list on the previous page contains both brand name products, such as a Dux bed, and markets, such as "automobile," instead of a specific car, such as a particular Lexus model with a particular list of options, someone might argue that because there are substitutes for everything, meaning that we do not "need" any particular thing, the list should have only individual items, not markets. Just as we cannot buy "food," we cannot buy "cold cereal." Therefore, shouldn't the list include Old Fashioned Quaker Oatmeal instead of hot cereal? The answer depends on the question being asked and who is asking it.

It may be accurate to say that no one can buy a "car"—that he or she can only buy a particular BMW model, for example. Even so, economists generally talk about markets, where each market is made up of many individual products

---

[19] Although we could use the term "free market," to follow convention, we are using the more accurate term, "private market."

or brands. Although we can only buy or sell particular items, such as a J. Crew cotton shirt, much of the knowledge economists seek is found by examining markets, such as the market for shirts, not individual products.[20]

That is why Plato used markets, such as food, dwelling, and clothing (things with no acceptable substitutes), when he created an argument about "needs," but when he wanted to show the danger of excessive consumption, he used specific things, such as gold, ivory, etc. (things that are trivial, because they are not "needed" and because each has substitutes). It is also why economic discussions about national defense can either be about total spending or about a particular model of tank; why discussions about money spent on roads can be about a total annual budget or about the benefits and costs of building a particular road; and why some questions are about the automobile industry and some are about Porsches.

If you work as an economist or a psychologist for GM, you will probably work in one particular division—Chevrolet, Cadillac, Buick etc.—because GM has to make decisions for each brand, each model, each option, each color, and so on, including pricing and financing plans. If you work in the Buick division, there are a lot of questions and answers that apply specifically to Buick. However, some of the most important questions can only be answered by understanding the overall market for automobiles and of Buick's position in the automobile market, or the market for "family cars," or whatever classification makes sense, given the question being asked.

The same is true for an individual consumer trying to buy a "car." He or she has to look at individual cars and options, because he or she can only buy an individual car. However, there are market factors that may be more important, or, at least, cannot be ignored, when making a decision as to which exact make and model to purchase. Gas prices can be a factor in deciding which models to look at. Interest rates may affect the decision to buy or not to buy at all.

Therefore, although the differences between particular choices are important to the economist or psychologist working for GM (in the Buick division) and to the consumer trying to buy a car, economics is different from disciplines such as psychology that work more with individuals. Economics works with markets and national issues. As such, economists do not claim to be

---

[20] "Market" is a vague concept that can best be defined as a category of goods or services that has both sellers and buyers—supply and demand. It is not a physical location, but an abstract concept. There is a market for automobiles. There is also an automobile dealership, where you can purchase a particular car.

able to make explanations or predictions regarding the actions or reactions of a given individual. A psychologist might be able to tell GM which colors or options it should offer on Buicks in order to help sales. An economist is more likely to look at the impact on sales of Buick's price relative to other market prices. Economists also accept the fact that an individual may do something economists (or psychologists) consider irrational, knowing that the behavior of a few "irrational" individuals does not affect the ability to explain and predict the results of changes in any market.

5. The fuzzy line.

Although you may have a mixture of Ps, Gs, and Ns on your list, you probably felt that something was wrong every time you wrote down a P, or a G, or an N. If so, it is probably because you already know that such designations are not really accurate.

In the first place, if you think of markets, rather than brand name products, you know that some things are provided by both private markets and government. Examples are education and mail delivery. We have both public and private schools, and public and private mail delivery (the Post Office, FedEx, UPS, etc.).

In the second place there is virtually nothing that we buy, use, or even know about, that does not have inputs from private markets, government, and nature. If you have city water, the water that comes out of your faucet comes from nature, is treated and stored by government, flows through government water pipes and then through the water pipes in your house before it comes out of your faucet. Your faucet was manufactured by a private company, using a number of other natural resources, and it was probably installed by a union plumber working for a general contractor, each of whom uses trucks and tools purchased by private manufacturers, and each of whom works under government regulations, whether they are fair trade practices or the right to join a union. Such a description could go on for pages.

The same is true for the water that runs out of your drain. It goes from your privately produced and installed sink, through your privately owned and installed pipes, into a city sewer, into a city sewage treatment facility, and then back into nature.

National defense is no different. Although it is easy to say that national defense is provided by government and paid for with taxes, military equipment is provided by private markets, and the production of each piece of equipment, as well as every action of the military, interacts with nature.

Therefore, to be accurate, each item on the list should be followed by a P, a G, and an N. But, if that is true, what is the point of the list?

The point of the list is to make it clear that people with strongly held political ideologies like to distinguish between private markets and government production and interference.

Conservatives believe that private markets should be left alone and that government should not provide anything other than protection of private property, especially not social benefits, such as welfare or Social Security or public schools. Conservatives also believe there is too much government regulation, especially environmental regulation.

Liberals argue that government can provide many things, including social programs or services that are good for the country. Liberals also believe it is not right that producers and consumers can use the air people breathe as a place to freely dump their toxic waste.

Which brings us back to the list. The point of the list is to make it clear that there is virtually nothing you can buy or use that is not the result of an interaction of nature, private production, and government regulation or production. Therefore, the real issue is not private markets versus government. The real issue is how to determine the mixture of private production, government production, government regulation, and nature that can maximize the wealth or well being of the nation while protecting an individual's right to life, liberty, and the pursuit of happiness.

The argument, heard on right-wing radio day after day, is that government is interfering in almost everything we do. That is true. It is virtually impossible to find even a single market in any advanced, industrialized country with absolutely no government regulation. Government has taken on the role of protecting consumers, workers, markets, and the environment from potentially fraudulent or dangerous production and sales practices, whether it is to protect markets from monopoly power, consumers from misleading or false claims about a product's or service's benefits, or the environment from harmful pollution. Therefore, there are no "real" Ps on our list. Some think that is good. Others do not. If you can think of something that is provided with absolutely no government regulation, put a star by it.

The proponents of laissez faire would like to see a lot of stars. They believe that government is producing too many things and interfering in too many private markets; and that government controls and regulations distort what they call "free market" prices. They see laws requiring people to wear seat belts or motorcycle helmets as examples of over-regulation and an attack on individual freedom. Liberals tend to think seat belt and motorcycle helmet laws are good, even if the purpose is simply to protect people from themselves. Conservatives tend to think they are bad. And because not everyone understands the economic argument behind such laws—an argument that dismisses the false individual freedom argument and replaces it with a "not wearing a seat belt or motorcycle helmet may do bad things to others" argument—the result, from a political standpoint, is a fuzzy line between things some think should be regulated and others do not. And it is that fuzzy political line that leads to disputes between those who think government regulation helps individuals and the economy and those who believe government regulation hurts individual freedom and the economy.

There is, however, no fuzzy economic line. If, in the process of doing something to benefit himself or herself, someone does good or bad things to others, economic knowledge says there are reasons to examine the possibility of making individuals and society better off by implementing government regulations that either discourage or encourage the activity; or that lead to a change in how it is performed. That does not mean it is easy to determine the best way to regulate something, or that any particular regulation should not be subject to debate. In order to reduce theft, laws are passed that make stealing illegal. In order to reduce cigarette smoking, taxes are imposed on cigarettes, based on the idea that if cigarettes are made more expensive, fewer will be bought. In order to support agriculture, government subsidies are paid to farmers. In order to improve air quality, emission standards are imposed on automobiles. In order to protect fish populations, quotas are imposed.

In each case, the fact that we know society *may* benefit from some sort of regulation does not mean we always know the "best" form of regulation to use, or if regulation will be a net benefit to society. As such, reason would dictate that each market should be examined to understand the exact regulations that exist today and to determine if individuals and the economy would benefit if there were more or less regulation, or a different kind of regulation. For example, there is a long-standing idea that legalizing drugs would reduce the economic impact of the illegal drug market and create a better alternative to laws that simply make certain drugs illegal. It is not a very good argument, but it has been around a long time.

Government regulations on automobiles include safety requirements, emission controls, mileage numbers, and fair trade practices, which include accurate and truthful pricing and financing information. Although many manufacturers now use the safety features in their cars as selling points, when the federal government first required the industry to add minimum safety features to all automobiles—a result of Ralph Nader's 1965 book, *Unsafe at Any Speed*—manufacturers argued that if they had to add seat belts to every car, they would go bankrupt. Regulations on food items are also based on consumer protection. Look at a box of cereal. Health claims on the box must be cleared with the FDA, all ingredients must be listed in order of their percentage of the total product, and the product's nutritional value must be clear.

The bottom line is that things provided by private markets are done so not because everyone believes private markets do anything perfectly, but because private markets can do some things better than government.

Things provided by government are done so not because anyone believes government does anything perfectly, but because government can do some things better than private markets or because government can do some things private markets cannot do at all.

Things provided by both government and private markets are things that some, but not all, people can do for themselves. They are things the private market can, and does, provide, but not well enough for everyone. Although mail delivery is handled by the Post Office as well as by private firms, such as FedEx and UPS, many laissez faire proponents claim we would be better off by closing the US Post Office and letting private firms handle all mail delivery. Even if it were true that private firms are more efficient than the Post Office at overnight delivery, no one requires overnight delivery for all their mail. Taking away the opportunity to mail letters for less than fifty cents rather than having to pay $18 to $20 would decrease the nation's wealth.

Regardless of the issue, at the center of most political fights is the idea that government-is-bad versus the idea that government-is-good.

Conservatives believe government is providing too many things.

Liberals believe government could be doing even more.

Conservatives believe there is too much government regulation.

Liberals believe that individuals and society would be better off if there were more, not less, government regulation, such as increased controls on pollution that negatively impacts the environment and the economy.

Conservatives would like to "privatize" many things currently provided by government, such as Social Security. Liberals do not like the privatization idea.

Therefore, it is not surprising that there are so many arguments, based on political doctrine, about what government should and should not provide, and what government should and should not regulate.

6. A line in the sand.

Imagine a Boeing 747, filled with a bunch of people, including a few economists, cruising along above the clouds. Inside the cabin, the passengers who are not economists are sitting in either the left or right row of seats. As each entered the plane, each was asked by an attendant if he or she thought government was good or evil. Those who said government is evil were seated on the right side of the plane. Those who said government is good were seated on the left. On the movie screen in front of each seat is a marked-up list like the one you just made. The passengers are in a heated debate, yelling at each other across the aisle about the items on the list.

Outside the cabin, standing at the end of the left wing, is Karl Marx. Outside the cabin, standing at the end of the right wing, is Ludwig von Mises. Each is jumping up and down, waving his arms, trying to get everyone else on the plane to climb out on his wing. They have some success, as some people and some politicians crawl out and join them.

Plato, Adam Smith, Thorsten Veblen, Paul Samuelson, Milton Friedman, and a few other economists are walking up and down the aisle, trying to get the seated passengers to listen to economic logic instead of yelling slogans based on political doctrine.

The economists are trying to convince the passengers that, not only is it dangerous to go out on one wing or the other, but that if everyone climbs out on either the left or right wing, the plane will veer off and crash. They are also trying to make it clear that if everyone moves to either the left or right side of the cabin, the plane might lose its balance and be unable to maintain its course.

The economists are hoping to keep the plane on course and to prevent it from crashing, but the passengers are not interested in what the economists have to say. In an attempt to stop the economists from disturbing the passengers, one flight attendant is trying to get them to sit down in the left row of seats; another is trying to get them to sit on the right. After a while, the economists accept the fact that the passengers are bored by what they have to say, and they give up. Each sits down on either the left side or right side of the plane. As soon as they sit down, they stop talking as economists and join in the political "discussions."

Milton Friedman, when he is in the aisle, offers up ideas about replacing the ineffective and expensive welfare program with what he calls a negative income tax; about having government correct market failures and neighborhood effects; and about school vouchers as a way to improve the quality of education. Each idea requires government action and funding, which means Friedman is not recommending that government stop collecting taxes, providing goods and services, and imposing regulations. He simply wants the tax money spent in more effective ways, sometimes by private companies. He explains that privatization is not the same as private markets. Privatization means giving tax money collected by the government to private, for-profit, companies. Private markets mean that the government is not involved.

Friedman also explains why tax cuts do not help the economy. He offers the same argument he used to dismiss the Kennedy tax cut in the 1960s. It is simple. Tax cuts give people more money to spend; so when they spend part of their extra money, the economy gets a boost. However, tax cuts also create deficits, and when the government sells bonds to cover its deficit, interest rates increase. And when interest rates increase, spending falls. The end result is a wash, unless the Federal Reserve buys a bunch of government bonds with new money it creates, thereby keeping interest rates down but risking inflation.

After sitting down, on the right side of the plane, Friedman tells everyone who will listen, "I have long said, I never met a tax cut I didn't like, though I would go on to say that I like some better than others."

Friedman's newfound love of tax cuts is not the result of bumping his head while sitting down. It is his political opinion, rather than his economic, opinion. He simply likes the idea that tax cuts can be used to cause a reduction in the size of government, which is his personal political objective.

When passengers on the right side of the plane hear Friedman, they think he is supporting the government-is-evil argument.

Passengers on the left side of the plane, based on what Friedman said before he sat down, think he is supporting the government-is-good argument. The same happens with Adam Smith. Passengers on the right think he supports the government-is-evil argument. Passengers on the left think he supports the government-is-good argument. As a result, the yelling and screaming escalate.

And with everyone yelling and jumping around, the plane begins to shake.

That is when the pilot comes out of the cockpit.

The pilot says he has been listening to the racket on the intercom, and that he has had enough. He says that everyone on the plane is going to the same place, and that his job is to make sure they get there, without having their conflicting political doctrines put the plane in danger. He says he has an idea. Here it is:

He says he is going to draw "a line in the sand," and on a piece of paper. The line will separate two distinctly different definitions of the role of government in a free society.

The right side of the line is for conservatives; the left side is for liberals.

He hands out sheets of paper with the "line in the sand" diagram and tells the passengers that it is time to stop yelling and start thinking.

He tells the Conservatives to list, on the right side of the line, things that government is currently providing but which they would like to do without, or things they want less regulated, or things government is doing, but could do better. He explains that items on this side of the line might be chosen because they meet President Ronald Reagan's pronouncement that, "Government can't solve our problems; government is the problem."

He tells the Liberals to list, on the left side of the line, additional things that government should provide, things that should have more regulation, and things government is doing, but could do better. He explains that items on this side of the line might be based on President Abraham Lincoln's statement that government is "to do for the people what needs to be done, but which they cannot, by individual effort, do at all, or do so well, for themselves."

He says no one will be allowed to leave the plane until the lists are completed, compared, and discussed. He says it is time for people to back up their dogma with reason and to talk with each other.

A LINE IN THE SAND

| A list of things liberals would like to add to what government does. | A list of things conservatives would like government to stop doing. |

A LINE IN THE SAND

3. What We Know

When Milton Friedman argues that tax cuts do not help the economy, it is an economic argument using logic and reason. When he says he never met a tax cut he did not like, it is a political argument using dogma instead of logic. Why would the person who first explained that tax cuts do not improve economic performance then say he likes tax cuts? Because tax cuts reduce government revenues, which means they may lead to a reduction in government, which is the political doctrine Friedman chose to believe in.

As Friedman shows, by the contradictions in his published work, conclusions based on political dogma and doctrine can be significantly different from those based on economic facts and reason.

The question is: How can anyone expect economic logic to stand up to political dogma in the real world when someone as smart as Milton Friedman cannot do it in his own life?

First, by using what is known about markets to dismiss or diminish the importance of political dogma.

Second, by focusing on solving problems.

If the focus is switched from political arguments about ideology to solutions for real problems, reason can replace dogma.

The education debate is an example.

The political argument over education is really an argument about government inefficiency versus private market greed. Conservatives favor the privatization of education because they believe government is too big, because they believe "government cannot solve our problems, government is the problem," and because they believe free markets and competition can solve all problems better than government. Liberals argue for the continuation of the current public school system because they do not believe private markets can solve all problems.

Aside from the vague idea that competition and government are either good or bad, the political argument has little to offer in the way of actually improving the quality of education.

The truth is, we have known for a long time that if education is limited only to those who are willing and able to pay for it, the nation's wealth is diminished, because not enough people are educated. Even so, extreme proponents of the laissez faire doctrine believe the nation would be better off by closing all public schools and letting private firms handle all education. Of course, they do not propose that their privatized schools be supported solely by tuition collected from students; their plan is to have the government collect taxes and then give the money to private businesses that want to run schools. In fact, all "privatization" proposals require the government to pay for them with tax money. None are self-supporting. Therefore, none can be called a "private market solution."

In its purest form, the laissez faire political argument for privatizing education is that competition will automatically increase the quality of education. So far, the results of one form of privatization—charter schools—are mixed.

A more "economic," but still government-funded laissez faire idea, is the school voucher program that Milton Friedman wrote about and tried to promote. Although Friedman's argument is that vouchers will generate competition in elementary and secondary education, thereby creating new and better schools while also forcing existing schools to improve, the results of vouchers are also mixed. The reason for the mixed results should not be surprising. Anyone who looks honestly at private markets will see that there are no private, competitive markets that turn out uniformly high quality goods or services. Competitive markets turn out all sorts of items, with a huge variability in quality.

The laissez faire proponents are correct in arguing that a total lack of competition, such as what occurs in communist economies, turns out low quality, sometimes useless, products. But that does not mean competition turns out only the highest-quality products. It does not. So why should anyone expect competition in education to do what it does not do in any other market? The laissez faire side thinks it will at least be better, because it likes to equate public education with communism, and if someone equates a public school with a communist factory, then he or she is likely to believe that replacing a communist factory with any kind of competition will inevitably improve quality. If public schools were run like communist factories, the laissez faire argument would make more sense. But they are not.

The difference between a public school and a communist factory is that the consumers of public education normally have the ability to demand that the schools they pay for meet certain standards or expectations. Unfortunately, the ability to make such demands is related to the income and education of the parents, which is why wealthy communities tend to have good public schools while inner city communities tend to have poor or inadequate schools. It is also why Friedman argued that vouchers, which give inner-city parents and students increased economic power, would force inner city schools to improve, a result that seems to be supported by at least some trial programs.

In terms of the public versus private (or privatized) education debate, it is common knowledge that some of the best schools in the country are public schools. Of course, the top public elementary and high schools are found mainly in suburbs, but not always. Both Minneapolis and St. Paul, Minnesota have city schools that send more graduates to Ivy League colleges than their suburban counterparts. When it gets to the university level, where there is a nationwide competition for students, any top ten or top twenty list of universities includes both private and public schools. The same would most likely be true for the bottom twenty, although logic might lead us to conclude that the bottom twenty might contain more private than public colleges.

Therefore, the expected result of competition in education, or in anything else the laissez faire people want to "privatize," should be that it will look like any other private market—a range of products from barely adequate to excellent. That does not mean the current public education system could not be improved by introducing more competition. Given current results, it is difficult for any reasonable person to defend the education system that exists. However, that does not mean alternatives that are not carefully thought out will automatically improve quality.

Lobbyists who represent corporations that stand to gain if the government hands them money to run schools try to get politicians to move toward privatization plans.

The huge education lobby tries to get politicians to protect the existing education system that benefits those currently employed in the public school industry. Neither side does much to examine the existing system and to look for honest ways to improve it.

Too many conservatives want to privatize education not because they have a good plan that will improve quality, but because the conservative doctrine is that government should be minimized, and privatizing education fits the dogma.

Too many liberals want to prevent the privatization of education not because the current education system is doing such a great job, but because they want to protect the status quo in education.

But if the political debate is replaced by demanding that both sides focus on the problem of improving education, political dogma and self-interest might be replaced with reason. Imagine someone walking into a room with twenty conservatives and twenty liberals and asking, "Who here wants to improve the quality of education?" How many will raise their hand? How many will not? If everyone who does not want to improve education is asked to leave the room, how many will be left? Odds are, there will still be forty people in the room, because virtually everyone wants to improve the quality of education.

Therefore, if someone were able to hold a discussion that does not allow arguments based on political dogma or self-interest, it might be possible for forty people to discuss solutions that could truly improve education.

Whether it is education, or any other problem, given what we know of history, it is difficult to claim that what we believe to be true today will never change in the future. However, that is not an acceptable excuse for failing to use what we know to do the best we can. In terms of this text, that means using what we know to avoid doing too many unwise things.

What do we know today?

We know the earth is not flat.

We know the sun does not revolve around the earth.

We know that President Ronald Reagan said, "Government can't solve the problem; government is the problem."

We know that President Abraham Lincoln said government "is to do for the people what needs to be done, but which they cannot, by individual effort, do at all, or do so well, for themselves."

We know that, just as science is said to be a record of dead religions, facts and reason expose the false basis of political dogma.

For example:

1. Economics does not support the laissez faire doctrine.

The laissez faire dogma of Ludwig von Mises defines away the perfect-competition standard of real economics and replaces it with the premise that real world markets are perfect as long as they are not disrupted by price distortions caused by government regulation or intervention. As such, the laissez faire doctrine accepts the price distortions caused by imperfect markets and by the lack of markets. By claiming that whatever happens in imperfect markets is good, von Mises is led to the utterly false conclusion that policies that allow monopolization and other market abuses to take place and prosper are good for individuals and the nation. Such policies *are* good—for the monopolist and for others who gain by exploiting imperfect markets or the lack of markets. They are not good for the people, the economy, or the nation's wealth.

According to economic thought, competition leads to an efficient allocation or use of resources only if there are no market failures and no externalities (or neighborhood effects).

Market failure occurs when there is imperfect competition, such as when a single firm takes over a market (monopoly), when a few firms take over a market (oligopoly), when firms make deals to restrict output or divide up market share (a cartel), or when a small number of firms, each with a somewhat different product, dominates a market (monopolistic competition). Monopolistic competition means that the products of a few large companies that dominate a market are similar, but can be told apart, such as Coca Cola and Pepsi Cola in the soft drink market, or Ford and Chevrolet in the automobile market. Most U.S. industries fall into the category of monopolistic competition, because virtually every product has its own brand name, which is why advertising is such a large part of the American economy.

Market failure also occurs when the supply of inputs is controlled (monopsony), such as when a labor union restricts the supply of labor.

In each case, market failure leads to a restriction in the quantity sold in order to raise market prices; and, in each case, the result is a reduction in economic efficiency and, therefore, the wealth of the nation.

Externalities exist when someone who is producing or consuming something imposes benefits or costs on others.

Looking at the real world, it is obvious that there are no perfectly competitive markets, because there are no markets that are free of either market failure or externalities.

And, if there are no markets that are free of either market failure or externalities, then real-world private markets cannot allocate resources in a way that maximizes the nation's wealth or well being.

That is why it is logically and factually impossible to support the laissez faire doctrine if the goal is to maximize the nation's wealth and the freedom of individuals.

2. Economics does not support the communist doctrine.

The logical fallacies in the labor theory of value, which is the cornerstone of Karl Marx's argument for capitalism's unavoidable exploitation of workers, dismiss the theoretical foundation of communism.

Historical evidence dismisses the communist claim that total government control of the economy benefits the people.

The fact is: Markets work, even without perfect competition.

Even without perfect competition, consumers, choosing how to spend their money in a way that is best for themselves, create a demand for goods and services, and producers, choosing what to produce, how to produce it, how to sell it, and what price to charge, in order to maximize their own profits, create a supply of goods and services.

As long as consumers are willing and able to buy more at lower prices and less at higher prices, while sellers are willing and able to sell more at higher prices and less at lower prices, the invisible hand of supply and demand pushes markets into a stable equilibrium.

The conditions for a stable equilibrium are clear.

A market is stable if, whenever the market price is above the equilibrium price, sellers try to sell more than consumers are willing and able to buy, thereby creating an excess supply in the market that causes sellers to lower their prices, and whenever the market price is below the equilibrium price, buyers try to buy more than sellers are willing and able to sell, thereby creating an excess demand in the market that causes sellers to raise their prices and sell more.

These price adjustments bring markets into equilibrium, where equilibrium is defined to be a situation where the quantity consumers are willing and able to buy is equal to the quantity sellers are willing and able to sell at the market price. Although standard textbooks discuss the conditions that would lead to unstable markets, so far, no one has found an unstable market in the real world.

Therefore, it is not possible to use either economic logic or facts to support the idea or practice of communism, even if it is known that every market exhibits some form of market failure or externality.

3. Specialization and industrialization create wealth.

Plato's explanation of how specialization increases the wealth or income of individuals still stands. Instead of making everything they need by themselves, people can choose a specialized occupation, such as a pin maker, and then use the money they earn from making and selling pins to buy much more stuff than they could ever make as self-sufficient individuals. Using Adam Smith's example, Plato's pin maker might make as many as 20 pins a day, which, when they are sold, would yield an income that would allow the individual to buy more than he could have if he made everything he wanted or needed, including pins, all by himself.[21]

Adam Smith, who wrote at the time that factories were replacing Plato's small-scale world, explained how industrialized specialization does even more to increase the wealth of the nation. Using Smith's numbers, if Plato's individual pin makers are moved into factories where each specializes in making only one part of a pin, the nation gets 48,000 pins a day from ten workers, instead of 200. The result is a huge increase in the nation's wealth.

Of course, regardless of the monetary benefits of specialization, some people, believing they will be happier with less stuff and less stress, might prefer a self-sufficient lifestyle, or as close to self-sufficiency as possible, or even Plato's version of specialization, to a life spent working in a pin factory. Most, however, will choose more stuff and what is, in most cases, an easier way to obtain it.

As such, neither logic nor historical evidence is on Marx's side.

4. Specialization is the best argument for foreign trade.

The specialization idea, whether it is Plato's or Smith's, also describes the benefits of free trade. Of course, "trade" is a misleading term, because nations do not trade stuff for stuff. In the real world, we make stuff that we sell to people in other nations, and people in other nations make stuff that they sell to us (and to others). And, just as it is not difficult to compare the quantity and quality of stuff we can obtain by working as totally self-sufficient farmers with what we can buy with money earned from a job, it is easy to compare the quantity and

---

[21] In his discussion, Plato assumes there are some things that we need and some things that we simply want.

quality of stuff a nation can have, with and without the opportunity to buy and sell in international markets.

Unfortunately, all the old (but still used) free trade theories are actually based on trading stuff for stuff, not on the reality of buying and selling stuff. Therefore, the fact that someone may benefit from buying stuff made in other countries does not mean that people in other countries will want to buy the stuff he or she makes. If you can buy a television set for less money from a foreign producer than a domestic producer, you are better off—as a consumer. You get a TV set, and you have money left over that you can either save or spend on other things. On the other hand, your country will then lose jobs to foreign TV makers. And, in order for your country to come out ahead, it needs new jobs to replace the lost jobs. Of course, there is no guarantee that will happen, because the money you save on a TV set might be spent on other things made in your country, or on other things made in other countries. There is no question that consumers benefit from foreign commerce; but if consumers are also workers, it is possible that the benefits of cheap imports are more than offset by a decline in incomes.

The assumption that the money saved on imported TV sets will automatically be spent in a way that creates new jobs to replace the lost jobs is the major weakness in all "free-trade" theories. As soon as it is understood that the political arguments for free trade have nothing to do with reality, it is then easy to understand how Japan and then China became economic miracles by promoting exports while restricting imports. It is not magic. It is simply economics.

5. Specialization eliminates some independent craftspeople.

Adam Smith's example of the pin factory shows exactly what specialization does. If the ten workers in his factory can turn out 48,000 pins a day, or 4,800 pins per worker per day, and an independent pin maker, working alone, can make maybe 20 pins a day, the independent pin maker cannot stay in business. Therefore, the independent pin maker may end up working in Adam Smith's pin factory, where he earns wages that keep him "very poor."

Would any society choose to outlaw specialization and factories in order to protect independent pin makers? Probably not. For one thing, instead of having the independent pin maker turning out twenty pins a day, by himself, he can be giving society 4,800 pins a day; and the ten workers can give society 48,000 pins each day instead of 200. For another, the independent pin maker may make more money working in the pin factory than he did working alone, even if he is still poor. Of course, for ten people to switch from being independent pin makers making a total of 200 pins a day to working in a factory making 48,000 pins a day there has to be a demand for 48,000 pins a day.

No one can deny that specialization and industrialization change societies. Some say for the better. Others say for the worse. Some argue that the historical evidence supports the laissez faire doctrine. Others argue that it exposes capitalism's weakness. But because few want to go backwards, political ideology is less important than attempts to make wise decisions that move society forward.

6. Economic efficiency is not an absolute.

The textbook definition of economic efficiency, which says that under certain conditions competition can cause resources to be used where they are valued the most, is also based on a given distribution of income and the existing tastes and preferences of consumers. It does not mean that the goods and services demanded and supplied are what society would like to see bought and sold.

The markets for goods and services that Albert Einstein called the "trite objects of human efforts—possessions, outward success," can, in theory, meet the conditions of economic efficiency.

As such, the concepts of competition and economic efficiency should be seen for what they are—useful textbook definitions—not as a stamp of approval for any particular good or service or any given equilibrium. The definition of economic efficiency includes the often-overlooked assumption that supply and demand represent the true value and cost to society of buying and producing things. But because the demand for something is defined as the quantity buyers are willing and able to buy at various prices, the demand for any particular thing is a function of the existing distribution of income. If incomes are redistributed, then the demand for things from people whose incomes increase will increase while the demand for things from people whose incomes decrease will decrease.

Therefore, economic efficiency is not an absolute; it is a function of the existing distribution of income. A policy that reduces taxes for the middle class and raises taxes for the wealthy will cause the demand for things middle-class people buy to increase and the demand for things wealthy people buy to decrease.

However, for any given distribution of income, whether or not you like it, competitive markets with no market failure or externalities would allocate resources in a way that is economically efficient. But, because John Stuart Mill, in the 1800s, "proved" that it is possible to redistribute incomes without adversely affecting economic efficiency, it is not necessary to accept the claim that the existing distribution is best, or that "leaving it to the market" is a policy that benefits individuals or the nation, whatever "it" is.

7. There is no "inherent good" in a market equilibrium.

A market equilibrium is what it is—a condition where supply equals demand. A market is stable if, when the market price rises above the equilibrium price, an excess supply of stuff causes sellers to lower the price, and if, when the market price falls below the equilibrium price, an excess demand for stuff causes sellers to raise the price.

Thinking there is some "inherent good" associated with a particular equilibrium, beyond the fact that stable markets are better than chaos, runs the thinker into a logical wall. Take the market for cigarettes…Please! An equilibrium in the cigarette market means that, at the existing price, the quantity of cigarettes consumers are willing and able to buy is equal to the quantity sellers are willing and able to sell. Is that good? Or bad? Your answer depends on what you think about cigarettes. If you think they are bad, then there is nothing good about an equilibrium that means a lot of people are buying and smoking cigarettes. If you think they are good, then you might think it is good that a market exists so that people can buy them. Which is why, because we do not all agree on everything, many issues lead to an inevitable interaction of economics and politics. Should cigarettes be outlawed? Or taxed to raise the price?

The laissez faire argument is that government should not pass laws or regulations intended to protect people from themselves. It is, of course, a terrible argument. It is a terrible argument for many reasons. One is that cigarettes, like heroin, are addictive. Therefore, it is legitimate to ask if individual freedom is protected or destroyed by allowing the free sale of cigarettes or heroin on the grounds that everyone has a "Constitutional" right to do whatever he or she wants, even if the addictive aspect of the product affects his or her decision. A second problem with the "freedom" argument is that people who use cigarettes and heroin do, in fact, affect others. A third problem is that some laws intended to protect people from their own stupid actions are based on facts. Without laws requiring children to stay in school until a certain age, many would quit. The same is true for seat-belt laws. Without laws, many people will not use seat belts. Of course, instead of a law requiring the use of seat belts, society could decide that anyone who is in an automobile accident while not wearing a seat belt should not receive medical attention.

4. Eight Market Problems

Although free-market economics does not look favorably on communism, neither does it consider government production or regulation undertaken by democratically elected governments to be a communist activity.

Economists, including Milton Friedman, no longer argue about totally free markets versus communism. Economists know that pure free markets do not exist. They also know that communism is a failed promise.

Instead of debating the good and bad aspects of extreme ideologies, economists focus on solving problems, beginning with the fact that virtually all economies are "mixed," meaning they have both private markets and government production and regulation; and given the fact that no matter what anyone thinks, we will wake up tomorrow with essentially what we have today.

Therefore, solving problems does not mean looking to either communist or laissez faire doctrine for answers; it means looking for ways to move incrementally forward, which requires being able to explain where we are today and to use what we know to solve real problems.

There are two broad categories of economic knowledge: the kind that fills up standard textbooks, which is of use primarily to academic economists, and the kind that can be used to solve the real problems that affect our lives on a daily basis.

Although the typical textbook can be daunting, as well as heavy, the truth is that virtually every real-market issue falls into one of eight categories. Once it is understood that imperfect markets exist, it is easy to explain and predict the consequences of market failure and externalities as well as to come up with possible solutions to the problems they create.

Since virtually all market issues or problems fall into one of the following eight categories, there is not a lot to learn if the objective is to understand how to solve market problems. Not only is there a short list of problem categories, there is also a short list of economic solutions to the problems in each category.

1. The public goods problem.

"Public goods" are things that, when they are provided to one person, are also available to others, whether they pay for them or not.

The most obvious example is national defense. If national defense is provided for one person, it is provided for everyone. No one can be excluded from its benefits, even if they do not pay.

There are other examples where, if something is provided for one person, others, but not necessarily everyone, get to use it as well. Roads, parks, food inspection, a lighthouse, sidewalks, and so on. It is, in truth, a long list.

The problem is that private markets cannot provide such goods at all, or at least not at a level that is best for society. The reason the private market cannot provide such goods is that it is impossible for private sellers or providers to collect payment from everyone who uses them or benefits from them.

Solving the public goods problem.

If there are good things that the private market cannot produce, because when they are provided to one person they are also provided to others, then it might make sense for the government to produce them. But only if doing so adds to the nation's wealth.

In many cases, a technique called benefit-cost analysis can be used to compare the expected benefits to society from a project, such as a dam, with the cost to society of building and maintaining it. Benefit-cost analysis is a procedure that "discounts" future benefits and costs so that the present value of net future benefits can be compared with the initial cost of a project.

In other words, the fact that public goods exist does not mean politicians should be given a blank check so they can spend taxpayers' money without thinking. It does mean, however, that there are legitimate economic reasons for government providing or producing things the private market cannot.

The fictional story beginning on page 53 points out the folly of believing that government is worthless. Or that there is some great, unspecified benefit to be obtained by blindly calling for a reduction in the size of government. Or that government cannot create wealth. Or that people can spend their money better than government can. The truth is, the best bargains people get are the public goods provided by government. People can buy their own SUVs, but they cannot drive very far on the roads they can pay for by themselves.

Even so, it is easy to point out individual examples of government waste. And because government spending is paid for with taxes, legitimate government spending is defined to be spending that provides things that are worth more to the people than the taxes they give up to pay for them.

2. The negative externality problem.

Negative externalities exist when the production or consumption of something does bad things to others.

An example is air pollution caused by driving a car. Driving the car is good for the driver. Lowering the quality of air others breathe is bad for them.

No one owns the air, so there is no market for air quality, which means no one can legally stop someone else from polluting the air they breathe (a negative externality). The result is that those who use *our* air as the least expensive way to dump *their* waste, end up making production or consumption decisions based on distorted prices. If we do not have to pay for the damages we cause to others, those costs are not taken account when we make decisions. And whenever we do not have to pay for something, we may use too much of it, meaning that we may reduce the wellbeing or wealth of the nation by using the air as a place to dump our waste.

Solving the negative externality problem.

If there is no market for air quality, because no one owns the air he or she will be breathing, it is foolish to argue that "The free market can control pollution without government intervention."

If there were a market for air quality, people would be able to buy and sell the right to pollute. But no one can buy and sell something he or she does not own in a market that does not exist. That is why, when markets do not exist, the price system cannot provide an efficient allocation of resources.

In the case of pollution, the result is too much pollution.

How much pollution is too much pollution? The answer is: More than the optimal amount. What is the "optimal" amount of pollution? It is the amount that would exist if those who cause pollution were forced to pay damages to everyone they harm with their pollution. It is not zero. And it is not what exists today. It is somewhere in between.

According to economics, if those who cause pollution had to pay everyone who is damaged an amount of money equal to the true (no lying) damages they cause, society would end up with an optimal amount of pollution.

Therefore, the economic solution is "simple." Do what the market would do if a market existed—make polluters pay for the damages they cause. Obviously, it is a solution that is simple only in theory, not in practice, which is why it is seldom tried.

However, if the logic of emulating a free market is used to solve pollution problems, it is clear that some kinds of pollution would not exist at all. The reason being that there are cases where polluters would not be able to pay enough to compensate the losers and still continue to pollute. Examples are lead in gasoline and leaf burning. In a true free-market, there would be no lead in gasoline and no leaf burning in cities and towns. Which is why laws that ban lead in gasoline and leaf burning in populated areas are justified by economics.

Do legal bans or fines on certain activities adversely affect the rights of polluters to do whatever they want to do? Of course. Just as an absence of laws or fines allows polluters to trample on the rights of those they hurt. So, which side should we support?

On a political level, politicians often make decisions to defend or help those on their side. On an economic level, the answer is to simply do what a free market would do if a free market existed. In what appears to be an odd conclusion, it does not matter if those who cause pollution are required to pay off those they damage, in order to continue polluting, or if those who are hurt are allowed to pay off those who are damaging them in order to get them to stop. The reason it does not matter, from the standpoint of society, is that, in the end, the actions of polluters will be determined by the true damages they cause versus the true costs of stopping the pollution. If the true cost of the damages is greater than the cost of stopping the pollution, the pollution will stop, because it will be cheaper for the polluter to stop the pollution than to pay off the damaged parties. If the true cost of the damages is less than the cost of reducing or stopping the pollution, the pollution will continue, because it is cheaper for the polluter to pay off the damaged parties and to continue polluting.

Some think "paying-to-pollute' schemes are a silly idea, because they allow polluters to simply pay a little money and continue polluting the air, ground, or water. If that happens, it is not because it is a bad policy, but because the damages are not great. When the damages are severe, the fines will be high enough to either end or reduce the activity that is causing pollution.

Although there is a wide rift between the conservative and liberal views of economic and environmental interaction, the economic solution of imposing fines on polluters that are equal to the damages they cause is both a free-market solution and an effective way to protect the environment.

The only catch is that the solution requires government to stand in for the free market by doing what the market would do if a market existed.

Global warming is an extreme example. Liberals believe global warming has been accelerated by human actions, and that it is necessary to restrict certain emissions (greenhouse gasses) in an attempt to save the world. Some conservatives believe the global warming issue is a hoax, and that restricting emissions hurts the economy. If global warming is a reality, it is unlikely that the economy will be helped if New York City and all of Florida are flooded. The main problem with the conservative global-warming argument is that it is based on a fear of government regulation, not economics. It is similar to what happened when the government required automakers to add basic safety features to their cars. Although automakers initially claimed that if they had to add seat belts to every car, they would go bankrupt, as it turned out, instead of hurting the automobile industry, safety became a major selling point.

More important, the global-warming issue is an example of how economic solutions must be based on real science. At the core of the global warming debate are two simple questions: One is whether or not the climate is changing; the answer to that question seems clear: all the evidence shows that the earth is warming. The other is whether or not the warming is part of a natural cycle or man-made; the answer to that question has been handled poorly.

The undeniable scientific evidence is that the earth has gone through ice ages and warming periods. But the changes are not cyclical, like the seasons or day and night. Each dramatic change was set off by an isolated event. The climate change that destroyed the dinosaurs was not part of a cycle. The dinosaurs did not exist for millions of years, under a suitable climate, then disappear when the climate entered a new part of its natural cycle, and then come back when the suitable part of the climate cycle returned. And so on, over and over again. The dinosaurs existed, then they disappeared, and they are not coming back.

After millions of years, something happened—a meteor hit the earth, throwing up a dust cloud that blocked the sun, destroyed plant life, and killed off the dinosaurs. Or the dust cloud was caused by extraordinary volcanic activity. Or it was a combination of meteors and volcanic activity. But while scientists continue to investigate the exact trigger, there is no question that the climate change that caused the extinction of dinosaurs was not part of a natural cycle. It was, however, caused by natural forces. And once the change is triggered, it is clear how natural forces accelerate the change. For example, as the earth warms, the polar ice caps melt. As the ice caps melt, the ice that reflects the sun's heat is replaced with bare ground that absorbs the sun's heat, thereby increasing the earth's temperature even more. As the oceans warm, huge quantities of methane gas that is trapped at the bottom of the oceans by cold water is released into the atmosphere.[22] There is more. It is actually frightening to read the scientific explanations of climate change—not a climate cycle—because it makes it clear how fragile our climate is and how it can change because of events that are out of our control.

The point is that before man existed, natural events triggered massive climate changes. Not as part of a natural cycle, but as isolated events. And once climate change was initiated, it fed on itself, pushing the earth into either an ice age or a warming period.

Therefore, the current debate about global warming can lead to successful policies and actions only if it begins with the fact that there is no natural climate cycle, only isolated events that cause sometimes-massive climate changes. Given the fact that there is no natural climate cycle, the question is: If the earth is warming again, what is causing it this time?

3. The positive externality problem.

Positive externalities exist when someone's production or consumption of something does good things to others.

An example is education. People who are educated are more productive, which means that when someone spends the time and money to become educated, he or she does good things for others. As President John F. Kennedy and then Congressman Jack Kemp pointed out, "A rising tide lifts all boats."

But, because there is no market for the external benefits of education, all those who benefit when someone else is educated do not have to help pay for that person's education. Therefore, if only those who can pay for a private education are educated, society will have too little education, which is why, if

---

[22] Methane gas is ten times more damaging, in terms of its impact on global warming, than the greenhouse gasses currently being spewed into the atmosphere.

education is left entirely to the free market, the nation's wealth is diminished. The tide does not rise as high.

Very simply, private markets cannot provide a sufficient quantity of things with positive externalities, because private suppliers cannot collect payments from everyone who benefits from their product.

Solving the positive externality problem.

Positive externalities (or positive "neighborhood effects") occur when markets do not exist for external benefits. When markets do not exist for external benefits, it is not in the interest of producers to provide things they cannot get paid for. The result is that not enough of those things are produced.

What is not enough? Not enough to maximize the nation's wellbeing or wealth.

If pure private schools could collect money from everyone who benefits from the education they provide to students who pay, they would educate everyone, without charging any tuition. They would educate everyone because they would get paid for each student who attends. The problem is, private schools can only collect money from the students or parents of students who attend their schools, because markets do not exist for the benefits they provide to society by educating those who attend their schools. The result is that a pure private school system will not educate enough people.

The solution is to have government provide education for everyone and to pay for it with taxes collected from society as a whole, which is exactly what the private market would do if a market existed for the benefits society receives when someone is educated.

According to economics, if everyone who benefits from others being educated has to help pay for that education, society can end up with an optimal amount of education.

Therefore, the economic solution is, once again, "simple." Do what the market would do if a market existed—make society pay for the benefits it receives. And, once again, the solution is simple only in theory, not in practice, because while public education may deal well with the "quantity" issue, it does not do as well as we might like with the "quality" issue. Which is why there are constant arguments over how to improve the quality of education.

Which brings us back to Milton Friedman's voucher idea. It may be wrong to claim that public schools are not doing as well as we would like, simply because they are run by bureaucracies rather than by profit-seeking private businesses, because we already know that private markets seldom, if ever, give us the best possible quality. Even so, the benefits of competition cannot be ignored.

The easiest way to "prove" the benefits of competition in education is to look at America's colleges and universities. America's elementary and high schools do not fare well in international comparisons. But America's colleges and universities are the equal of those in any country. And America's graduate schools are the best in the world.

Why the disparity? The economic explanation is that as we move up the education ladder, more and more competition is introduced into the education system. There is little or no choice for most elementary and high school students; with few exceptions, they go to the public school in the district in which they live. The only competition for public schools is from private schools that only a few can afford, which means there is no real competition. Colleges and universities compete with each other for students in their state and from all across the country, as well as from around the world. The competition is limited somewhat by large differences between in state and out-of-state tuition and also by the fact that many undergraduate students prefer to stay relatively close to home. When it comes to graduate schools, the competition among universities is severe. Graduate schools compete with each other to get the best students, and few graduate students worry about staying close to home.

If you are thinking that the "positive externality" problem sounds a lot like the "public goods" problem, you are correct. Public goods are an example of a positive externality. Therefore, the theoretical solution to each can be the same: Government either provides the good or service, or uses subsidies to encourage the activity, such as grants or tax breaks for private schools.

As such, the concerns are the same. Is the government doing the best it can to solve the problem? Would the results be better if some form of competition were introduced into the solution?

The fact that everyone seems to agree about the need to improve the quality of public education at the elementary and high school level does not mean public schools do not work at all or that they should be handed over to private companies. The fact that charter schools and voucher programs have had mixed results does not mean such ideas should not be looked at more closely.

Three things are clear: One is that successful solutions will not occur by blindly supporting the existing education bureaucracy. The second is that legitimate solutions will not occur by blindly believing that any so-called competition will automatically improve education. The third is that successful policies regarding education must begin by defining what it means to "get a good education" and explaining how to do it. There is no reason to expect either public schools or "privatized" schools to succeed if they do not know what they are trying to accomplish and how to do it. The simple reason as to why most truly private schools do a good job of educating students is that they do have to compete—with public schools and other private schools—and they have to deliver what their customers pay for.

4. The common property resource problem.

Common property resources are resources that no one owns until someone takes them. Some are renewable; others are non-renewable.

No one owns the fish in lakes, rivers, or oceans. They are owned only after they are caught. Therefore, without laws, anyone can take as many fish as he or she wants, on a first-come-first-served basis. The result is that fish populations can be harvested to extinction. Even if a group of fishermen decides to restrict its catch, in order to protect the population, it cannot legally stop others from taking whatever they can.

The same is true for other species, such as whales, elephants, tigers, ducks, etc., all of which are "renewable" resources, meaning that their populations can grow or shrink over time (sometimes quickly).

The problem with non-renewable resources, such as oil, is that if no one owns the oil in the ground, then no one is able to manage its extraction over time in a way that is best for society.

Very simply, renewable common property resources will almost always be depleted to levels that increase the cost of production, and possibly to extinction. Non-renewable common property resources will almost always be used up too fast. In both cases, the result is a disruption in economic efficiency and a decrease in the nation's wealth.

THE EIGHT PROBLEMS

Solving common property resource problems.

As is always the case, economic efficiency cannot exist if markets do not exist.

In terms of common property resources:

The private market cannot manage a fish population in a way that is best for society, because there is no market for fish in the ocean, lakes, and rivers. There is no market for fish in the water, because no one owns the fish until they are caught.

In most cases, the environment imposes a natural limit on the size of a population. And, in most cases, the annual rate of growth of a population is a function of its overall size. If a population is reduced to zero, there is no growth—it is gone. If a population reaches its natural maximum size, which is sometimes measured in numbers, sometimes by weight, the growth rate is also zero—because it cannot grow any larger. In between a zero population size and the natural maximum, there is a function that describes the growth rate of the population as a function of population size. For fish populations, the function is normally a parabola. The importance of the function is that it describes not only the growth rate of the population, but also the "sustainable" harvest or yield. The definition of sustainable yield is the catch that can be taken each year that will leave the total population unchanged. If the sustainable yield can be described by a parabola, it means there are two different population sizes that can yield the same annual catch. It also means there is one population size that yields the maximum sustainable annual yield.

According to economic theory, as well as a lot of real-world evidence, all valuable renewable resources that are not owned are in danger of being harvested to extinction. In terms of a fish population, if the actual annual catch is larger than the annual sustainable yield, the population decreases. Over time, if the actual catch remains above the sustainable yield, the total population can be depleted. The good news is that if the actual catch is limited to less than the sustainable yield, the population can increase, unless it has already been reduced to a size that cannot survive.

As such, economic policies intended to solve renewable common property resource problems must be based on real science. There are two ways such resources can be managed for the good of society. One is for the government to impose limits on the harvest, or catch, such as the daily quotas on sport fish in lakes and rivers. The other is for the government to impose taxes or fines on the catching of fish, or other resources, that would, at least in theory, equal the price that would be charged by the owners of fish in the water if there were owners.

If a fish population were owned, owners would regulate the sale of fishing rights in a way that would maximize their profits over time. In almost all cases, that would mean maintaining a healthy population level rather than selling off all the fish for a short-term profit. That would be accomplished by selling the rights to catch the sustainable yield. It also means that, if a parabolic function describes sustainable yield as a function of population size, the owners would maintain the population at the larger of the two levels, because it is cheaper to catch a given quantity of fish from a larger than a smaller population, which means the owners could charge a higher price for fishing rights.

In theory, emulating the free-market solution that would occur if fish were owned would generate the most economically efficient solution. In practice, it is much cheaper, and possible more effective, to manage the resource with quotas. In either case, the solution requires understanding the "population dynamics" of the resource, meaning the relationship between population size and growth rates and the possible lower limit of a population, which is the level, below which the population cannot recover.

The same solutions apply to non-renewable resources. And, again, legitimate economic solutions require real science, so that quotas or charges yield a use of the resource that maximizes the wealth of the nation.

5. The exclusion problem.

There are some good things that not everyone is willing and able to pay for.

In any market equilibrium, some consumers do not get to buy any of the good or service. That is because in every market, some people are excluded because they are not willing *and* able to pay the market price. On one level, that does not matter. On another level, it might be important. It depends on the definition of "market."

Does it really matter if someone is willing, but not able, to buy a Cadillac SUV? Most people would say, no. But, it might matter if a person is willing, but not able, to buy any car. The same is true for Cheerios. Does anyone care if someone is not willing and able to buy Cheerios? Probably not. But what if that person is not willing and able to buy any food at all? That is why, when Plato wrote about necessities, he named food, dwelling, and clothing, not a particular food. Meanwhile, textbooks claim that there is no thing that is needed, because there are always substitutes for any particular food item. The textbook idea comes from market to be for individual products, not a category of product.

Who is correct: Plato or the textbooks?

The answer depends on who you are. If you are the manufacturer or seller of a particular product, the fact that no one needs any particular *thing*, including your product, is true. If you are a consumer who is willing and able to buy a new car, the fact that you do not need any particular *thing*, such as a particular car, is true. But, if you are someone who cannot afford food at all, the fact that Cheerios and Corn Flakes are substitutes does not mean you do not need food.

The economic idea that we do not "need" any thing is true if we mean that we do not need any thing, and not that we do not need anything. It is true that we do not need any thing, meaning any particular thing, because there are always substitutes. But it is also true that we do need categories of things, such as Plato's food, dwelling, and clothing.

We do not need a particular box of corn flakes.

We do need food.

The textbook argument, that we do not buy food, that we buy corn flakes or Cheerios or eggs or whatever, is true, but it is not a functional truth to someone who cannot afford food, meaning that he or she is willing but not able to choose between various brands of corn flakes and Cheerios,

Solving the exclusion problem.

This is the most political of the eight issues, because it is difficult to argue against someone who believes that if people cannot take care of themselves, that is their problem.

A market reaches an equilibrium when, at the market price, the quantity of the good or service that consumers are willing and able to buy is equal to the quantity sellers are willing and able to sell.

Given the demand for any good or service, when a market reaches equilibrium, there will be some consumers who do not get any of that good or service, because they are not willing and able to pay the equilibrium price. That is not an opinion or a judgment. It is a fact. And it does not matter if the market is perfectly competitive or not.

In some cases, we can say, "Who cares? If someone is not willing and able to pay for something, so what?"

But there is an important difference between the terms "willing" and "able" that economists use to define how much of a thing people will buy. If someone is not willing to pay for a gold Rolex, does it matter? Or if they are willing, but not able (they do not have enough money), to buy a gold Rolex, does it really matter?

By the same token, if someone is able but not willing to pay for health care, we can say, "So what? It's their choice."[23] But what if someone is willing, but not able, to pay for health care? In a totally private-market solution, he or she is excluded because he or she is not able to pay. If society believes that is an acceptable result, then everything is fine (except for the person in question). If society believes it is unacceptable, then society can look for ways to fix it—to change the free-market equilibrium, even though the equilibrium might be considered, by definition, to be economically efficient.

If such exclusions are seen as political or social issues, any and all remedies will be debated in terms of political ideology or individual values. Some liberals tend to think society has an obligation to help those who cannot help themselves. Some conservatives tend to think that because they were able to succeed without any help from anyone, then everyone else should succeed on their own, without any help from government social programs.

If such exclusions are seen as an economic problem, the negative impact of such exclusions, which includes increased crime and less productive workers, leads to economic solutions, such as Milton Friedman's negative income tax, as an alternative to the ideological political arguments.

Unfortunately, because of the power of political dogma, every time politicians, either liberal or conservative, brought up Friedman's alternative welfare program, it was shot down.

Although there are huge political fights over whether or not government, using taxpayer money, should help those who cannot help themselves, or provide things to those who are unable to pay for them, few people, no matter how conservative they are, argue that roads, education, national defense, and so on should be limited only to those who can pay for them. The reason is simple. Even the wealthiest individuals know they cannot go very far driving on their own private roads or survive in business without government protected contracts, patent, and copyright protection.

Therefore, the economic solution is to determine whether or not the nation's wealth can be increased by providing things to people who, on their own, may

---

[23] Negative or positive externality arguments show that such decisions affect others. Therefore, it is not accurate to say it is up to the individual.

be willing, but not able, to pay for them. It is already done with education, police and fire protection, laws and courts, and so on. The question is: Are there other things that, if they are provided to everyone, will increase the wealth of the nation. For example, if elementary and high school education is provided to everyone, what about a college education? Or health care? Politically, whenever universal health care is raised as an issue, people dig in their ideological heels. They also claim that the Canadian system is not so good. Maybe not. But what about the rest of the civilized world? Many European and Asian countries have health care systems similar to America's education system—a combination of public and private. They provide health care for everyone, and anyone who chooses to do so, can pay for private care.

Those who argue that such a system is no good, because government cannot provide anything of quality, have only to look at America's education system, where many public schools are equal or superior to many private schools. If government-provided health care were equivalent to going to Berkeley or the University of Michigan, would anyone turn his or her back on it?

6. The "bad things" problem.

There are some bad things that, whether people want them or not, they get.

Crime is an example. No one wants to be the victim of crime.

The private market cannot prevent crime, although some individuals may be able to protect themselves and their property.

Some who believe in the government-is-evil argument seem to think of themselves as part of the Old West, where individuals did not need government; where the good guys always whipped the bad guys. That was the movies. In reality, without laws, the fastest gun in the West can be shot in the back.

Solving the "bad things" problem.

There are a couple different solutions.

The political solution is to pass laws against bad activities, such as making it illegal to steal or kill.

The economic solution, which includes the political solution, is to include the relationship between crime and economic opportunity. People with a lot to lose, because they are making a lot of money, are less likely to commit crimes (the exceptions being crimes of passion and exceptional greed) than those with little to lose. It is an opportunity cost issue. What is the cost of going to prison? A lot if you are rich. Not much if you are poor.

In many states, one of the largest government expenditure is for prisons. Therefore, improving economic conditions for everyone is likely to reduce crime and also save taxpayers a lot of money.

7. The "bad things we buy" problem.

There are some things society may decide no one should have, whether or not they are willing and able to pay for them.

Heroin, cigarettes, alcohol, and so on.

The private market cannot prevent such things from being bought and sold, because if people are willing and able to pay for them, there may be money to be made. If supply and demand exist for some item, there is a market for the item, whether it is good or bad for the buyer. And if there is money to be made, it will be sold.

Solving the "bad things we buy" problem.

There are two ways of dealing with "bad" things:

Pass laws making such things illegal.

Impose fines or taxes on "bad" things in order to make them less attractive to buyers.

Of course, society sometimes changes its collective mind about such things. At one time, alcohol was legal. Then it was made illegal. Then it was made legal again.

Heroin is still illegal.

Cigarettes are still legal.

Of course, making something illegal does not make it disappear. It simply creates an illegal market.

Prohibition did not eliminate alcohol; it put distribution in the hands of criminals. Making drugs illegal did not eliminate drugs; it put distribution in the hands of criminals. The same is true for prostitution and other goods or services that society, off and on, decides are bad for us.

Sometimes, it is easy to identify bad things, such as heroin. Sometimes it is not, such as when communities ban books like *The Catcher in the Rye*. In some cases, things considered bad in one society are acceptable in others, which means the determining factor in deciding whether or not something is good or bad can be personal beliefs or values, not scientific evidence. In some cases, things are declared to be bad, and made illegal, because they pose a threat to those in power; such as laws in the 1300s against Bibles written in a language the people could understand.

One of the arguments against such laws is that society should not pass laws to protect people from themselves.

Another is that it might be cheaper and more effective to discourage the purchase of bad things by imposing taxes on them, which is currently done with cigarettes. Some think this is a good policy, because it also raises a lot of money for government, Others think it is not so nice to keep an addictive and harmful product on the market just so manufacturers and the government can make money.

A third argument against making things illegal is that it might be better to legalize or decriminalize certain activities or products, such as some currently illegal drugs. There is, in fact, a long-standing economic argument for legalizing drugs.

The argument is that legalizing drugs will decrease the demand for drugs by eliminating the enormous profits made by drug dealers. The assumptions are that if drugs are legalized, pushers will be put out of business and that pushers are the main reason for creating the demand for drugs.

The argument also assumes that the supply of drugs will increase, because the excessive costs of illegal drug production and sales will be replaced with lower-cost legal production.

The truth is: It is unclear what will happen to the supply of drugs. It could increase if the above assumption is true. It could decrease if it ends up costing more to provide drugs legally, which could happen if the cost of packaging, retail outlets (which may be more expensive than dealing drugs out of cars), and advertising offset any possible savings. Supply could also remain unchanged if the changes in costs and savings exactly offset each other.

Therefore, it is necessary to look a little closer at the assumptions behind the push to legalize drugs, none of which are very good.

The most problematic assumption is that the demand for drugs will decline without pushers. A more likely assumption is that if the legal sellers of drugs are free to advertise their product, the demand for drugs will increase.

Turning drug production and sales over to legal corporations is not likely to lower the costs of drugs. If producers can legally sell drugs for a profit, there will be competition and advertising. As with alcohol and cigarettes, advertising and packaging adds a substantial amount to costs. Then there are the middlemen—wholesalers and retailers—each of whom requires a profit margin and each of whom may have expenses greater than those currently selling drugs out of their cars. Along with adding to costs, advertising, if it is successful, may increase the demand for drugs, as it has for alcohol and cigarettes. And because drugs, like cigarettes, are addictive, once hooked, the customer is a long-time customer.

The other lesson to be learned from alcohol and cigarettes is that legalizing a "bad" product does not take the "excitement" out of it. As a result, legalizing drugs can increase both the costs of production and the number of users, which will add to, not subtract from, the crime necessary to pay for the goods.

An additional issue, which is seldom raised, is: What would the legal age limit for drugs be? Wherever the age line is drawn, the consequences are virtually certain. The old pushers, driven out of the adult business by legal sales, will turn even more seriously to the child market. In the end, the illegal pushers will still be in business, but they will be focusing on children. And if all the illegal pushers deal only with children, drug use by children could soar.

Legalizing drugs has always relied on "simplifying" the argument. As such, it is a good example of Saul Wurman's observation that "Simplification has led to the dumbing of America."

8. The market failure problem.

Competition does not maximize profits; competition reduces or eliminates profits.

Therefore, it is in the interest of producers to restrict competition in order to increase their profits.

And because markets cannot protect themselves from the abuse of power, there are no perfectly competitive markets in the real world. Perfectly competitive markets do not exist, because it is in the interest of sellers to monopolize markets or form cartels and unions.

The result of market failure is a reduction in the nation's wealth.

Solving the market failure problem.

Because markets cannot protect themselves from those with the power to eliminate competition, the only way to protect markets or correct market failure is with government regulation or control.

One solution is the anti-trust laws that are periodically used to break up large monopolies.

Another is to use regulations that force a monopoly to operate at a price and quantity that emulates a perfectly competitive market. Although such a solution sounds complicated, it can be implemented simply by setting a maximum price the monopolist can charge. Government-regulated pricing was standard practice for utilities considered to be "natural" monopolies, and it is still in use today. The utility, such as an electric power company, is granted a monopoly status, but its prices are subject to government approval.

There is, however, another side to the monopoly issue. It is that although it is easy to show how monopolies disrupt economic efficiency, thereby reducing the wealth of the nation, it can also be argued that large, monopolistic corporations can be key ingredients to economic growth. In other words, the "robber barons," and the trusts President Teddy Roosevelt broke up, contributed to the building of America. As such, the market-failure issue is not always as clear-cut as it might seem.

9. Conclusion

Private markets work if, when things are provided to one person, they are not available to others.

If you buy and eat a cookie, no one else can eat it. You paid for it and you are the only one to benefit from it. Of course, some might argue that cookies are not actually good for you. That may be true. But the economic issue is that there are many things that, when they are bought and consumed by one person, or family, or group, are not available to anyone else. And it is those things that private markets are good at providing, because if the one who pays is the one who benefits, then there is no problem collecting money from those who are willing and able to pay. These are also the things that some consider to be trivial. Which is true.

Virtually every *particular* good or service is trivial, in the sense that no particular good or service is *needed*. As long as consumers are willing and "able" to pay for it, and someone is willing and able to sell it, it is up to each individual to decide how he or she wants to spend his or her money. Exceptions are bad things, such as the heroin Bob sells.

Some might also argue that there are *categories* of things that are trivial, meaning there is no reason to care if someone has them or not. Snowmobiles, for example. Or SUVs. Or very green, weed-free lawns. Or books. Or Plato's "…dainties, and perfumes, and incense, and courtesans, and cakes…and gold and ivory and all sorts of materials." Or Albert Einstein's "…trite objects of human efforts—possessions, outward success, luxury…"

Others might argue, instead, that the things Thorsten Veblen labeled conspicuous consumption and Einstein called contemptible are the stuff of dreams—the snowmobiles that define civilization.

In *Walden*, Henry David Thoreau makes a case for the simple, meaningful life.

In *The Art of the Deal*, Donald Trump makes a case for wheeling and dealing yourself to the top of the money pile.

Regardless of your view of the simple life versus the good-stuff life, the economic argument is that the production and consumption of goods and services is economically efficient as long as there is no market failure and if the process of producing or consuming them does not do good or bad things to others.

In fact, the benefits of private production and consumption are so great that economics is willing to "allow" market failure and external effects to exist without correction, as long as their negative impacts on the nation's wealth are not too great. The economic argument for doing so is that it is not smart to spend more of a nation's wealth to correct a problem than it will gain by eliminating the problem.

For any given economic issue or question, the first step is to determine if it is something the private market can provide. Private markets should provide things that are good. Ideally, they will be produced and consumed without market failure or externalities. Of course, we already know there is always some form of market failure or externality. We also know that private markets sometimes produce bad things.

If it is a market failure issue—monopoly, oligopoly, monopolistic competition, or monopsony—the government can protect the market with antitrust laws or with regulations that force the monopoly to operate at the price and quantity that emulates a perfectly competitive market. When there are market failures or externalities, the nation's wealth may be increased by government regulation or control. But, real markets should not be expected to live up to the textbook ideal of perfect competition, because real markets will never meet the strict definition of perfect competition.

If it is a public good or externality or common-property resource issue, government can provide things the private market cannot provide at all, or as well as we would like. The questions are: Will the private market provide enough? Or too much? Or too little? Should the market be regulated? Should government provide some of the good or service itself? If so, how and how much? Benefit-cost analysis can often provide an answer. Sometimes, however, benefit cost analysis is not the tool to use. Sometimes, compassion is as important as economics in a civilized society, meaning that government might provide some things just because we, as a society, believe everyone should have them, at some level. Life, liberty, and the pursuit of happiness, for example. What can we do to ensure life, liberty, and the pursuit of happiness? Having the freedom to ask that question is at the heart of the American experiment. How the question is answered, day after day, determines the future of the republic.

If it is a bad things issue, such as crime, drugs, prostitution, or some books, government can try to reduce or eliminate the bad things with laws that make them illegal, with taxes or fines that discourage the activity, such as taxes on cigarettes or alcohol, or with bon fires. What does society think is bad? That is often open to debate.

On one hand, using what we know to examine or "solve" real-market problems is relatively simple. On the other hand, virtually any recommended solution or policy can be hotly debated on both political and economic grounds. Which brings us back to Whitehead's observation that "Education is the acquisition of the art of the utilization of knowledge." There is an "art" to using knowledge. And acquiring that art is what education is about.

5. Dialogues About Markets

Ideological debates about social and economic issues tend to be simple…and simpleminded. Government is good. Government is evil. By drawing a line in the sand, Democrats and Republicans, Liberals and Conservatives are driven to choose sides in a battle with virtually no middle ground. "Choosing" may be the wrong word, because it does not appear that anyone does much choosing once he or she decides to throw in with one political party or another.

In the U.S., the argument is as old as the nation. Actually it is older than that; it began when colonists came to a new land in search of religious freedom. With religious freedom came the desire for political freedom. The colonists grew tired of a monarchy that denied them representation in the decisions that affected their lives and of paying taxes that were used to finance England's wars rather than to help build the new nation.

1. The Declaration of Independence.

The Declaration of Independence, signed by the Continental Congress on July 4, 1776, helped create the United States of America. The first draft was written by Thomas Jefferson, who based the preamble on the Virginia Declaration of Rights written by George Mason, a neighbor and friend of George Washington. Jefferson then added a long and detailed list of grievances against King George III of England and the British people. When Jefferson's draft was given to Benjamin Franklin and the independence committee, they cut out a number of Jefferson's grievances and edited others, believing the public would be more likely to support a shorter and more easily understood document.

The Declaration of Independence was written after the war of independence had already begun. The first shot in the Revolutionary War was fired on the morning of April 19, 1775 at Lexington and Concord in Massachusetts, and, more than fourteen months later, the Continental Congress believed it was necessary to have a document that explained to the people the reasons for and purpose of the war that was already underway.

After "the shot heard round the world," and prior to The Declaration of Independence, the independence movement and the war were bolstered by Thomas Paine's *Common Sense*, a 50-page pamphlet printed in January 1776. In it, Paine wrote:

"First, the powers of governing still remaining in the hands of the king, he will have a negative over the whole legislation on this continent. And as he has shown himself such an inveterate enemy to liberty and discovered such a thirst for arbitrary power, is he, or is he not, a proper person to say to these colonies, 'You shall make no laws but what I please!'"

Independence, in the United States, still means the attainment of liberty and freedom from arbitrary power.

However, the Declaration of Independence, the document that made that statement to the King of England, is not an abstract document. It is a principles-based statement that contains specific examples of the abuses of power wielded by the King of England. Along with stating the ideals that formed the basis of this nation, the Declaration of Independence focuses on concrete complaints. It is a mixture of principles and details, a format that is as important today as it was when it was written.

Those who created this nation knew that gaining freedom from a king would not, by itself, secure freedom for Americans. They knew it was necessary to have laws that would allow the nation to protect itself from outside enemies. They also knew it was necessary to have laws that would protect individuals from the potential abuse of government power.

We have all read the Declaration of Independence. But, for most of us, what we remember is the preamble. We forget, or maybe never read, the specific complaints against King George III of England, because we thought they were dated; no longer relevant. Some are dated; but not all. Some could have been written yesterday. In either case, it is important to remember and to see that this nation was created with a specific understanding of the details. Neither the Declaration of Independence nor the United States Constitution was intended to simplify crucial principles by using a term such as "abuse of power" as a substitute for carefully identifying specific actions that were unacceptable.

Unfortunately, while the founding fathers' decision to limit the length of explanations given to the public lives on in today's sound bites and one-liner political slogans, the desire to buttress ideological arguments with facts has been lost in today's political world.

The Declaration of Independence was not the beginning of a call for freedom; it was a response to years of turmoil and repression. It cried out for a new beginning, but not a new beginning dreamed up by the few who wrote and signed it; a new beginning based on the realities of life and the thoughts of wise people.

In 1776, The Declaration of Independence helped set in motion events that would change the world. But no one involved with The Declaration of Independence, including the citizens it was written to represent, would have thought reasonable people should rely on political ideologies not supported by at least some reason and evidence. That is why The Declaration of Independence contained more than the statement, "The King is evil."

How can someone say, "Government is good," or "Government is evil," and expect a reasonable person to agree?

Only a fool would believe that everything government does is either good or bad. A reasonable person will look at what government does, has done, or could do, and decide, on an issue-by-issue basis, whether it was or is a good or bad idea or a good or bad execution of a good idea. Those decisions have nothing to do with being a Democrat or a Republican. They have to do with reason. Therefore, anyone who understands the ideological cornerstone of The Declaration of Independence should also understand that freedom and progress require a careful examination of reality. Ideology without logic and facts does not yield freedom, it creates cults.

In terms of current politics, a reasonable person should be depressed by all the straight party votes in Congress, because voting with your party does not require logic and facts; it requires only blind allegiance to an ideology.

For example, a laissez-faire doctrine would be more functional if it accepted the reality that all markets exhibit market failure and externalities. Given that reality, which should mean accepting the legitimate role of government in a democratic society, the laissez faire doctrine could be used to help ensure that things government does will benefit the nation.

And a Marxist doctrine would be more effective if it accepted the reality that even imperfect markets work and that business does not prosper only by exploiting workers. Given that reality, the Marxist doctrine could be used to help ensure an interaction of government and business that maximizes the wealth of the nation and the freedom of individuals. In many European countries, political parties on both the left and right accept these realities. The opposing argument, of course, is that the U.S. is better than everyone else and that our ideologies have served us well. There is some truth to the argument, but if the U.S. expects to be more than history's shortest empire, it has to get back to the practical application of logic and reason that is the true foundation of its success.

The practical application of logic and reason was the basis not only of The Declaration of Independence, but also of the United States Constitution, one of the greatest political documents ever conceived.

2. The Constitution of the United States

The underlying belief behind the Constitution of the United States is that government can make things better.

When the Constitution was written, it was intended to create a strong federal government, because individual states were acting like individual countries, to the detriment of each other and the nation as a whole.

The Preamble

We the People of the United States, in Order to form a more perfect Union, establish Justice, insure domestic Tranquility, provide for the common defence, promote the general Welfare, and secure the Blessings of Liberty to ourselves and our Posterity, do ordain and establish this Constitution for the United States of America.

The Constitution intended to make it clear which rights belonged to the federal government and which belonged to state governments. But, before it was ratified, in 1788, key figures demanded that it also include specific rights for individuals. Those demands were agreed to, and ten amendments were added to the Constitution in 1791. Those first ten amendments, called The Bill of Rights, were intended to protect individuals from abusive action by the federal government. The XIV amendment to the Constitution extended the Bill of Rights to states, so that individuals would also be protected from abuses of power by state government.

The United States Constitution, which is universally accepted as one of the greatest documents ever written, is ingenious. But it is not the result of a single draft, and it was not a completed document in its original form.

After the Bill of Rights was ratified in 1791, seventeen additional amendments were added, each of which deals with a specific issue or action.

Over the years, the Articles and Amendments to the Constitution have been tested and defined in cases brought before the Supreme Court.

3. The news.

Read any newspaper or watch the news on television. What you see are lots of events, problems, issues, and opinions. Sometimes you might like what is happening. Sometimes you might not. Sometimes you will agree with the opinions being offered. Sometimes not. Sometimes you might write letters to the editor of your newspaper. Sometimes you might make calls to talk-radio shows. Sometimes you might yell at your television set. In the end, the most important input most of us have is when we vote. It is when the people vote that we can say we have a government of the people, by the people, and for the people.

However, the less informed the people are, the more possible it is that they will vote for bad policies, or for candidates who promise to implement bad policies. Of course, no candidate campaigns on the promise that, "If elected, I will do everything in my power to do really bad things." Instead, he or she promises to do things that sound good to the voters—in many cases, things that appeal to base values. But because we do not all have the same values, not everyone chooses to vote for the same political party or candidate. And because some people believe their values are God's values and other people's values are the devil's values, political campaigns have become more and more brutal and less and less concerned with real solutions to real problems.

On a political level, whenever the party in power believes it has the right to do whatever it wants—ignoring minority and individual rights and disregarding the protections provided to individuals by the Constitution—then the republic to which we pledge allegiance is at risk.

On an economic level, doing too many unwise things risks bringing an end to the greatest economic miracle the world has ever seen.

How long has the United States been a superpower? How long has it been the number one economy in the world? Some would say since the end of World War I. Others would say since the end of World War II, when the U.S. was the only country with an atomic bomb. Still others might say since the collapse of the Soviet Union, when the U.S. became the sole superpower. Regardless of which point in time someone picks, it was less than 100 years ago, a flash in the pan compared to the Egyptians, the Greeks, the Romans, the Spanish, the Aztecs, the Incas, and others. Therefore, no one should believe that just because the United States has been on top for a few years that it will remain there if we are not careful about the decisions we make as a nation—both political and economic. Empires that lasted for a thousand years declined and disappeared. Therefore, there is no reason to assume that we can do one wrong thing after another and not cause one of history's shortest empires to slip into a difficult-to-reverse decline.

Back to the news. When we read, listen to, or watch the news, there is no order to the problems or issues presented. Stuff happens. Some of it ends up on television or in newspapers. Some does not. In either case, issues are not presented in a neat, orderly, textbook format or in the form of exam questions, where it is obvious which pieces of knowledge are needed to answer the exact question you are given. In fact, it is not always obvious what the question is.

What we do is read and watch an endless stream of disjointed and disconnected descriptions of and stories about our changing world. In the age of information, we have a lot of information, but not much knowledge. And an overload of information, without the knowledge needed to make sense of it, leads people to look for quick solutions to sometimes complicated problems and to vote for politicians based on one-liner attacks and policy prescriptions.

Once, while complaining about the press, Karl Rove, the political strategist behind President George W. Bush, explained that it is "wrong to underestimate the intelligence of the American voter, but easy to overestimate their interest. Much tugs at their attention." Rove understood that when voters do not have the time and energy needed to truly understand issues, it is the job of the politician, with the help of his or her staff, to do people's thinking for them, which means creating one-line pronouncements that describe "the sizzle," not "the steak" for each issue in a way that appeals to voters. Done honestly, such one-liners can convey a candidate's true position on issues. Done dishonestly, they can be used to deceive voters by leading them to believe a candidate is going to do something he or she has no intention of doing.

When it comes to economic issues, it seems even more difficult for politicians to tell the truth, either because they do not know the truth or because they believe economics is too difficult for the average person to comprehend. It is not.

4. A few dialogues.

Following, with apologies to Plato, are a few economic "dialogues." They were transcribed from fictional Sunday morning political talk shows.

(1) Perfect competition.

Privatizing government functions supports the free market.

No it doesn't. Neither does supporting abusive market power, or preventing government from correcting market failures. What such policies do is destroy the free market and reduce the wealth of the nation. Competition is not the same as perfect competition.

What's the difference?

Perfect competition refers to markets in which no firm or consumer is large enough to affect the market price. No one is big enough to have any influence on the market price.

What else?
No externalities.

What do perfectly competitive markets do?

Perfectly competitive markets lead to economic efficiency, which is an economic term meaning that society gets the maximum possible level of satisfaction from the given quantity of inputs and technology.

But perfect competition does not exist if someone is big enough to affect the market price, or if there are externalities.

That's right. And because there aren't any markets in America that are free of externalities or that are not affected by imperfect competition, there are no perfectly competitive markets.

What does that mean?

It means that no one can use economics to defend the claim that whatever happens in the private market is justified by economics. It is not.

So, perfect competition does not exist, either because of externalities or because some buyers or sellers are large enough to affect prices. And if markets are not perfectly competitive, there is no economic justification for the doctrine that says that whatever happens in private markets is justified by economics.

That's it. In the first place, economists have always known that the incentive to maximize profits leads to imperfect competition in virtually all markets, such as when a single firm takes over a market (a monopoly), when a few firms take over a market (an oligopoly), when firms make deals to divide up market share or restrict output (a cartel), or when a small number of firms, each with a somewhat different product, dominate a market (monopolistic competition). Under monopolistic competition, the products of each large company are similar, but can be told apart, such as Coca Cola and Pepsi Cola in the soft drink market, Ford and Chevrolet in the automobile market. Most U.S. industries fall into the category of monopolistic competition, which is why advertising is such a large part of the American economy.

Therefore, if someone wants to claim that markets are perfectly competitive, in order to argue that whatever private business does is economically efficient and, therefore, *justified*, they have to find a market without brand-name products and with no externalities. And there aren't any.

(2) Externalities.

What exactly do you mean by *externalities*?

It's economic jargon. According to economists, *externalities* are the byproducts of production or consumption that pass on benefits or costs to someone not involved in the activity.

Like what?

Like the benefits to society as a whole that occur when someone is educated or inoculated against a contagious disease. In each case, the action taken by individuals to help themselves also has positive effects on others. It's called an *externality* because it is *external* to the person or firm doing the activity. It is called a *positive externality*, because a benefit is something positive.

And what do you mean by costs?

The cost to society of pollution is one example. Pollution from production or from driving an automobile imposes costs on people other than those doing the activity. Again, it is called an *externality* because it is a cost that is *external* to the person or firm doing the activity. In economic terms, it is called a *negative externality*, because costs are a negative.

How do externalities destroy economic efficiency?

In a market economy, producers and consumers use prices to decide how much of each thing to buy or sell. If prices reflect the true benefits and costs to society of making or consuming things, then the free choices made by individual producers and consumers will maximize the satisfaction of society.

So, if either positive or negative externalities exist, prices do not represent the true social costs or benefits of individual actions, and producers and consumers, acting on market prices, will make decisions that do not maximize the wealth of the nation.

(3) Protecting the environment hurts the economy.

According to economics, environmental regulations and controls hurt business, disrupt the free market, and damage the economy. Therefore, regulations on pollution should be reduced, and the environment should be opened up to business, because the more money business makes, the better the economy will be.

What makes you think protecting the environment hurts the economy?

What makes you think that environmental protection and pollution control do not hurt business?

They obviously affect the profits of polluters. But *business* is not the economy. Some may still believe that *the business of America is business*. But the business of the economy is not business. The business of the economy is people.

What does that have to do with handing the economy over to tree huggers and whale watchers?

What makes you think you can rationalize wealth-reducing environmental policies by calling people names? Economists know—with certainty—that a market will *always* produce too much of any good whose production or consumption creates costs that are borne by someone not producing or consuming it.

    Doesn't economics say that the more we produce, the better?
    Who told you that?

    It's common knowledge.
    According to economic knowledge, negative externalities disrupt economic efficiency. If external costs exist, then prices do not reflect true social costs, because social costs are equal to internal costs *plus* external costs. If perfect competition existed, prices would steer producers and consumers to use resources in a way that maximizes the satisfaction of society. But because producers and consumers do not have to pay external costs, the existence of negative externalities means that prices cause producers and consumers to do too much of activities that impose costs on others. Too many resources are used to produce and consume goods with negative externalities, and too few resources are used to produce and consume other goods. The result is a decrease in the nation's wealth.

    You are ignoring the fact that the greatest accomplishment of competitive markets is that they allocate resources in the best possible way, so that the right quantities of things are produced and bought.
    You are ignoring the fact that your statement is true only for competitive markets with no market failure and no externalities, something that does not exist. Do you know the difference between competition and perfect competition? Or that your statement is true only for a perfectly competitive market, because that's the only time market prices yield an equilibrium where the value consumers place on a product is equal to the true social cost of producing it. When external costs exist, market prices cause too much to be produced.

    How does it cause too much to be produced?
    The lower the price, the more will be bought. It's the law of demand. When producers or consumers decide how much to produce or consume, they make their decisions by considering the prices they actually pay. Polluters, who pay only part of the cost of their actions, produce or consume more of it than if they

had to pay the total social cost—internal plus external costs. That is why, whenever producers or consumers are not responsible for all costs of their actions, the result is a reduction in the nation's real wealth.

That's your opinion.
No it's not. It's textbook economics.

(4) We can't stop all pollution.

People pollute the air when they breathe. They breathe in good air and breathe out bad air. Do you want to kill everyone in order to stop pollution? You're talking about taking away free choice.
Would you like to freely choose to be locked in an eight-foot by eight-foot by eight-foot airtight room for a week?

That's ridiculous. I would die. No one in his or her right mind would choose to do that. Besides, what does that have to do with pollution?
Okay. Would you like to freely choose to drink water that will make you sick, or possibly kill you in a few years?

Of course not. Why would I?
Okay. Would you like to freely choose to breathe air that will make you sick, possibly kill you in a few years?

Of course not. Who would? You are not making any sense.
Okay. Let me ask it a different way. If you were being led to the airtight room, to be locked up for a week, would you be willing to pay someone to let you go?

No one has the right to do that to me.
What if they did have the right?

Then I would obviously be willing to pay to get out of it.
How much?

A lot. Maybe everything I have.

And if someone could force you to drink water or breathe air that would make you sick? Would you be willing to pay to not have to drink it or breathe it?

Of course. But no one has the right to make me drink bad water or breathe bad air.

Yes they do. Polluters are affecting the water you drink and the air you breathe every day. And they have the right to do it.

No they don't.

Of course they do. Do you have the right to drive your car whenever you want? Do you have the right to use chemicals on your lawn that pollute lakes, rivers, and ground water?

That's different.

Why? Because *you're* doing it? Because you are exercising your *free right* to damage the water and air others use? The truth is: No individual can legally stop you from damaging his or her water or air.

The free market will take care of it.

How? You said you would be willing to pay someone so you wouldn't be forced to drink bad water or breathe bad air. Who would you pay?

You're making a big case out of nothing. Our air and water are clean. Our pollution isn't causing any real problems.

That's one of the differences between liberals and conservatives. If someone mentions pollution to a liberal, he or she seems to think of something serious, like being locked in the airtight room. If someone mentions pollution to a conservative, he or she thinks of something with a minor or nonexistent effect on our lives. The truth is: We are all locked in an "airtight" world with limited resources. And if we don't manage our resources correctly, the satisfaction of society is diminished.

What's your point?

The point is simple. You said you would be willing to pay to avoid being killed in an airtight room or to avoid drinking poisonous water or breathing poisonous air. The problem is: there *is* no one to pay, because individuals do not own the resources that are polluted—water and air. Therefore, someone has to step in and take your side in the issue; to stand up for what you would be willing to pay for, but cannot. All negative externalities, including pollution, exist because of a lack of property rights. If individuals do not own the air or the rights to air quality, they cannot legally prevent someone from polluting the air they inhale.

But all pollution isn't life threatening.
That's true. But it doesn't have to kill you to adversely affect your life. It becomes an economic problem if you are willing to pay to reduce or eliminate it. And you said you were.

And you have a way to fix it?
There are some possibilities. One is to create property rights, or ownership rights, for resources, so they can be handled by the market or in the courts. Another is to impose a fine or tax on those causing the damage, where the tax is equal to the dollar value of the damages caused to others. A third is to pass laws that make the activity illegal.

How would property rights for something like air solve anything?
If everyone had property rights to air quality, then each damaged person could take everyone who is polluting his or her air to court. The result would be fewer goods produced and consumed that damage others by polluting the air. Litigating all the cases, however, would use so many resources that it could cause an even greater loss to society. Imagine all the cars driving on a freeway during rush hour, each of which is polluting the air and reducing the air quality for many people. If each driver had to make legal arrangements with each damaged party before driving to work, the cost would be uncontrollable. Therefore, legal solutions to negative externality problems can work only if a small number of people are involved. Otherwise, the solution itself might reduce the nation's wealth.

What good would another tax do?
A tax or fine imposed on a polluter—if it is equal to the value of the damage caused—makes the producer or consumer responsible for the total costs of what they do. It's the *ideal* economic solution for dealing with negative externalities. Because after the tax is imposed, the market can solve the problem.

But polluters could pay the tax or fine and continue to pollute. What would that solve?

Polluters *could* pay the tax and continue to pollute the air, water, or earth. But if that happens, it is a result that is best for society, because whether or not polluters are able to pay the tax and keep on polluting depends upon the value of the damages they are causing, as well as on the costs of reducing their pollution.

You're not making sense.

Yes I am. Once a tax is imposed, a polluter has three choices. Pay the fine and go on with business as usual. Spend the money to change the production process in order to stop or reduce polluting and avoid or reduce the tax. Go out of business if it is too expensive to either pay the tax or stop the emissions. If a tax is levied on an individual automobile driver, to take account of the air pollution caused while driving through town, the choices are the same. Pay the tax and continue driving. Avoid or reduce the tax by purchasing a car that does not pollute the air or that puts out less pollution. Drive less, or stop driving altogether if the tax or an alternative vehicle are not affordable.

Why is that an economic solution?

Because it takes account of all the factors that affect society's wellbeing. But the tax should be imposed on *units of pollution*. Instead of a tax on owning a car, the tax would be imposed on driving. The tax could be on miles driven or it could be added to the price of gasoline. But, if an electric utility company has to pay a tax or fine for each ton of high-sulfur coal burned, it will simply pass the fine on to consumers. It will pass on part, but not all, of the fine to consumers through higher prices. But that is what should happen.

So you want consumers to pay? It sounded like you were against big business.

I'm not against big business. I am in favor of policies that help the nation, not just certain elements of society. It isn't about business versus the economy. It's about the economy—in total—with business being one important part of it. That's why both producers and consumers should be held responsible for the environmental damage caused by generating electricity. After all, if consumers were not using electricity, there would be no production, and no damages. If the damage caused by the production of electricity is severe, the utility company will have to charge a high price for its product if it can't solve its pollution problem. The higher the price of electricity, the less will be consumed and produced, and the lower the environmental damage will be.

I still don't understand what happens if the polluter simply pays the tax and continues polluting.

It means that the cost of fixing the pollution is greater than the damage it is causing. In terms of using resources in the best possible way, that is the solution economics wants.

What if the polluter fixes the pollution problem instead of paying the tax?

Then that's good. It means the cost of stopping the emission is less than the damage it is causing. Again, in terms of using resources wisely, it is what economics wants.

What if both the tax and the cost of controlling emissions are so high that the firm is forced to close down?

Then that's the best solution for the economy. It means that the people who are buying that product are not willing and able to pay for the true social cost of its production—internal plus external costs. Once the tax is imposed, whatever solution comes out in the market, it's best for society.

How could it ever work?

Making automobile drivers responsible for the pollution damages they cause can be relatively easy. A tax on gasoline, based on damages, makes the decision to drive take account of external costs, not just private costs. The problem with automobiles is similar to that of a factory. People drive too much if they are not responsible for the true costs of driving. The result is that some resources used for driving would add more to the wealth of society if they were shifted to alternative uses. However, the idea of imposing a tax must also consider the cost of the program. In some cases, it is relatively inexpensive to impose a tax on a polluter, although it might be expensive to estimate the actual damages.

What about the third choice—making an activity illegal?

Sometimes, that is the best solution. Let me tell you how a small town in Wisconsin decided to deal with the problem of leaf burning. Whenever someone burned leaves in the fall or spring, the smoke affected others in the community. There was no law against burning leaves, so those who were damaged by the smoke could not stop the burning. No one owned the rights to air quality, because there are no property rights for air or air quality. So no one, even if the smoke hurt him or her, could legally prevent others from burning leaves. The City Council was wise enough to recognize and understand the problem: A person decided to either burn leaves or bag them based on his or her private costs. If the cost of burning, including the value of the burner's time, was less than the cost of bagging and dumping, the leaves were burned. Each person with leaves made a decision that was in his or her own best interest, which is what should happen in a free-market economy. Unfortunately, the results of those decisions were not very good because people did not have to consider, or be responsible for, the smoke damage they caused to others. As a result, the community was upset. Many people felt their quality of life was being diminished. After a long debate, the City Council adopted an ordinance that banned the burning of leaves.

Sounds like more government regulation.

It's pure economics. If the decision had been to make individuals responsible for the total costs of their actions by imposing a tax on burning that is equal to the *external* costs of their activity, the tax would be calculated by determining the damage to the total community caused by burning leaves. The tax, or fine, would vary with how many leaves were burned, from zero if there is no burning to the estimated damages caused by greater and greater levels of burning. Instead of outlawing burning, the tax would give each person with leaves the ability to make a choice between burning and bagging, given the fact that he or she is now responsible for all costs of his or her actions. Then, whatever decision people with leaves make, whether it is to stop burning or to continue burning, society comes out ahead. No matter what happens, the real wealth of the community is increased. If the tax the burner has to pay to burn leaves is greater than the cost of bagging leaves and bringing them to the dump, the burner will bag the leaves and bring them to the dump, because that would be his or her cheaper solution. Burning the leaves and paying the tax would cost more than bagging. If the tax—the damages—is less than the cost of bagging, the burner would continue burning, because burning and paying the tax would cost him or her less than the cost of bagging.

You sound like a typical environmentalist. You have a solution that doesn't fix the problem.

Oh, but it does. And it is the solution economics wants, on the grounds that it is wrong to spend more to fix a problem than the damages are worth. Although people have a choice of burning leaves and paying the tax, or not burning and not paying the tax, the *only* way leaves would continue to be burned is if the *true* damages to others are less than the cost of fixing the problem—which is the cost of bagging the leaves.

So why was the City Council right to outlaw leaf burning instead of using a tax?

Because it would have been too costly, in terms of resources used, to first calculate the damages and to then impose and collect the taxes. That is why prohibiting leaf burning was the best economic solution. According to economics, a ban is the best choice if it yields the same result as a tax. In other words, a tax on burning leaves, calculated by adding up the real damages caused to everyone else, would be so high that no one would be willing to pay for the right to burn leaves. Therefore, from the standpoint of resource use, it's more efficient to have a law that yields the same *ideal* result: no leaves burned. And because no resources are needed to constantly measure damages and impose taxes, society gains even more. As a rule, if it can be shown that the result of imposing a tax on offenders will lead to a total elimination of the activity, it is cheaper and easier to simply make the activity illegal, because it uses fewer resources. Examples are: taking lead out of gasoline and paint, requiring emissions controls on automobiles, eliminating some food additives, outlawing the use of certain chemicals, and so on. In some cases, it is assumed that if manufacturers are forced to provide complete information on the contents or side effects of a product, consumers can make a rational decision as to whether or not they want to use the product. In other cases, where the negative effects are certain and unavoidable and high, society comes out ahead by banning the product or activity.

I was right. Your solution is to save the environment is at the expense of the economy.

You are back to the beginning. Back to one of the biggest economic fallacies dumped on the American people. Environmental problems are the result of market failure. And if we want to maximize the wealth of America, we have to correct the situations where the market lets us down.

I have a question about the tax idea. How do we know that a tax imposed on a polluter will be used to clean up the pollution?

The purpose of the tax is to force the market to take account of *all* costs. It is not to collect money to be used to clean up pollution. The market will take care of that on its own—once everyone is responsible for the true costs of their actions. Choosing the best place to spend the money is a separate issue.

But what if the pollution is really harmful? Paying a tax to have the right to kill people doesn't sound like a very good policy.

The greater the damages, the higher the tax would be. If the damages are severe, the tax will be very high. The economic-tax idea supports the bans that have been placed on leaf burning, DDT, and lead in gasoline and paint. The same logic can be used to prosecute people for murder. In that case, the "tax" could be time in prison or, possibly, the death penalty. It also supports government mandated improvements in automobile safety, required reductions in auto emissions, required increases in fuel economy, bans on dumping raw sewage and toxic chemicals into rivers and lakes, and so on.

Those things are already in place.

I know. But they are not in place because of the free market. They are in place because of government regulations. And we still elect a lot of politicians who want to reverse the environmental regulations we have. That is why it is important to understand that protecting the environment is not bad for the economy. The opposite is true. Protecting the environment to protect the health and wellbeing of the people increases the wealth of the nation.

Let me get this straight. A production or consumption process that pollutes the air, ground, or water, imposes costs or damages on someone else—external costs. And if the producer or consumer is not responsible for costs imposed on others, those external costs are not considered in the decision-making process, even though they are real costs to society. The result is that he or she will produce or consume more of that product than they would if they had to pay for both internal and external costs. Resources are misused, and the wealth of America is diminished.

That's it.

(5) Government should not produce goods and services that can be provided by the private sector.

Private, profit-making businesses can always provide a better quantity and quality of goods and services than government. This is a standard economic argument. The free market is always better than government at providing goods and services. The profit motive drives private business to give people what they want. And competition improves quality. The government is not concerned with profits; therefore it makes decisions based on bureaucratic goals, which are not in the best interest of the people. As an example, look at the poor quality of education in America.

You want private businesses to take over our schools?

That's right. Just look at how bad they are. A private business could do much better. I would love to run a high school.

Do it. Go ahead and start a private, profit-making school. This is a free country. There's no law against setting up a private school in America.

But there's already a private school in my town.

Start another one. If you know how to offer a higher quality education, it should be successful. Anyone who wants his or her children to attend your school simply has to pay whatever tuition you want to charge—if they are willing and able to pay what you want to charge.

But there aren't enough students that can pay what I would have to charge. Most students are in the public high school, and their parents are paying taxes to pay for it.

What if we close the public high school and let you have a chance at all the students?

That's what I'm talking about.

Of course, if we do that, we will also have to stop collecting the taxes that are now being used to pay for the public high school.

But how will I get paid?

Parents who no longer have to pay property taxes for the public high school can spend their tax savings on tuition at your new school.

But that won't be enough. Each family would save only one or two thousand dollars. We can't run a high school with that kind of tuition. The only students we could get would be those that can afford to pay what we have to charge. Most of the kids wouldn't get to go to high school at all. That doesn't make sense. We would all lose. Every business in town would suffer if our kids didn't get at least a high school education. Crime would go up. Social problems would increase. It would not be good.

So how do you want it to work?

Collect property taxes from everyone—not just those with kids in school—and give us the money. Then I will show you what I can do.

So you don't really want the government out of it. You want the government to collect taxes from everyone and give you the money. How is that privatizing the high school?

It's letting me make a profit.

I'm supposed to hand you tax money collected by the government so that you can make a profit? That doesn't sound like free enterprise or the free market at work. And you certainly wouldn't be adding competition to our school system.

Well, how else can everyone get a high school degree?

There *is* no other way. If the government did not collect taxes from the population in general, we would not have public education. Your plan is still public education, because you still want everyone to pay for it—not just the parents of students that are in school. The only difference is that you think a private business can do a better job managing or running a school. So far, there is no evidence that you're right. Not if you look at what has happened in cities where your scheme has already been tried.

Maybe not. But it would work if we had vouchers, and a bunch of private schools for students to choose from.

And how would vouchers work?

Simple. It's a perfect free market solution. Each child gets a voucher that can be used to pay tuition at any school he or she chooses to attend, with their parents' consent, of course. And because the schools would have to compete against each other to get students, they would be forced to offer high-quality education.

How is that different from the private school I said you could start anytime you want? What is the difference between a voucher and someone simply paying tuition?

The vouchers would be worth more than individuals could afford to pay. Maybe even more than the current system spends per student.

And where would the voucher money come from?

From taxing everyone. Just like we do now.

So, it's still public education. The government collects money from the community and uses it to pay for the education of all children. I assume you would let everyone into your school, whether or not they're good students.

I might want to be more selective than that. More like a real private school.

I suppose that's one reason why you could expect to do better than the public high school. You wouldn't have to deal with bad students.

But the key is competition.

No, it's not. Government is the key. If the government doesn't collect taxes from the community in general and use the funds to educate the community's children, we would have exactly what you said would happen if we shut down the high school and let you run a true private school. Some children could afford to become educated. Others could not. And the entire community would suffer. The question is: On what grounds can you justify taking money from people without children in school to pay for the education of those who are in school?

Because we all benefit from the education of the children in our community.

Economists call that a *positive externality*. When someone becomes educated, some of the benefits of that education are shared with others. Society as a whole gains, because educated people tend to be more productive, thereby increasing the wealth of the nation. However, as you already explained, if we had a true free-market education system, in which those who gained from the increased education of others did not have to pay, the market would provide too little education, as measured by its contribution to the nation's wealth.

Okay, you're right about quantity. But, what about quality? Our public schools are not doing very well. Private, profit-seeking businesses can do a better job than government.

As I said, so far, there is no proof of that. Public schools that have been handed over to private businesses do not have very good track records, which is not surprising For one thing, they are not true private schools, because they do not have to compete with other good schools for students. In fact, they don't have to compete at all to get students and tuition. They get all the students in the district and they take money from the government to run the school. So the government is still involved. So, the competition you claim will improve quality doesn't exist.

Where are you going to draw the line on taxing the community in order to provide a free education for anyone who wants it?

Maybe there shouldn't be a line. It makes economic sense at all levels. Every state has public colleges and universities, supported partially by general tax revenues, so that more students can afford to attend. If public universities did not exist, education in America would be at a terrible level.

How far do you want to go to provide subsidized or *free* education past high school?

Farther than you might think. One of the great stories is the GI Bill that paid for veterans of World War II to attend whatever colleges or universities they were admitted to. It is an example of how far we can go. Although the cost of the GI Bill was significant, the program earned a *profit* for the government. The difference between the income taxes actually paid by those who received free tuition and the estimated income taxes they would have paid had they not received a college education, was a multiple of the cost of the program. But that was only a small part of the benefits received by society. The education of that group of people played a major part in the scientific and business advancements that propelled the United States to its leadership role in the world.

So, you would probably argue against cuts in education.

We all benefit personally from receiving an education. And we all benefit from the education of others, because the more education we get, as a nation, the wealthier the nation will be. The GI Bill is just an example of how profitable education is to America. No matter who manages our schools, we should make certain they are funded at a level that will maximize the wealth of America.

Education is one of the greatest examples of the rising-tide argument.

Okay. I admit that government should be involved in education. But, that's an exception to the rule that says the private sector is better than government at providing goods and services.

It's great that you feel free to make up *rules* whenever it suits your purpose. Education is an important example of a positive externality. But it's not the only example. There are many cases where, according to economics, the government must be involved in order to ensure that the quantity of such goods and services is sufficient to maximize the wealth of America.

You mean other cases where, when someone does something, others benefit?

Right. *Positive externalities* exist in all areas of the economy. And we know, with certainty, that the market will *always* produce too little of such goods.

Why?

Because there is no market for the positive benefits given to others. And if there is no market for those benefits, those who receive those benefits will not help pay for the production of the good or service. Therefore, there is always less of those goods and services than the quantity needed to maximize the satisfaction of society, unless they are provided by government or subsidized by government.

Like what?

Like cures and inoculations for contagious diseases. They create positive benefits not only for the treated individual, but also for everyone who is spared from contracting the disease. In order to maximize such benefits, public health programs are established. Improvements in technology and new inventions provide profits for the inventor, but also for many others. In a totally free-market economy, such innovations would not be protected. Anyone would be free to copy and use what someone else did, thereby eliminating the profits that may encourage such work. In order to promote and encourage innovation, patent rights were created. Patents give inventors rights that prevent the copying of their ideas for a specified length of time, allowing the inventor to earn a profit and giving others the incentive to be creative. The pharmaceutical industry is an example. In each case involving a positive externality, if the government does not step in and find a way to increase the consumption or production of such goods, the wealth of the nation is reduced. That is one reason why anyone who says that the government should hand over much of what it does to private, profit-based corporations is wrong. The market *always* produces too little of goods whose production or consumption yields benefits to those who do not pay for it, such as education. Unless the government produces or provides such goods, the wealth of America is reduced.

What about my neighbor's flower garden that gives me, and other neighbors, pleasure? Are you saying that the government should subsidize my neighbor's gardening? Or pay to paint the house down the street?

The economic *test* as to whether or not government should use general tax money to help pay for something that has a positive externality is: Would others be willing to pay for it? For example, from what you have said, I know you would be willing to pay for education. And I believe you would be willing to pay to avoid the possibility of coming in contact with a contagious and deadly disease, and possibly for a program that would increase national health, because you obviously know healthier workers are good for business. On the other hand, I doubt that you, or any of your neighbors, would be willing to pay someone to plant more flowers. Therefore, the government shouldn't either.

(6) **Government is too big**.

That's what free-market economies are all about. The forces of supply and demand in private markets ensuring that the *best* quantity is produced and consumed in each market. When the government produces things, it disrupts the free market.

What do you want the government to stop doing?

I don't have to be that specific.

Why not? Why don't you have to be clear when you make a statement? The truth is, there are important things that private markets would not provide at all.

Your opinion is that the market doesn't work?

It's not my opinion. It's standard economics. And it is not just that sometimes markets don't work; it is that sometimes there are no markets. The question is: What do you want to get rid of? The police department? The fire department? The court system? Maybe you want to trust your home or your life to whomever you can pay for protection. Maybe you would like to trust justice to a court being run to make a profit.

That's not what I mean.
What do you mean? Maybe you and your profit-making friends want to go into the lighthouse business.

How could anyone make a profit running a lighthouse?
Charge fees to all the ships that benefit from your light.

No one would pay.
Why not? You would be providing a valuable service.

We could never keep track of all the ships that are protected by our light. And those we did know about wouldn't pay anyway. They would just say that they don't care about our light. Then they would benefit anyway, because we couldn't stop them from seeing it
I suppose that's why lighthouses had to be provided by government.

Okay. But we don't use lighthouses any more, anyway. We have new technology that can be sold to each ship. If someone doesn't buy it, he or she is not protected. So we don't need the government. And your argument is false.
No it's not. Before those products were available in the market, ships relied on lighthouses. If the government hadn't built them, there would have been countless shipwrecks that could have been avoided.

This sounds like a positive externality idea. You want me to admit that the free market will not provide enough of things like lighthouses, police protection, or fire protection. But the lighthouse example shows that the private market is better than government.
No it doesn't. It shows that technology is constantly changing how markets work. But I doubt that you can prove that ship owners would have chosen to operate without lighthouses while they waited for the introduction of a technology they could buy.
But the private market could provide some police and fire protection—

through profit-making private companies.

That's true. The private market will provide some, but not enough. A lighthouse is an example of an extreme form of positive externality that economists call *public goods*. The line separating public goods from other goods with positive externalities is fuzzy. In fact, some economists do not even make a distinction. Public goods are goods whose benefits cannot be excluded from those who do not pay for them, and which can be provided to additional people at no additional cost. The thing that separates public goods from other goods with positive externalities is that the market may not provide them at all. They might not exist if the government did not provide them. Some examples, along with lighthouses, are national parks and national defense.

Everyone cares about national defense.

It doesn't matter if they care about it or not. National defense cannot be bought and sold in the market. And it cannot be provided for with patriotic donations.

Why not?

If someone came to your door, asking for a contribution to pay for national defense, how much would you voluntarily give?

Probably a lot.

I doubt that. No one is that stupid. The only rational response is to give nothing.

Not if you care about national defense.

That has nothing to do with it. There are three reasons why a rational person will refuse to pay. One is that whether people pay or not, they know they will receive the benefits of being protected. The second is that they know their contribution is meaningless, because the donation the average person can give cannot affect the level of national defense for the country. The third is that, even if someone ignores the first two reasons and thinks about paying what he or she believes is his or her *fair share*, there is the reality that, 'If no one else pays, I will have given my money for nothing.'

What's your solution?

The same as for all positive externality issues. The government must take care of it. The government must provide national defense and pay for it out of general tax revenues. Of course, there is still the question of what constitutes an *adequate* or *necessary* level of defense. The economic argument that the government must provide national defense does not say that the government should provide more defense than we need, or that defense spending should not be closely examined. But without government control, that question would never have an opportunity to be debated.

Okay. There are a couple things that would not exist without government.

Maybe your friends would like to get into the private freeway business. They could build freeways, and other private roads, for profit.

No one can make a profit building and owning private freeways.

Does that mean you want to close all our roads? How about getting into the national park business?

You're picking extreme examples. That's not what I'm talking about.

Well, the examples we just discussed make up a large part of the federal government's budget. So, what should government do that's different?

I don't know. The government has already gone too far. Things like national parks are a drain on the economy. Too much money is being spent on things that only a few people care about. And the only value of wilderness areas is the resources that can be extracted by business, which is why environmental protection is bad economics.

No, it's not. Environmental protection is good economics, because real economics says that the value of things such as national wildlife areas and ancient forests goes beyond the value placed on them by the people who go there. Or the market value of extracted resources. It must include the value they give to people who may never see them.

That doesn't make sense.

Have you ever been to the Grand Canyon?

No. But what does that have to do with it?

Do you care that the Grand Canyon exists. Or that it is a protected site that will be a part of America's future?

Of course. But I still doubt that I will ever see it in person.

You don't have to. The question is: Would you be willing to pay something just to know that its existence is assured?

I think everyone would.

That's what real economics is about. Along with the prices we can see in the market, economics takes account of the value that people place on things they may never see. Back in the 1980's, we sold off one of the last stands of ancient trees in Alaska to Japanese lumber mills for $2 a tree. I know I could have collected more than $2 a tree by getting small contributions from each of the millions of Americans who liked the idea that such trees still existed in America. But the benefits those trees offered to millions of Americans did not show up in the market, because there is no market that includes the total value all of America would have been willing to pay to keep them. And because no such markets exist for other resources or wilderness areas, such resources cannot be allocated by the free market.

(7) Government should stop trying to manage natural resources and let the market do it.

The market always does a better job than government of deciding how to use natural resources. It's another textbook issue. It's what free-market economics is all about: The forces of supply and demand yield an equilibrium quantity in each market that is best for the nation's wealth. Government regulations that affect how business uses natural resources disrupt the free market.

Actually, textbooks do not say private markets are the best way to allocate all natural resources. Textbooks say that we will *always* overuse resources that are not owned. And if the government does not regulate the use of un-owned resources, the nation's wealth is diminished. Resources, such as fish in lakes, rivers, and oceans, that no one owns until someone takes them. Without laws, licenses, and quotas, anyone has the legal right to catch all the fish he or she wants. The result has been the extinction of many species.

Why would anyone want to cause the extinction of a fish population they fish for sport or profit?

Imagine you are a commercial fisherman, heading off to catch fish. Which of the commercial fishermen in your fleet get the fish?

Whoever gets them, I guess.

That's right. There is no market to allocate fish in the ocean to those who are willing and able to pay the most for the right to catch them, because no one owns the fish in the ocean. Therefore, fish are taken by whoever gets there first. If you were a commercial fisherman, how many fish would you take on each trip?

As many as I could. The more fish I get, the more money I make.

And the other fishermen?

As many as they can.

But if everyone catches as many fish as possible, won't the fish population decline?

I suppose it will.

And the fewer fish there are, the more time, effort, and money it will take to catch any given quantity. In fact, if you keep going, there might not be any fish left at all.

I suppose. But if I knew that, I could stop catching so many fish. If I caught fewer fish, then the population of fish could continue to exist, and I could keep fishing.

The trouble is, you *don't* know. On top of that, if you don't catch them, someone else will. No one *wants* to exploit the fish population to extinction, but that's what happens when no one owns the fish in a lake or an ocean. Anyone can take all he or she wants, as long as there is no law against it. And when overfishing reduces the size of a fish population, others who want to catch fish have a more difficult and costly time doing so.

Sounds like a negative externality argument.

It is a type of negative externality. The economic issue is: If un-owned resources are not managed correctly, they will not be used in a way that maximizes the wealth of the nation. Un-owned resources, which economists call *common property resources*, do lead to a type of negative externality, because one person's use of the resource negatively affects others. But there are some unique issues related to common property resources. One is that a lack of property rights means non-renewable common property resources, such as oil in the ground, will be used up too quickly, causing a reduction in the nation's wealth. Another is that renewable common property resources, such as fish or whales, are always in danger of being exploited to extinction. And it doesn't do any good for one or a number of fishermen to voluntarily limit their catch, because that won't stop others from over-fishing.

I suppose you have a solution.

There are three economic solutions to this kind of market failure. One is to assign property rights to the resource so that it can be traded in the market. A second is to impose taxes on those who use it, so that fishermen, for example, are responsible for the true costs of the impact they have on other fishermen. A third is to set physical quotas.

There goes the free market.

What free market? Common property resources aren't traded in the market, because there is no market. No one can buy or sell something that isn't owned. So if the government doesn't manage such resources, they will not be used in a way that maximizes the satisfaction of society or the wealth of the nation.

Your solutions sound impossible to use.

It *is* difficult to assign ownership rights to fish in the ocean. It *is* also difficult to impose taxes on catching fish. And there *are* long-standing debates on the size of an optimal quota for most commercial fisheries. As a result, there are fewer examples of successful intervention than there are of populations exploited to extinction.

But sport fish in lakes and rivers have been protected for years.

That's right. They have been protected by requiring fishing licenses and setting daily limits on catch. If that had not been done, there might not be any fresh-water sport fish left today. Unfortunately, ocean species, including mammals, such as whales, have not been managed as well, partly because no nation has the ability, on its own, to set fishing or whaling limits on the high seas. However, international agreements have led to the comeback of some species that were on the verge of extinction.

Any other success stories?

One of the best is the successful regulation of the Alaskan Salmon fishery. An annual quota was calculated that would maintain the population at a healthy level. The quota is divided into parcels that are assigned or sold to individual fishermen. Each fishing boat is then allowed to freely catch its given quota. The result is a successful and profitable industry that can exist for many years. On the other side of the country, it is estimated that there are little more than 100 wild salmon left in New England.

So you're saying that if government gets involved, common property resources can be productive far into the future.

Only if government does what is right. And there is no guarantee it will. In fact, it was the government that put together the terrible program that was the final blow to wiping out the Cape Cod fisheries—once the most productive fishing grounds in the world. After years of over-fishing, fish populations were run down to levels that virtually eliminated any profits for fishermen. Instead of finding a way to regulate fishing so that the fish populations could recover, an absolutely terrible program was put in place. The program financed, at zero down and close to zero interest, the purchase of larger, more efficient fishing boats. The result was predictable: Giving fishermen bigger boats to catch fish from a dwindling population wiped out what was left. Fisheries that had been in danger were eliminated. The boats were not paid off. The nation's wealth was reduced. Cape Cod fishermen lost their jobs. Only the boat builders won.

No matter what you say, I do not want the government telling me what I can and cannot do. The government does not have the right to set limits on what I can do. This is America. And I can tell you that I know a lot of people that see limits or quotas as government attacks on the freedom of individuals and on the free market itself.

That's what the Cape Cod fishermen thought. They did not want the government involved—although they thought it was okay for the government to use tax money to give them deals on boats. Now they have the freedom to do a lot of things, except the freedom to make a living fishing. Whenever common property resources are involved, the lack of a market allows individuals to do what is not good for the nation or for themselves. Individuals who believe they are exercising their free rights to make a living any way they choose, may end up having their jobs eliminated along with the resource.

And your answer is government control or regulation over the exploitation of common property resources?

For the good of the nation, as well as for the good of those who exploit such resources for sport or profit.

(8) Price supports help farmers.

When the government sets minimum prices for agricultural products, farmers get to sell their products for at least that price, instead of the market price; and, if they get to sell at a higher price, they make more money.

Some will. Some won't. The reality of supply is that sellers want to sell more at higher prices; less at lower prices. The reality of demand is that buyers are willing and able to buy more at lower prices and less at higher prices. Therefore, if the government sets a minimum price above the market price, farmers will grow and try to sell more, while buyers are willing and able to buy less. Total production increases, but total sales decrease. The result is a surplus. Farmers pay to produce more, but they sell less. And because total sales are less than they were before, farmers who are able to sell what they produce at the minimum government price earn higher incomes, but farmers who cannot sell everything they paid to produce earn smaller incomes, or no income at all.

Is that why we hear about farmers dumping their produce?

That's it. The only other possibility is for the government to buy the surplus at the new, higher price, in order to artificially support the price in the market and to save farmers the cost of dumping what they can't sell. But, then the government has to dump it or store it. And that costs more money. In the end, some farmers win, some lose. Consumers buy less and pay higher prices. And taxpayers pay for the government to buy and store, or dump, the surplus it created with its price support program.

So, price supports transfer income from taxpayers to some farmers, while other farmers lose. That doesn't sound so good. What can we do if we want to help small farmers survive?

Give them money. If you want to support them in their profession as farmers, it is cheaper for taxpayers and consumers if the government just gives them money. It is more honest, and it will not reduce economic efficiency.

(9) Price ceilings help consumers.

Many people think government can protect consumers by setting maximum prices in markets. Rent control laws are an example.

Rent control laws do not negate the reality of supply and demand. If the government tries to help consumers by setting a maximum price in a market that is below the market price, the reality of supply is that less will be offered for sale, and the reality of demand is that buyers will want to buy more. The result is a government-created shortage. And shortages that are not allowed to be handled by the market create black markets. Rent control leads to fewer rental units being offered while also leading to more rental units being demanded. The result is that some who cannot find rental units at the controlled price will offer bribes to landlords or property managers in order to be given preferential treatment. Others who cannot find rental units, but who are unwilling or unable to pay bribes, incur the costs of waiting to find a suitable unit or the costs of moving out of the rent-controlled area to find housing. In the end, some people are forced out of the rent-controlled area while others pay both the controlled rent and bribes, which can total more than the uncontrolled rental price.

So, who wins?

Those who are lucky enough to get housing at the controlled price without having to pay bribes win. But, even for them, laws that set prices below the market price cause the owners of rental units to spend less on upkeep and repairs. And because there is a long line of potential renters waiting to find units, renters are in no position to demand that owners take better care of their property. Also, below-market rent prices cause fewer units to be built in the future, making the shortage even worse over time.

This sounds like an example of government interference that disrupts economic efficiency and reduces the nation's wealth.

It is. It is an example of how government interference can hurt those it is intended to help, as well as damage markets and the nation as a whole.

(10) Economic laws.

So, economic laws run the markets.

The law of supply and demand runs private markets, but not always in a way that maximizes the wealth of the nation, because the law of supply and demand cannot protect free markets from those with the power to profit by limiting competition and from price distortions caused by market failure and externalities. Therefore, other laws or regulations are needed to protect the free market. Without such laws or regulations, we give everyone the right to degrade or destroy the environment while being immune from prosecution for the damage they cause to others. Some may think economic laws are less important than civil or criminal laws. They are not. On the other hand, laws intended to help people by setting minimum or maximum prices in markets not suffering from market failure tend to disrupt economic efficiency while hurting those who are supposed to be helped.

THE ECONOMY

1. What Do We Want?

One of the basic rules of any civilized society is that no one should have the right to make himself or herself better off at someone else's expense. Do whatever you want to make yourself better off, but do not hurt someone else in the process.[24]

We do not believe that society gains by allowing muggers to make a living stealing purses from little old ladies. Therefore, we have laws against stealing. Of course, passing laws against stealing does trample on the "rights" of muggers. But the civilized world decided long ago that the right to walk down the street in safety is more important than the right to make a living by mugging little old ladies. Now, if all we had to do to get what we want or to not get what we do not want were to pass laws, the world would be much simpler. Unfortunately, making it illegal to steal does not stop everyone from stealing.

We believe that the threat of potential punishment will prevent most, but not all, people from committing crimes. For some, the potential rewards from crime seem greater than the punishment they might receive if they are caught, if they are prosecuted, if they are convicted, if they are sentenced, and if they actual serve the potential sentence. For others, committing a crime is a "spontaneous" act, not a thoughtful decision that weighs the benefits against the consequences.

We need laws and rules. But we need more than that. We also need societies and economies organized in the "best possible" way. For example, one way to make crime not pay is to improve the alternatives. In other words, the more you have to lose, the less crime pays. That does not mean there is some simple economic solution to all crime. That would be absurd. However, there is a strong correlation between crime and low economic expectations. Therefore, by improving economic possibilities, the attitude that leads to "thoughtful" crime will decline; it may even reduce spontaneous crimes.

---

[24] The economic exception to this rule is that it is okay to "hurt" someone else if the harm is the result of actions taken in free markets where the damage is caused by changes in prices.

1. The best of all possible worlds.

In *Candide*, Voltaire satirized the "technocrats" of the 18th century who thought they had the knowledge to create "the best of all possible worlds." But Voltaire's low regard for other thinkers did not prevent him from believing that he had ideas that could make the world a better place to live.

From the beginning of civilization, thinkers and doers have tried to improve the world, and although history is full of horrors committed in the name of spreading good, we like to believe that we are moving forward. Whether we are or not is, of course, a question that must be asked constantly.

Hopefully, we will never run out of people who believe that the world can be improved and who are willing to devote their energies to what often seems like an impossible task. But the fact that we never have all the answers should never be used as an excuse to accept the status quo.

2. Weighing the winners against the losers.

The one unanswerable question confronting anyone who hopes to make the world a better place is: How do you judge a change that helps some while hurting others? If a proposed change is expected to help 1,000 people at the expense of one, is it a good plan? If you happen to be one of the 1,000, chances are it will sound pretty good. But if you are the one who is to be sacrificed for the good of the many, you might not think it is such a good idea.

But what if you are neither? What if you are simply an outside policymaker trying to do your best? How would you judge such a policy? Would you say that the total gains to the 1,000 would obviously be greater than the losses suffered by one? Or would you recognize that if the objective were to maximize society's *total* happiness that it is possible for one person's loss to be greater than the happiness gained by the 1,000?

If you could actually measure happiness, and if maximizing total happiness were your goal, then you could, in theory make a decision. But if you admit that it is impossible to make such a measurement and also that it is possible for one person's losses to outweigh the gains of many, then you will understand why this is an unanswerable question.

3. The economic solution.

Economists have devised two ways to avoid this unanswerable question. After all, if you cannot find a way around the question, there really is not much you can do.

One is to say that a policy or a change is good if it helps at least one person without making anyone else worse off. That is a good idea, in theory, but you will not find many chances to put it into action.

The other is to avoid the question altogether, by claiming that economists cannot make such decisions.

That way, instead of trying to make an unsupportable decision, an economist can simply explain who the winners and losers will be and let someone else decide what to do.

That might sound like a cop out, but it is not. Once an economist has analyzed a problem and identified the potential winners and losers, his or her job *as an economist* is finished. The next step—deciding whether or not to implement the change—is not an economic decision, it is a personal decision. An economist does not have any more to say about the matter than anyone else. As people, economists can have opinions. But when those opinions cannot be supported with economic logic, then it must be clear that the economist is talking as a person and not offering an economic solution.

Of course, when no one wants to take the responsibility for such decisions, it is easy to point at economists and say that they are not doing their job.

But if you understand the distinction between an individual as an "economist" and as a "person," you will not only understand the limits of economic analysis, you will also understand why economists are cautious when making policy statements. Rather than shirking their responsibility, they are trying to avoid making judgments that others may believe are based on economic logic instead of personal opinion.

4. Models.

In order to help understand what went on in the past, is going on now, or is expected to go on in the future, economists create models.

Some models, such as those using market supply and demand, are used to explain individual markets.

Others, such as the one that follows, are used to explain the economy as a whole.

In all cases, the value of models is that they are able to use a small number of variables to explain and predict the values of other variables and to help us understand complicated situations.

The INDIVIDUAL MARKETS section of this book looks at individual markets.

The fictional story that follows presents a unique and useful model that can be used to explain and predict changes that affect the overall economy.

2. An Economic Story

1

The first Friday in May opened with a warm spring sun that promised a new beginning. A gentle wind buffeted the still-new leaves, and as the sun moved higher in the sky, the wind picked up; not like the kite-flying breezes of April, but stronger than the mild currents that would soon mark mid-summer.

It was a day, like spring days throughout history, that should have raised spirits and hopes as nature proved, once again, that winter leads to a renewal. But, for some, that did not happen on this particular day.

David Peterson walked out of the elevator, turned right, took nine steps, and pressed his thumb against the remote entry button on his Lexus key. The lights on the big V-8 sedan flashed against the wall of the underground parking garage. Another right turn, four more steps, and his left hand found the handle on the driver's door. Then he stopped. Instead of opening the door, he stared over the roof of the black car, without focusing on anything in particular.

Thirty seconds later, he blinked; then he looked down as his hand squeezed the handle. He pulled the door open and sat down, placing both hands on the leather-covered steering wheel. Then he paused again, staring at the wall that was one foot away from the front bumper. His name was stenciled on the concrete in neat blue letters:

DAVID PETERSON, VICE PRESIDENT.

A few seconds later, he pushed the key into the ignition. As he did so, he thought about the meeting he had just left. His company had to make a stop-or-go-decision about a major project, and he was responsible for determining if economic conditions were right to go forward.

He had spent the previous three months reading everything he could find about the state of the economy and talking to as many people as he could. Because of his senior position and the size of his company, he had access to top-level people in and out of government, as well as the budget to obtain reports from highly respected economic think tanks.

But he had a gnawing knot in his stomach as he announced at the meeting that he was certain the current economy would support the multi-million dollar investment. And it took all the nerves he could pull together to force a smile when the others had congratulated him on his outstanding presentation.

What he did not say to anyone was that he had poured over countless pieces of contradictory predictions and had listened to experts with views that were all over the board.

And here we go, he thought, as his thumb and forefinger tightened on the key. *It was a stop or go decision, and I said go.* He turned the key and the Lexus hummed quietly. As he pulled into the street, he thought, *I might as well have flipped a coin.*

Brian Jones rolled over for what seemed to be the millionth time in a night filled with demons. The demons were variations of the authors whose ideas he would be expected to use in a few hours. The leader of the pack was the professor who was giving him a 9:00 a.m. final exam on practical economics, a required course in the MBA program at his prestigious university.

Of all the courses Brian had taken during his six years in universities—as an undergraduate and now as a graduate student—the ones that made the least sense to him were the economics classes, none of which he would have registered for if it had not been required.

But, like it or not, understand it or not, he was facing one last economics final. The problem, the thing that was keeping him awake, was that he was going to be asked to demonstrate his expertise by discussing or explaining the economics behind a number of current issues. He would have slept much better if the exam were based on material he could have memorized. His only solace was that this was the last time in his entire life he would ever have to think about economics.

Or so he wanted to believe.

The Questions

Kevin and Karen Elmwood leaned back against the starboard seat of the old Pearson Ensign they had totally restored two years earlier and let the ten knot southerly wind push the twenty-two foot day sailor out into the bay.

The Elmwoods, who were in their thirties, loved sailing in May, before the heat of high summer and the sometimes still days left them becalmed for long periods of time, sometimes making it necessary to start up the small Johnson outboard hanging off the stern of the full-keel boat.

They were doing well financially, partly because they had put off having children until they felt more secure.

Normally, when they sailed, they did not talk business. Business, to them, meaning their jobs, their investments, their housing plans, and their family plans, was not part of sailing. Today was different. Today, they were both worried about what the economy was doing—what the economy had been doing for the last few years.

It was obvious to the experts in the media that the economy was not okay, but they did not know exactly what that meant. They watched television and read major newspapers and business magazines, but it was difficult to get a grip on what was happening, because it was virtually impossible to find anyone who talked about the economy without having his or her pronouncements affected by his or her political affiliation. From what they could see, there was Republican economics and Democratic economics, but no economist economics.

No wonder they call economics the dismal science, they thought. *Under some circumstances, the politicizing of economics and economic facts might not be a big deal; it was how the world worked. But when you are overwhelmed by uncertainty, it would be nice to have the chance to use non-political economic knowledge to help make decisions and plans that might affect the rest of your life.*

Economics in the Park

2

At exactly 11:52 a.m. on September 27, a medium blue 1964 Austin Mini turned off Lincoln Street onto the narrow dirt path that led to the bandstand in the center of Jefferson Park. It was not the old Cooper S model famous for sweeping races against the world's most exotic automobiles; it was the basic model with an only adequate supply of horsepower and front windows that opened and closed by sliding back and forth on a track, like miniature patio doors, not by rolling down into the door. Still, it was impossible to ignore. Not because it was so small, but because it was pulling a trailer. Not just a trailer, but a wooden-floored flatbed trailer holding a bathtub.

The single-unit parade stopped in front of the bandstand, and a man in his forties, wearing a tweed sport coat and khaki trousers, climbed out of the small vehicle. He brushed back his long, graying hair and smiled at the crowd that was gathering. After their initial surprise, the spectators noticed a sign on the side of the trailer. The sign read:

Rubber Ducky Economics

There was a crowd in the park that day because of a small notice that had been placed in the newspaper. The notice read:

ECONOMICS IN THE PARK
September 27th at noon
The Bandstand in Jefferson Park

So everyone in the crowd was taken aback when an old Austin Mini pulling a trailer holding a bathtub stopped at the bandstand. They were expecting an economist, not a…whatever this was. Still, the man with the tweed sport coat looked pretty smart. And the sign on the trailer did say Rubber Ducky Economics… whatever that meant.

Among the spectators were David Peterson, Brian Jones, and Kevin and Karen Elmwood.

David Peterson was in the crowd because he was, once again, in the middle of making a stop-or-go recommendation on another very expensive project and he did not trust any of the coins in his pocket to make the right decision. So, when he saw the notice in the paper, he thought he might as well have lunch in the park.

Economics in the Park

Brian Jones was in the park because, after receiving his MBA in June, he had accepted a good, but high-pressure, job that, contrary to his hopes of a few months earlier, required him to deal with the economy on a daily basis. Although he had received a B on the economics final that kept him awake all night, he had been spending a lot of his time after graduation trying to find someone or something that would give him a basic understanding of how the economy works.

The Elmwoods were there because they were hoping to find some help in dealing with the strain on their marriage caused by not knowing how to handle economic and financial uncertainty.

As David Peterson was about to discover, September 27th would be his lucky day.

It would also be Brian Jones's lucky day.

And Kevin and Karen Elmwood's.

"Do you think we are in the right place?" Karen asked. "This isn't what I expected."

Kevin looked around at the crowd, and then at the trailer with the bathtub. "I don't know," he said. "I don't know if these are the kind of people who would come to an economics in the park lecture, or not. But the sign on the trailer *does* have the word *economics* on it."

A man in his fifties, standing next to Kevin, turned to them and said he was pretty sure they were in the right place.

He was correct.

As soon as Kevin turned back to Karen, the man standing beside the trailer began speaking.

"Good afternoon," he said. "Welcome to the first ever *economics in the park* meeting. Before we begin, I want to make certain that everyone who is here belongs here."

The people in the crowd looked around at each other, wondering who might not belong.

While the people were wondering who might and might not belong, the speaker continued.

"The question each of you has to ask yourself is, 'Do you know why you are here?'

"Let me explain what I mean. When asked why they climb mountains, some mountain climbers answer, 'Because they are there.' Others say, 'If you have to ask, you won't understand.'

Economics in the Park

"It is the same with wanting to understand the economy. If someone is asked why he or she wants to understand the economy, the answer should be either, 'Because it is there.' Or, 'If you have to ask, you won't understand.'

"So, if there is anyone here who thinks he or she has to ask the question, you should probably be doing something else."

Kevin smiled at Karen.

"I am very serious," the man continued. "If there is just one thing everyone should understand about economics, it is that there is no such thing as a free lunch. Which means there is no such thing as a free lecture. No one had to buy a ticket to be here. But by being here, you are giving up the opportunity to be somewhere else or to be doing something else. And the value to you of the most important thing you have to give up to be here is a very real cost to you. Economists call it *opportunity cost*. And it is the foundation of virtually all economic theory. So take a minute to think about your options. If you do not already know why it is more important to your business life, your investing life, and your personal life to understand how the economy works than to be doing something else, then the cost to you of being here is too great. For everyone who does know, I want to welcome you again."

Brian Jones knew. He knew, without a doubt, how important it was for him to understand the economy. In fact, he came prepared to record whatever transpired in the park, even though he had no idea what it would be.

And that is what he did. He recorded everything on a small, digital recorder. When he returned home, he transcribed it all. He did not use quotation marks to identify the speaker's remarks, because he wanted a clean manuscript. But he did add notes, in italics, to describe some of the action and the questions others asked.

What follows is Brian's transcript of what the man who drove the Mini into Jefferson Park said, or, as Brian titled it:

"Rubber Ducky Economics"

3

The speaker began:

Welcome to the first-ever economics in the park meeting. Although some of you may think economics is difficult, that it is based on some strange, or secret, way of thinking, it is not. Economics is pure common sense. It is, at its core, little more than pointing out and organizing the obvious.

Of course, like many things we eventually end up knowing, sometimes it helps to have someone else point out what is obvious.

That is why I am here. To introduce you to a series of economic ideas, which, once you hear them, should lead you to say to yourself, "I knew that."

The first idea I want to give you is that the economy is a bathtub.

Well, it's not really a bathtub. But it can be represented by a bathtub. That is why I have this wonderful prop sitting on this trailer.

This bathtub is a model. It is a model of the economy that is just as useful as the complex, mathematical models found in textbooks. In fact, it can be more useful, because it is easier to understand and easier to use.

All of which you will understand by the time our little economics in the park meeting is over.

When you get home, your own bathtub will be a reminder of today's discussion. If you do not have a bathtub at home, it doesn't matter; as long as you know what a bathtub is and how it works, you know all you have to know. That is about as complicated as we are going to get.

In other words, if you can understand how a bathtub works, you can understand how the economy works.

Now, I am not talking about all the plumbing needed to hook up a bathtub; I am talking only about how a bathtub works.

There is a faucet and a drain. And we, hopefully, control both. We control how much water goes into the tub by turning the faucet handles. We control how much goes out by adjusting the stopper on the drain. Of course, we do not have total control. No matter how much we turn the handles there is a limit to how much water will flow into the tub. And no matter how much we open the drain there is a limit to how fast the water can flow out of the tub. But, we can set the inflow from zero, meaning it is turned off, to some maximum flow; and we can set the outflow from zero, meaning the plug is in, to some maximum outflow, depending on how much we open the drain plug.

Given these facts about bathtubs, we know the following. If we pick a given period of time, say thirty minutes, and we turn on the faucet and open the drain, water will flow into the tub and water will flow out of the tub. Then, depending on whether the inflow is greater or less than the outflow, after thirty minutes, the tub will be overflowing, or empty, or it will have some water in it; the actual quantity being a function of the inflow relative to the outflow.

That's it. That is how a bathtub works. It is also how the economy works.

While he was talking, the speaker connected a hose from a faucet on the side of the bandstand to a threaded pipe at the front of the bathtub on the trailer. Then he opened the faucet on the bandstand and the faucets on the bathtub so that water ran into the tub. He left the drain partially open, so while water was going into the tub, water was also flowing out, onto the ground. At this point, it was not clear if the people in the crowd thought the speaker, who was jumping on and off the trailer, was crazy, or if he were offering them something truly clever. The one thing that was clear was that everyone was saying to each other, "I knew that."

Then the speaker put up a sign that said, "It's all about the GDP."

Okay. Now that we know how a bathtub works, we can use that knowledge to understand how the economy works, because understanding the economy is just as simple as understanding a bathtub.

In other words, if you can understand how the quantity of water in a bathtub is determined by the inflow relative to the outflow, you can understand how the economy works and how economic activity is measured. All we have to do is assume that the water in the tub represents production during some time period, which is normally called Gross Domestic Product.

Of course, the economy is more than water; it is all the things that are produced and consumed. Unfortunately, while it is easy to see, or visualize, how we can measure the quantity of water in a bathtub, if we had a giant tub filled with everything that was produced or bought during some time period, we would be looking at a giant junk pile. Well, not really a junk pile; a huge pile of good things. In any case, there is no real way to measure, in physical terms, how much stuff is in the tub. We can't add up all the things that are produced and sold during a given time period by weight or by volume, because neither measure would mean much. Or, to put it another way: As we all learned in grade school, you can't add apples and oranges.

In other words, imagining a huge bathtub filled with all the good stuff we, as a nation, made or bought last year might be a great image, but there is no physical measure we can use to add all the Fords that were produced to all the corn that was produced to all the computers that were produced to all the apples that were produced to all the oranges that were produced and so on.

So, we add up their dollar values instead. We add up the market values of all final goods and services produced inside the country during some time period. And we call that number

Gross Domestic Product.

When we, meaning the government statisticians, add up all the spending numbers, they are separated into four categories: consumer spending, investment spending by business, government spending, and net exports, which are exports minus imports. Some of you may be wondering why I am switching back and forth between two different terms: production and spending. The answer is that when we measure spending, we are also measuring production, because whatever is bought had to be produced. You may also be wondering why the definition of Gross

Domestic Product is for final goods and services. The reason is to avoid double counting; we do not want to count steel and then the cars the steel was made to produce, and so on.

There are a few other rules that are followed when calculating Gross Domestic Product.

One is that the investment number is for gross business investment, which means that depreciation of the nation's capital stock is ignored. If depreciation is accounted for, the final number is called Net Domestic Product, because it uses net instead of gross investment. Pretty smart.

Another rule is to count only goods and services produced inside the country. It doesn't matter if the stuff is produced by domestic or foreign companies, as long as it is produced inside our national boundaries; therefore, everything produced and sold by U.S. companies operating in other countries is excluded.

A third rule is that we can adjust the GDP number to take account of inflation.

That's pretty much it. There is nothing magical about GDP; it is simply a definition. But it is a useful definition, because it offers a logical way of measuring the economy.

By following the definition of Gross Domestic Product and all the rules, we end up with a number—GDP—that is used by the media, the government, and private economists, to describe the state of the economy at a point in time, to compare different economic time periods or different economies, and to estimate economic growth.

Very simply, GDP is calculated by adding up four items:
>Consumer spending,
>Investment spending by business,
>Government spending, and
>Exports.

And subtracting one item:
>Imports.

And that's it.

Someone in the crowd asked, "What do you mean, 'That's it?'" The speaker answered, "That's it. That is what you have to know." Then he continued.

Once you know what GDP is and how it is measured, everything else falls into place. The economy becomes simple.

The Model

4

He put up a new sign: "The water in the tub is Gross Domestic Product (GDP)."

Now that we all know what GDP is, and how it is measured, we can look at our bathtub economy.

> We have a bathtub; and the water in the tub is Gross Domestic Product.
> The water flowing in is:
> > consumer spending,
> > investment spending,
> > government spending, and
> > exports.
> The water flowing out is:
> > imports.
> The actual quantity of water in the tub, after some given time period, depends on how much is coming in and how much is going out.
> Whatever that quantity is, it represents Gross Domestic Product.
> In order to make it even simpler, imagine that the tub has marks on its side, like a measuring cup, so that we can easily know the quantity of water in the tub by looking at the water level.
> And, finally, to make the whole thing—our bathtub model—as visual as possible, imagine there is a rubber ducky floating in the tub.

As he said this, he threw a little rubber duck into the tub. The rubber duck bobbed along on top of the water.

> And, so that you will never forget what we are doing here today, I am giving everyone his or her own rubber ducky to bring home.

He took a bag out of the little Austin Mini. The bag was filled with rubber ducks, and he started throwing them into the crowd. When he saw that everyone had one, he continued.

> Just remember—the higher the rubber ducky is floating, the greater our GDP is.

The Model

As you can see, I already opened the faucet and the drain on our tub.

I opened the faucet because the water flowing into the tub represents consumer spending, investment spending, government spending, and exports.

I opened the drain because water flowing out of the tub represents imports.

If I had opened the faucet more, while leaving the drain alone, there would be more water in the tub. If I had closed the drain more, while leaving the faucet alone, there would also be more water in the tub. In other words, the level of water in the tub, or GDP, is determined by the inflow and the outflow.

Of course, if we want the water gauge to measure the real quantity of water in the tub, we have to adjust for inflation, because inflation can artificially raise the water level without increasing the actual quantity of water in the tub.

And that is our model.

Except for one more thing—money.

Our model represents a market economy with money, not a barter economy. In a barter economy, people trade things for things. In a market economy people use money to buy goods and services and they receive money for the goods and services they sell, including their labor.

Barter economies are inefficient because it takes time and resources to find someone who is willing to trade something that you want for something you have. In fact, it may require many intermediate trades before you end up with what you want.

Market economies with money are more efficient, because people simply use the money they have to buy what they want.

In terms of our model, for the inflow and outflow to work efficiently, the entire plumbing system must be in tip-top shape. Therefore, we can use a master plumber to represent the monetary authorities.

If the plumber has the system running perfectly, we will not even think about the mechanics of the inflow and the outflow.

It is the same for the money supply. If the money supply is handled correctly, we will not even think about it.

But if the plumber lets us down, the flow of water in the system will not be efficient.

And if the monetary authorities let us down, by putting too little or too much money into the economy, the economy will not be as efficient, and GDP will suffer.

If they put too little money into the economy, interest rates will be too high, and the economy will not work as efficiently as it can.

The Model

If they put too much money into the economy, we can end up with inflation.

Therefore, just as it is the responsibility of the master plumber to keep our plumbing system in order, it is the responsibility of the monetary authorities to keep the money supply in order—to ensure that we have just the right amount of money in the economy.

In our model, the job of the master plumber is to make sure the system is working smoothly—to make sure all the pipes and faucets and drains are in order.

In the real world, it is the responsibility of The Federal Reserve to manage the money supply in order to ensure that the economy is working smoothly, which normally means stable prices, acceptable economic growth, and an acceptable level of employment.

Someone asked the speaker if he weren't simplifying economics too much. "Simple is not the same as simplification," he said.

If you think I am using a bathtub to simplify economics so that everyone can understand something not worth understanding, I want to make it clear that I am not.

Our bathtub model does virtually everything a mathematical model does: It represents the real economy in a way that lets us understand how it works, and it allows us to explain and predict the results of changes.

No matter how many "experts" are standing around the tub talking about the value of complex theories, in the end, it all comes down to: Is the water level acceptable? Or is the water level too low? Or are there other water problems?

In other words, no matter how many "gurus" are standing around the tub, waving their hands and making great pronouncements, all you have to do is keep your eye on the rubber duck.

A woman standing next to the bathtub asked the speaker if he were going to use charts and graphs and numbers. She said that she took two economics courses in college, and all she remembered were charts, graphs, and numbers. He said, "None of that is necessary. As you will see, all you have to do is watch the rubber ducky."

The Right Amount of Water

5

He then held up a new sign that read, "More is better."

Okay. Water has been running into and out of our tub for about ten minutes. According to the water gauge, we have eleven and a half gallons in the tub.

The speaker was standing on the trailer, next to the bathtub. He motioned for everyone to come up and take a look. "Well, what do you think?" he asked. "Looks right to me," someone said. The speaker laughed. "I don't mean, did I read the gauge correctly. What I am asking is: Do you think we have a good quantity of water in the tub?" Someone said, "Wouldn't more be better?" And the speaker said, "Very good. If the water is Gross Domestic Product, why wouldn't more be better?"

We would obviously have more water in the tub if we increased the inflow relative to the outflow. But, no matter what we do, we are limited. There is a maximum quantity of water that can flow into the tub, and the most we can do to the drain is close it completely. So, if I had opened the faucets completely and closed the drain, there would be more water in the tub. Let's say that if I had done that, there would now be fifteen gallons of water in the tub.

The speaker then asked what everyone thought about fifteen gallons versus eleven and a half gallons. "It has to be better," someone said. "Right," someone else said. "Very good," he said.

Fifteen gallons must be better than eleven and a half gallons, because GDP is also a measure of national income. Therefore, the higher GDP is, the higher total income is. But our bathtub model shows us another obvious truth, which is that the level of GDP for a given time period is limited by the available natural resources, technology, and work force.

Therefore:

Anything that leads to an increase in the inflow relative to the outflow will increase GDP.

Anything that leads to a decrease in the inflow relative to the outflow will decrease GDP.

As GDP increases or decreases, the rubber ducky will be bobbing higher or lower.

And we need just the right amount of money in the system, because the supply of money can affect both the inflow and the outflow.

But, no matter what we do, there is a limit to the level of Gross Domestic Product for any time period.

The speaker then asked if there were any questions. There were. Following are the questions and the answers.

GDP and Employment

6

What about GDP and employment?

The more water we have in the tub, the more employment we have.

Aside from knowing that more national income is better than less, the fifteen gallons of water show us something else that should be obvious. If GDP is the market value of all final goods and services *produced* inside the country during some time period, then it obviously requires more workers to produce fifteen gallons of water than to produce eleven and a half gallons.

But is it enough?

Will fifteen gallons of water give us full employment?

In the old days, meaning the days before the Great Depression, it was assumed by economists and, therefore, by others, that if we wait long enough, a market economy will eventually reach an equilibrium with full employment if it is just left alone, even if there are temporary periods of low production and high unemployment.

The full-employment assumption came from an argument made by the French economist J.M. Say (1767–1832), which was that if there are high levels of unemployment, we just have to wait until the forces of supply and demand cure the problem.

In other words, if there are seven gallons of water in the tub, and seven gallons of water results in a high level of unemployment, we should not do anything to adjust the inflow or outflow, because the water level will rise on its own as markets clear, and because trying to fix the problem will only make it worse.

A second part of the argument was based on the assumption that production, not consumption, drives the economy. That assumption led to the original supply-side economics argument, which was that if government wants to improve the economy, it should give breaks to business, not consumers, because if business profits increase, the incomes of workers will eventually increase as well.

7

What about GDP and unemployment?

If there is not enough water in the tub to give us full employment, we end up with unemployment, which is sometimes referred to as an unacceptable level of employment.

Although the full-employment assumption from the good old days is now seen as either false or useless, it was accepted by mainstream economists for many years—until the Great Depression made it clear that even if an economy might eventually recover on its own, it can be painful or costly to wait. Although many economists, even during the darkest days of the Great Depression, continued to argue that everything would eventually be okay, that in the long run, markets would clear, production would increase, and unemployment would disappear, others pointed out that, "In the long run, we are all dead."[25]

In other words, the Great Depression led to a revolution in economic thinking. Instead of continuing to believe that market economies are driven by production, it now seemed obvious to most economists that market economies are driven by spending, which means that if there is an unacceptable level of employment, we should look first at how to improve spending, not production, because if spending increases, then production and employment will follow. The corollary is that "supply-side policies"—policies that increase business profits are less likely to increase production, employment, and the nation's wealth.

Of course, it is production that creates the actual jobs, which means it is a mistake to minimize its importance.

---

[25] John Maynard Keynes

8

How does GDP affect happiness?

An important goal of economics is to maximize the happiness, or wellbeing, of society. Unfortunately, no one has yet figured out how to measure happiness or wellbeing. So we measure real income instead, and assume that a higher GDP and higher real incomes mean greater happiness.

Obviously, that is not always true, because, as we all know, there are many factors, other than money, that affect happiness; things such as health, safety, security, family, friends, art, education, meaningful employment, and the environment are just a few.

Therefore, in order to use GDP as an indictor of society's happiness or wellbeing we have to be clear what we mean. First, we mean that an increase in GDP will increase the wellbeing of society if, when GDP increases, no other factor or factors that affect happiness decline, or do not decline too much. Second, we mean that if GDP remains the same, or even increases, while other factors that affect happiness decline, then happiness may decline.

Two conclusions come from these facts. One is that economics does not claim that happiness can be measured solely in money terms. The other is that if it is understood that there are many factors that affect happiness, it is possible to explain or predict how changes in any of them, including GDP, affect the happiness or wellbeing of society.

And that brings us to the true purpose of economics, which is to first explain and predict what is happening or is expected to happen, and then, if what is happening or is expected to happen is not good for society, try to fix it.

The current view in industrialized nations is that when unhampered market forces do not create acceptable levels of profits, wages, and employment, then someone should do something to fix it. Of course, there are only two "someones" that can help: the government and the central bank, which, in the U.S., is now The Federal Reserve System.

Although there are only two institutions with the power to affect the economy, many individuals, businesses, and groups stand to gain or lose by the actions taken by either the government or the Federal Reserve. As such, the concept of using "pure" economic ideas to make the economy better sometimes takes a back seat to the special interests that make their "needs" and desires known to those in power.

Putting the possibility of corruption aside, by the time World War II brought an end to the Great Depression, virtually all rational people believed that if we could adjust the faucet and the drain to get more water in the tub, we should do it.

Of course, as Shel Silverstein pointed out in one of his children's poems, where a little blue engine fails to chug to the top of a hill, even though it thinks it can, *"Sometimes, thinking you can just ain't enough."*

In terms of our bathtub, the question is: If we want to alter the quantity of water flowing into and out of the tub, can we do it just because we think we can?

Given the fact that GDP is equal to consumer spending plus investment spending by business plus government spending plus exports minus imports, the question is: Is it possible to intentionally change the values of any of the variables?

Consumer Spending

9

What determines the level of consumer spending?

Consumer spending is a function of two main factors—after-tax income and interest rates.

    If after-tax income increases, consumers spend more.

    If interest rates increase, consumers spend less.

    Therefore, an increase in after-tax income or a decrease in interest rates increases the inflow, which means that if we can change real income or interest rates, it is possible to intentionally change consumer spending and the quantity of water in the tub.

    Consumer spending is also affected by how we handle government spending, monetary policy, market failures, positive externalities, negative externalities, unowned resources, and public goods.

Tax Cuts

10

Do tax cuts improve the economy?

Probably not. On one hand, tax cuts increase the inflow. On the other hand, tax cuts reduce the inflow.

A tax cut gives its beneficiaries more after-tax income. And because the main determinant of consumer spending is after-tax income, those who receive tax cuts will probably spend more money, which means the inflow of water into our tub increases.

On the other hand, a tax cut creates a government deficit. And because the government covers its deficits by selling bonds, an increased deficit leads to an increase in bond sales, which leads to an increase in interest rates, which leads to decreases in consumer spending and investment sending, which means the inflow of water into our tub decreases.

In the end, the increase in the inflow due to a tax cut is offset by a decrease in the inflow caused by higher interest rates.

While one hand is opening the hot water faucet, the other is closing the cold water faucet.

Which is why a tax cut may not increase the water in the tub.

A woman in the front row complained that the speaker was getting political. "The reason my husband and I are here," she said, "is because we wanted to hear an economist, not a politician, talk about the economy. And you are taking the Democratic position on tax cuts, saying they don't work."

The speaker smiled.

"That is the economic position," he said. "Tax cuts are always political, because they are handed out by politicians. The problem is that politicians seem to pass tax cuts that help their own friends, which is why Republicans don't like Democratic tax cuts and Democrats don't like Republican tax cuts. When Democrats pass tax cuts, claiming they are helping the economy, Republicans say they won't work. When Republicans pass tax cuts, claiming they will help the economy, Democrats say they won't work. The argument I just gave you is the non-political, straight economic argument. But it is not my argument and it is not a Liberal argument; it is an argument that was first made by Milton Friedman, a conservative economist, in response to the Kennedy tax cut in the 1960s."

Tax Cuts

Then he continued.

In the 1960s, the Democratic argument for the Kennedy tax cut focused on the increased consumer spending it would generate, while totally ignoring the fact that it would also create a deficit that would lead to higher interest rates.

A few years after that tax cut was implemented, there was a famous debate between Walter Heller, one of the architects of the Kennedy tax cut, and Milton Friedman, one of America's leading conservative economists. Heller claimed that the growing economy proved that the tax cut worked. Friedman claimed that Heller was misreading the facts. The facts, according to Friedman, were that the tax cut added to consumer spending, but that it also created a deficit and that the deficit should have led to higher interest rates that would have then decreased consumer and business spending, thereby nullifying the expected benefits of the tax cut.

Heller said that did not happen; he said that spending and the economy did, in fact, improve.

Friedman said that was true; that the economy did improve, but that it improved only because the Federal Reserve prevented interest rates from rising by using newly created money to buy government bonds in the open market.

Heller said that did not matter; all that mattered was that the economy improved after the tax cut.

Friedman said it did matter. He said that the economy would have improved without the tax cut if the Federal Reserve had just increased the money supply, thereby lowering interest rates.

Years later, Milton Friedman wrote what, to some, seemed to be a refutation of his earlier argument:

> "I have long said, I never met a tax cut I didn't like, though I would go on to say that I like some better than others.
>
> "The reason for my flat, unhedged statement is neither the Keynesian attribution of an economic stimulus to a tax cut, which I believe is generally wrong, nor the supply-side attribution of favorable incentive effects to a tax cut, which I believe is generally correct. It is, rather, the effect of tax cuts on government spending."

Friedman did not change his mind about the economic benefits of tax cuts, deciding that they would boost the economy after all; he liked them simply because they could be used to diminish the size of government, which is a political objective, not an economic objective. Friedman's positive feeling for "supply-side" tax cuts is also political, not economic, because supply-side tax cuts create the same deficits he claimed would negate the benefits of a tax cut given to someone other than big business.

In other words, Friedman's initial argument is based on economic logic; his later statement is not. It is a political argument. And although everyone is free to follow their political beliefs, when it comes to business, financial, and personal decisions that are affected by the economy, it is almost always better to stick with economic logic and facts.

Unfortunately, it is often difficult, or impossible, to separate straightforward economics from political beliefs and realities. For example, there is one other way a deficit caused by a tax cut may not lead to higher interest rates that will choke off consumer and business spending. It is if foreigners or foreign governments buy substantial quantities of U.S. bonds. In that case, it means trading a current problem for a potentially much more serious future problem, because when foreign governments hold vast quantities of U.S. bonds, they hold great power over the U.S. economy. Whether or not that power is ever misused, a massive dumping of U.S. bonds would cause interest rates to soar and impose untold damage to the dollar and to the U.S. economy.[26]

---

[26] A counter argument is that the resulting high interest rates would then attract new foreign investors, thereby leading to a decline in interest rates. It is a logical argument, but it assumes that foreign investors have faith in the future of the U.S. economy.

Fiscal Policy

11

Can fiscal policy improve the economy?

Probably not. Changes in government spending and changes in taxes are the two actions that make up what is called fiscal policy—the government's options for improving economic activity and employment.

But we already know that tax cuts may not work.

And increased government spending has many of the same problems that negate the expected benefits of tax cuts.

It should be clear that increased government spending increases incomes. And because the main determinant of consumer spending is income, those who receive additional money from the government will spend some, or all, of that money, which means the inflow of water into our tub increases.

On the other hand, an increase in government spending creates a government deficit, just like a tax cut, which means the government will sell more bonds, which will increase interest rates, which will cause a decrease in consumer spending and investment spending, which will decrease the inflow of water into our tub.

Again, while one faucet is being opened, the other is being closed.

Which is why an increase in government spending may not increase the water in the tub.

There is, however, one difference between tax cuts and increased government spending. It is that when the government spends money, the money goes directly to people or companies. Instead of waiting for a tax cut to lead to an increase in spending, government can hire workers or buy stuff directly. That difference, however, does not negate the negative impact of the deficit and higher interest rates.

Nor does it negate the potential problems of foreign governments owning substantial quantities of U.S. bonds. Aside from what could happen if those bonds were dumped on the market, the interest payments on those bonds, paid for by U.S. taxpayers, are sent out of the country; and when foreign-owned bonds mature, the total value of the bonds is also sent out of the country. In other words, when the government sells bonds to cover current deficit spending, it is, in effect, charging that spending to a credit card. And if the credit card "company" is foreign, the payments and interest go to foreigners, lowering the quantity of water in our tub in the future.

Monetary Policy

12

Can monetary policy improve the economy?

Yes. Monetary policy means changing the money supply and interest rates in order to change consumer spending and investment spending. It changes the inflow into the tub, because increasing it does not create a deficit to offset the positive impact of lower interest rates. And the Federal Reserve can change the money supply and interest rates immediately, without waiting for a Congressional debate.

Although textbooks go to great lengths to present the arcane process economists cooked up to explain how the money supply is increased or decreased through the commercial banking system, the fact is that the way the Federal Reserve increases or decreases the money supply is very simple. If the Federal Reserve wants to increase the money supply, it purchases bonds in the open market with checks it writes from its own account, which means it is creating new money. If the Federal Reserve wants to decrease the money supply, it sells bonds in the open market, taking money from the purchasers.

Checks are money; bonds are not money. Therefore, when the Fed buys bonds, it puts something that is money, Federal Reserve checks, into the economy and takes out something that is not money—bonds. When it sells bonds, it puts bonds into the economy and takes money out.

The results are clear. If the Fed increases the money supply, it lowers interest rates, which increases consumer spending and investment spending. If the Fed decreases the money supply, it increases interest rates, which decreases consumer spending and investment spending, which decreases the inflow into our tub.

That's it. It is just that simple.

There are, however, potential problems.

One is that if the Federal Reserve increases the money supply too much, it will cause inflation; and if it decreases the money supply too much, it will cause a recession.

The second is that the Fed can make mistakes. For example, if the Fed reduces the money supply to fight inflation when the real problem is a recession, the Fed will make the recession worse. And, if the Fed increases the money supply to fight a recession when the real problem is inflation, the Fed will make the inflation worse. Could the Federal Reserve ever make such mistakes? It has, more than once.

13

Can regulating monopolies improve the economy?

Yes. Market failure, such as the monopolization of markets, distorts prices and reduces economic efficiency. It lowers real incomes and consumer spending, thereby reducing the quantity of water in the tub.

Imagine what would happen if a single company took over the water supply in our bathtub model. By controlling the entire supply, that company, as a monopolist, can limit the supply of water in order to get us to pay higher prices, in order to increase its profits. We lose happiness, because we have to pay more for water than we would if someone had not taken over the market for water. We also buy less water and we may buy more or less of other things than we would if prices were not distorted by the monopolist.

Therefore, correcting market failure with anti-trust legislation or price controls can increase economic efficiency, incomes, consumer spending, and GDP.

14

Can correcting positive externalities improve the economy?

Yes. Positive externalities are the benefits we receive when others spend their time or money to do something, but that we do not have to pay for. Examples are education and inoculations against infectious diseases. When someone spends his or her own time and money to increase his or her education or to be inoculated against infections diseases, others benefit. Positive externalities exist when there are no markets for the benefits we receive from the actions of others. Because, if there are no markets, we do not have to pay for those benefits. That is why they are called positive externalities.

And if prices do not represent the true benefits of consumption or production, too few resources are used for actions that cause positive benefits to others.

Imagine that someone pays a fee to take a bath in our tub. He is now cleaner and smells much better. He feels good, and so does everyone who comes in contact with him. Now, what if this person can afford to pay for only one bath a month? Would everyone who comes in contact with him on a daily basis benefit if he could pay for more frequent baths? Probably. Would each of them be willing to chip in a little money so he can take a bath every day? Probably. How much? That is a difficult question to answer. But if we know that each person would be willing to pay something, then we know that if we collected "taxes" from each of those people and used the money to pay for his daily baths, everyone would be better off.

That is why correcting positive externalities with government production or subsidies increases economic efficiency, real incomes, consumer spending, and GDP.

Negative Externalities

15

Does protecting the environment hurt the economy?

No. Protecting the environment can improve the economy.

Environmental damage, such as pollution that harms people, occurs when markets do not exist for things such as air quality, water quality, noise, and so on. When markets do not exist, people or companies that cause pollution are not financially responsible for the damages they cause to others. And whenever consumers or producers are not responsible for the total costs of their actions, they do more of those things than they would do if they had to pay or compensate the damaged parties.

Meanwhile, the damaged parties cannot, on their own, legally force the polluters to stop or reduce their pollution. The result is distorted prices that benefit polluters and negatively impact those who are hurt by the pollution—which is why economists call such negative externalities.

And when people and companies spend money in markets with price distortions caused by negative externalities, the nation's resources are misused. When prices do not represent the true costs of consumption or production, too many resources are used for actions that cause pollution, and too few for actions that do not cause pollution.

The result is that negative externalities reduce economic efficiency, which lowers real incomes, consumer spending, and the water in the tub.

Imagine that you want to take a bath in our tub. Just before you get in, you see that someone has dumped a bunch of dirt and garbage into it. You are upset, but you can't do anything about it, because they have a right to do it. The reason they have a right to dump their garbage in the tub is because you do not own the tub or the water in the tub. What happens to your happiness or real income? It decreases.

Why did someone dump garbage in the tub? Because it was the cheapest way for him to get rid of it.

What do you do? You either take baths in garbage-filled water or you do not take any more baths. In either case, you are worse off than if you could have stopped the dumping. If you owned the water, you could have made the dumper pay for the right to dump his garbage. How much? That depends on you. If you want to take baths in clean water, more than anything else, then there is no amount of money that the dumper could pay you for the right to dirty up your water. On the other hand, would you be willing to give up baths in return for $100,000,000? In a free market, there would be some sort of negotiation between you and the dumper that would arrive at a price you are willing to accept to give up clean baths in the tub and what he is willing to pay to dump his garbage in the tub rather than bring it somewhere else. When the negations are done, you will have either clean water or dirty water and a bunch of money. It is up to you. Of course, it is unlikely that he would be willing to pay $100,000,000. But in the real world, the numbers regarding damages and costs of cleanup get pretty large.

That is why correcting negative externalities with laws that outlaw activities or with fines and taxes that make polluters responsible for the damages they cause to others increases economic efficiency, incomes, consumer spending, and GDP.

Some believe that taxes on negative externalities, such as pollution, hurt the economy. That is not true. Taxes or fines based on the real damages caused by harmful actions will improve the economy, because one of two things happens. If the cost of reducing the damage is less than the true value of the damages, then the polluter will fix the problem and avoid the fine. If the cost of reducing the damage is more than the true value of the damages, then the polluter will pay the fine instead of correcting the problem. In either case, if the fine represents the true value of the damages, the economy wins. It is the true free market at work.

Common Property Resources

16

Does managing unowned resources help or hurt the economy?

It helps. Unowned resources, which economists call "common property resources," are resources that are not owned by private companies or individuals until they are grabbed or taken by someone. Examples are fish in lakes, rivers, and oceans. No one owns the fish, so anyone can catch as many as he or she wants.

The problem is that a lack of ownership for common property resources distorts prices and reduces economic efficiency, which reduces real incomes, consumer spending, and the water in the tub.

That is why correcting common property resource problems, with quotas, fines, or taxes, increases economic efficiency, incomes, consumer spending, and GDP.

Imagine that there are fish living in our tub. If we want to catch some fish every year, we could catch just the right quantity, so that we have a healthy population that will let us catch that quantity of fish year after year. But if we do not own the fish in the tub, someone else can come along and grab them all. In that case, the fish are used up all at once, and there is nothing left for the future. Who wins? The grabber? Maybe. Maybe not. Maybe the grabber would have preferred to have some fish every year rather than take all there are all at once. So, why doesn't the grabber do what we want to do—catch a few fish each year? Because he knows that even if he tries to be careful, some other grabber can come along and take all the fish. Or take so many that we have to catch fewer fish in the future if we do not want to fish the population to extinction. Therefore, we lose. We lose, because someone took all the fish, which means we no longer have the opportunity to catch fish as part of our overall consumption or spending plans.

How do we know we are worse off? There is a little test. Begin by recognizing the different possibilities. In this case, there were fish in the tub, and then there were no fish in the tub. Then look at the choices. When there were fish in the tub, we had two choices—catch some fish or catch no fish. When there are no fish in the tub, we have no choice—we cannot catch any fish. The question is: If, when there were fish in the tub, did we have the option of doing what the second possibility allowed, which is to not catch any fish? If the answer is: Yes, we did have that choice, but we chose to spend the time and money to catch some fish, then we must be worse off, because without any fish in the tub, we do not have the option of doing what we chose to do when there was a choice to either catch fish or not catch fish.

This test can be used for virtually all changes.

Public Goods

17

Does providing public goods help or hurt the economy?

It helps. Public goods are things that cannot be provided by private markets—either at all or in sufficient quantity to maximize the nation's wealth or wellbeing. Public goods can be provided only by government. And the failure of government to provide public goods reduces economic efficiency, which reduces real incomes, consumer spending, and the water in the tub.

Imagine that our bathtub is filled with a lot of good stuff that is ours for the taking, but the tub is five miles away from us. How do we get there to get the good stuff? We can use the car we bought with our own money. But what about the road? What if we can drive only on roads we pay for ourselves? Obviously, few people have the money to pay for their own five-mile long road. The rest of us are stuck, unless government collects a little money from each of us and uses it to build roads we can all use. If that happens, we all win.

That is why, when government provides public goods, such as national defense, police and fire departments, courts, copyright and patent protection, and protection of property rights, it increases economic efficiency, incomes, consumer spending, and GDP.

18

Can we improve the economy by increasing investment spending by business?

Yes. The Federal Reserve can intentionally change investment spending, because the Federal Reserve can change interest rates.

There is a negative relationship between interest rates and investment spending by business. If interest rates increase, investment spending decreases and the water in the tub decreases. If interest rates decrease, investment spending increases and the water in the tub rises.

The reason investment spending is inversely related to interest rates is that there are many different investment opportunities available, each with a different expected rate of return. If all possible investment opportunities were listed in order of their expected return, from highest to lowest, a line could be drawn at the current rate of interest. All investments with expected rates of return higher than the current rate of interest could be undertaken by borrowing the necessary funds, because each would yield a profit. All investments with expected rates of return less than the current rate of interest would be passed up, because borrowing the necessary funds at that current rate would result in a loss.

Therefore, as interest rates fall, the cut-off line moves lower, adding more and more investments to the profitable-to-do category. And as interest rates increase, the cut-off line moves higher, eliminating investments that were profitable at a lower cost of borrowing.

Government and Markets

19

Can government production and regulation improve the economy?

Yes. Intentionally increasing government spending to increase the water in the tub, in an attempt to improve a weak economy, is called fiscal policy (a macroeconomic idea). As discussed earlier, it is not as effective as some might hope. But government spending on public goods and to correct market failures and externalities (microeconomic ideas) does increase the water in the tub.

It cannot be assumed that fiscal policy will increase the water in the tub, because government actions that create deficits can cause interest rates to increase, which leads to decreases in consumer and investment spending. Therefore, as with other fiscal policy actions, such as tax cuts, while one hand is opening one faucet, the other hand is closing the other faucet.

In reality, the actual level of government spending is determined by politicians and is related to the health of the economy, along with a number of other factors, some of which are under our control, some of which are not.

During periods of high unemployment, government payments to individuals rise. During wartime, government expenditures can increase dramatically, which is why wars appear to add to GDP, sometimes making a not-so-good economy look better than it is, especially if the war is financed by borrowing (using bond sales instead of taxes).

And government spending on public goods, social programs, and subsidies, such as agricultural programs, changes as political parties change power.

In the end, the actual level of government spending is always a mixture of economic ideas, compassion (or lack of compassion), political doctrine, and favors to friends and special interests.

That is why, when government spends money on something a large part of the public does not like, such as an unpopular war, politicians prefer to not raise taxes to pay for it. They would rather sell bonds instead. But, just as they do not want the unpopular spending to be the cause of higher taxes, politicians do not want it to be the cause of higher interest rates. And if the Federal Reserve wants to help the politicians responsible for the unpopular spending, it can keep interest rates down by creating new money to buy a bunch of bonds. Foreign investors and governments also keep interest rates from rising when they buy U.S. bonds.

But the U.S. then has to send money to foreigners to pay the interest on those bonds and to redeem the bonds at maturity.

And if the Fed creates too much new money trying to keep interest rates down, it will cause inflation, which is what it did when the U.S. fought a war in Vietnam alongside a War on Poverty at home.

Most important is the fact that when government tackles what are normally called microeconomic issues (issues in individual markets), it can achieve great macroeconomic results.

Although those positive results assume wise government actions, dealing with individual market failures, including positive and negative externalities, adds to GDP. So can dealing with problems created by private markets, such as the "bursting of speculative bubbles" in investment markets or the markets for goods and services.

In other words, the Federal Reserve may be able to add to the water in the tub by using "macroeconomic" actions (changing the money supply and interest rates), but government can also affect individual investment markets through its use of regulations, tax laws, and incentives.

Exports

20

Can we intentionally change exports to improve the economy?

Yes and no. Many things affect exports, such as producing goods and services that people and businesses in other countries want to purchase, international trade agreements that make it easier or more difficult for U.S. producers to sell to foreign buyers, foreign exchange rates, and interest rates.

Interest rates are important, because of international capital flows. When interest rates increase, U.S. interest-bearing securities become more attractive to foreign investors, which leads to additional purchases of U.S. securities by foreigners. And foreign purchases of U.S. securities are counted as exports, because in order to buy anything from the U.S., including investments, such as U.S. bonds, foreigners first have to convert their currency into U.S. dollars.

However, an increased demand for U.S. investments increases the value the dollar relative to other currencies, thereby making U.S. products more expensive to foreigners, which reduces exports As such, rising interest rates can lead to an increase in exports—more foreign purchases of U.S. securities—but also to a decrease in exports, because the increased value of the dollar relative to other currencies makes U.S. goods more expensive to foreigners.

Exports and imports are determined by a number of factors, including trade agreements, the value of the dollar relative to other currencies, interest rates, and anything that makes the goods and services of one country look good or bad to consumers and businesses in other countries.

Our bathtub model separates exports and imports in order to focus on the importance of each in terms of its impact on GDP. Most models use net exports, which are exports minus imports. If we did that, there would be an outflow only if there were a trade deficit. But looking only at net exports covers up a lot of what is happening. Japan knew, and China knows, the importance of both exports and imports. Each built an economy by encouraging exports and minimizing imports. Neither followed the idea that unhampered "free trade" would maximize the nation's wealth.

There is, however, a side issue with increasing exports. It is that a large increase in certain exports, such as agricultural products, can raise prices at home. As a result, some of the gains from increased exports may be offset by higher prices for many goods and services.

Imports

21

Will a trade deficit automatically eliminate itself?

In theory, yes. In practice, not necessarily.

When people, especially politicians, talk about free trade, they are normally talking about the free importation of goods and services produced in foreign countries, either by foreign companies or by U.S. companies operating in foreign countries.

Limiting imports reduces the outflow from our tub, which, if it is accomplished without reducing exports, increases GDP. But, it may do so at great cost. If you have $1,000 to spend, does it matter how you spend it? Of course, it does. There are many ways to spend $1,000, each of which gives you a different level of "happiness." If you could spend it only on goods and services produced in your own country, you are not likely to be as happy as if you had choices from all over the world. That is the argument used to support what are called pure free trade policies—because few people would say that they do not like the idea of having as many choices as possible or the chance to buy an imported television set or kitchen appliance for less than they have to pay for the same items produced domestically. The counter argument is that it does not matter how cheap TVs are to someone who loses his or her job to imports.

Foreign commerce is complicated, which is why so many people choose to use simple free-trade "theories" created in the 1800s to support their free-trade policies. Unfortunately, the old free-trade theories are based on models using two goods, two countries, and one input—labor. What they show is that if each country uses different quantities of labor to produce each of the two goods, then, even if one country can produce both goods with less labor than the other country, each country can gain by specializing in the good it is relatively better at producing and then trading some of that good to the other country for some of the other good. Doing so gives each country a greater total quantity of the two goods than if each produced both goods by itself.

What do these theories have to do with a world where countless goods, each requiring many different inputs, are bought and sold, not traded, among a large number of countries? Nothing. They have absolutely nothing to do with real international trade, where countless things, each of which is made from a large number inputs, are bought and sold in a world with huge differences in wages and capital costs, as well as government regulations and subsidies. In the real world, the fact that your country buys things from other countries does not mean that other countries will buy anything from your country. And because exports do not automatically match imports, fast-growth countries, such as Japan in the twentieth century and China in the twenty-first, intentionally promote exports and limit imports.

Of course, limiting imports hurts the living standard of many people. The reason for the harm, or loss, is simple—much simpler than the bogus free trade theories. It is that the benefits of specialization are real. Whether it is the occupational specialization described by Plato in *The Republic* in 360 BCE or the industrial specialization described by Adam Smith in *An Inquiry Into The Nature And Causes Of The Wealth* in 1776, it is clear that self-sufficiency, even if it is a chosen lifestyle by some, drastically limits the real income or wealth of individuals and nations. That is a non-refutable fact.

But the fact that specialization gives individuals and nations more income and more stuff than self-sufficiency, does not change another fact, which is that the inflow to our tub increases as exports increase and decreases as imports increase.

Therefore, managing foreign trade is a complicated issue.

In terms of foreign trade, exports add to the water in the tub and imports reduce the water in the tub.

Even so, specialization makes sense for individuals and for countries.

Therefore, foreign trade policies must be addressed by accepting the fact that there are no free trade theories that make sense, which means that free-trade policies must be based on real results, not false theories.

Outsourcing

22

Does outsourcing jobs improve the economy?

We don't know.

Outsourcing jobs reduces some incomes and consumption. It also reduces investment spending. Each change reduces the water in the tub. And because payments to foreign workers are counted as an import, there is another reduction to the water in the tub.

On the other hand, outsourcing jobs reduces costs and increases profits for some.

The question is: Will the decrease in production costs lower consumer prices and add to GDP, or will the lost incomes lead to a decrease in GDP that outweighs the gains?

Part of the answer, of course, depends on where the savings are spent. Will they be spent on domestically produced goods and services? Or on more imported goods?

As with all other import savings, it is never clear that the savings will be spent in a way that adds to real GDP. Anyone who assumes that the savings will lead to an increase in GDP sees outsourcing as a good thing. Anyone who assumes that the benefits of the savings will be more than negated by lost incomes and profits sees outsourcing as a bad thing.

Who is right? No one knows. What we do know is that there is no reason to accept either side's assumption without evidence to back it up.

23

What about inflation?

There is a story about a man who was confused about what to do with his life, and who decided to seek the advice of a famous guru living on a mountaintop on the other side of the world.

The man worked for years, saving every penny he could, to finance a pilgrimage to see the guru. He did nothing but work and dream of his eventual journey.

Finally, when he had the money he needed, he quit his job and began his search. As he was spending the last of his savings, he discovered the mountain he was looking for. He then spent weeks struggling upward, nearly killing himself more than once.

When he reached the top, he found the guru he had thought of for so many years—an old man with a long white beard and long white hair—sitting by the side of a small pool of water.

The man fell on his knees and pleaded with the guru, "Please, tell me the meaning of life."

The guru stared out over the mountaintops for what seemed like an eternity.

Finally, he said, "Life is a fountain."

The man, who had given up everything to find this guru, could not believe what he had just heard. He sat still for a minute, lost deep in thought.

Then he jumped up screaming, "Life is a fountain?! What kind of nonsense is that?! I ruined my life and traveled half-way around the world to have you tell me that life is a fountain?"

Eventually, the man settled down. Exhausted, he slumped against a rock.

The guru, who had not moved until now, looked at the man and, with a puzzled expression, said, "Life isn't a fountain?"

What does this story have to do with inflation?

Simply that many people spend a lot of time looking for gurus to explain the meaning and the cause of inflation, and that the answers they get are as useful as the one in the story. Instead of treating inflation as a straightforward issue, many people see it as something mysterious and magical. Instead of listening to economists, they look for wisdom from self-taught analysts, the media, or politicians. But there is nothing mysterious about inflation.

Inflation

Someone asked the speaker for a definition of inflation.

The standard economic definition of inflation is: constantly rising prices over time.

And the most common measure of prices is the Consumer Price Index.

The problem is, there are two different reasons for the Consumer Price Index (or the Producer Price Index) to increase.

The CPI can be pulled higher if there is too much money in the economy. Or the CPI can be pushed higher by increasing costs of production, such as rising oil prices.

When the CPI is pulled higher by an excessive money supply, it is a signal of inflation.

But, when the CPI is pushed higher by rising costs of production, it is a signal of a possible recession.

As simple as this fact is to understand, the media, investors, businesspeople, and even the Federal Reserve, do not seem to comprehend the difference. The most likely explanation for the error is the old economic idea that there are two types of inflation—demand-pull and cost-push. Demand-pull inflation is assumed to be the result of a rising demand for goods and services that pulls prices higher. Cost-push inflation is assumed to be the result of rising costs of production pushing consumer prices higher.

Demand-pull inflation is real. Cost-push inflation is not. The term most often used to describe cost-push inflation, beginning with the soaring oil prices of the 1970s, is stagflation. It is a term that was created to describe an economy suffering from inflation and stagnation at the same time.

But it was, and is, a false description. When resource costs increase, the result is a recessionary pressure caused by higher costs of production; it is not inflation. Therefore, when oil prices cause increases in the Consumer Price Index, we should be prepared to deal with a possible recession caused by rising prices, not inflation.

On the other hand, increases in the Consumer Price Index caused by a rising demand that pulls prices higher is a signal of a true inflation. And the only thing that can create an increase in aggregate demand is an excessive increase in the money supply, normally the result of the monetary authorities creating money to finance deficit spending by government.

Therefore, a failure to understand the difference between an increase in the

Inflation

Consumer Price Index caused by rising costs of production and an increase in the Consumer Price Index caused by a rising demand due to excessive money creation, leads to poor decisions by the Federal Reserve, investors, and business.

Someone asked why there is still so much concern with inflation, given that the last time prices were increasing at a double-digit rate was back in the 1970s?

Because inflation takes a terrible toll on the economy and on individual living standards, and because the cure for inflation can hurt as much as the sickness.

Inflation's impact on personal savings and investments can be devastating. The American formula for success has long been to work hard and save for the future. But if wages and investment returns do not keep up with inflation, then living standards decline over time.

What causes inflation?

Some blame the people for inflation. They claim that inflation is the result of greedy unions, greedy businesspeople, and greedy resource owners. Others claim that inflation is caused by fast economic growth. And some believe that inflation is the result of too much money in the economy.

Who is correct?

The evidence, which is supported by the most logical arguments, says that the only possible cause of inflation is too much money.

Everyone knows that prices are determined by supply and demand. Therefore, it seems to make sense to argue that greed is a major cause of inflation. But, it is not that simple.

The greedy-union argument says that if a strong union negotiates a large wage increase, the industry that is affected will simply pass on the higher labor costs to its customers by raising prices. Then, as prices rise, unions want even higher wages. The higher prices climb, the more the union wants. And the more the union wants, the higher prices go. It sounds like a sensible argument. In fact, it is still included in some textbooks. But it has a serious flaw. It assumes that a business can protect its profits, even if its costs of production increase, simply by raising prices—an assumption that even many corporations believe to be true. But a corporation cannot pass on all such costs.

Anyone who sells something faces a demand for his or her product. If not, they would not be in business. But, when a seller raises his or her price, consumers buy less of that product. As a result, if a corporation increases its prices in an attempt to recover higher labor costs, it will not sell as much. It will then have to cut back on production, which means using fewer inputs, including labor.

When it is all over:

The prices of products produced with union labor will be higher, but output will be lower.

Part, but not all, of the increased labor costs will be passed on to consumers. Corporate profits will be lower, because less is being sold and production costs are higher. The cutback in production will lead to unemployed resources, including labor. And, as the unemployed resources look for new employment, wages and prices will fall in other industries.

All told, there will be higher prices for the products from the unionized industry and lower prices elsewhere. But that is not inflation. It is a change in relative prices.

How do you know corporate profits will fall?

That's easy. We know that the corporation, which is always trying to maximize its profits, had the option of selling less at a higher price before the increase in union wages, but it chose not to. Why? Because it chose the price that would maximize profits, not a higher price that would lower both the quantity sold and profits. So, if it now sells less at a higher price, *and* with higher costs, it must be worse off. It had that choice before, with lower costs, and turned it down.

But will the union workers, who can now spend more money, cause inflation?

Not necessarily. Union workers who still have their union jobs will have more money. But those who lose their jobs due to the cutback in production have less; so do those who cannot sell their resources for as much; and so do those whose incomes come from profits in the unionized industry.

The union workers who keep their jobs come out ahead. Others lose. And although there is a change in relative prices, the most important result is not inflation; it is a transfer of income.

Of course, if corporations could raise prices to cover all wage increases, then unions could be held responsible for inflation.

But if corporations could raise prices whenever they wanted, then why not raise them by more than enough to cover the higher wages? Even better, for the corporation, why not raise prices every day and add to profits no matter what the union does? Why pass up the chance to make billions of dollars by keeping prices low?

In other words, why don't greedy businessmen constantly create inflation by charging higher and higher prices? Because they can't; not if they want to make a profit and stay in business.

One of the basic assumptions of economic theory is that everyone—individuals, unions, small businesses, and huge monopolies—will always try to get the most they can. But there is a big difference between getting the highest price for something and making the largest profit. If any business could charge any price it wanted and sell all it wanted, anyone could open a business and make billions of dollars by charging one or two million dollars for each item they sell, whatever it is.

You could call yourself a consultant, charge one million dollars per hour for your services, and advise every financially troubled business to simply raise its prices. You could also advise every profitable business to raise its prices and make even greater profits.

These are obviously absurd ideas. So is the idea that a business has the power to charge whatever price it wants.

It is true that when resource costs increase (labor, oil, interest expenses, and so on) it is more expensive to produce products that use those resources, and the prices of those products will increase. But if we have to spend more for some things we buy, then we either have to buy less of them or less of something else. As a result, while some prices increase, others fall.

What about things we need?

Economists do not think we "need" anything. We need food to live, but we do not buy "food." We buy a certain kind of steak, a certain size and grade of eggs, a particular brand of orange juice or whole oranges, and so on. There is not one particular food item you, or anyone else, must have. So whenever some prices increase, economists expect less of those goods and services to be sold. They also expect people to look for substitutes and to cut back on some other purchases.

That is why it is impossible to present a logical explanation of how increasing resource costs create inflation. In each and every case, the upward pressure on prices is stopped by the fact that sellers face a demand for their product or service; and no one has yet discovered an instance where it is possible to raise prices and sell the same quantity.

Therefore, the only logical explanation for inflation is that it is caused by a constant increase in demand. Because if demand is increasing, then prices can be pulled higher and higher over time.

What can cause demand to increase?

Anything that causes a large increase in the money supply. It can be excessive government spending financed by money creation (the Federal Reserve purchasing bonds sold to cover the government's deficit spending), or bad decisions by the Fed, or, as happened in the past, banks printing "counterfeit" money.

Spending by consumers and business is limited by current incomes and the possibility of borrowing against future incomes or profits.

Spending by government is not. The government can spend whatever politicians choose to spend, within limits that might lead to being voted out of office. But because, whenever the government spends money, someone benefits, the government can do a lot of spending without touching off a voter revolution. In fact, the loudest screams are normally heard when the government cuts, rather than increases, spending.

Of course, the government has to get the money it spends from somewhere, and it has only three choices. The government can get its money from taxes, by selling bonds to the public, or by creating money out of thin air by selling bonds to the Federal Reserve Bank.

In terms of the government's impact on total spending and inflation, if government spending is financed by taxes or bond sales to the public, the money the government spends is taken away from the general public—individuals and businesses. Therefore, any increase in demand caused by government is offset by a decreased demand from others. Even so, some inflation can occur because the impact on aggregate demand from increased government spending can be greater than the decrease caused by reduced consumer incomes.

On the other hand, if increases in government spending are financed by selling bonds that are purchased by the Federal Reserve Bank with newly created money,

Inflation

then no income or wealth has to be taken away from the people. In this case, the increase in government spending is not offset by decreases elsewhere, and the result is a rising aggregate demand that can cause prices to increase over time.

Of course, as prices increase, it takes more money to buy what you are now buying. And only government can create more and more money for itself.

Very simply, then, inflation is caused when the government acts to outbid individuals and businesses for resources, and does so with money created out of nothing by the Federal Reserve.

The more the government gets, the less the people get.

And the less slack there is in the economy—the lower the unemployment rate and the higher the plant utilization rate—the greater the inflation will be.

Therefore, it can be argued that the higher the rate of inflation, the more intent the government is on taking resources away from the public. That is why the standard of living of America's middle class declines as the inflation rate increases. The average American is hurt not only by rising prices, but also by what causes prices to rise—the government's taking of resources.

Someone asked if inflation helps anyone.

Rising prices help debtors, because they get to pay back their loans with money that is worth less than the money they borrowed. At the same time, inflation hurts lenders, because when the loans they made are paid back, they receive money that is worth less—in terms of what it can buy—than the money they loaned out. Therefore, there is a longstanding difference of opinion between debtors and creditors concerning inflation. That is what was behind William Jennings Bryan's "cross of gold" speech.

In 1896, after more than twenty years of declining prices, Bryan gave his famous speech at the Democratic National Convention in Chicago. The ending, which was a rebuttal to those who wanted the nation's money supply pegged to gold, was, "Having behind us the producing masses of this nation and the world, supported by the commercial interests, the laboring interests and the toilers everywhere, we will answer their demand for a gold standard by saying to them: You shall not press down upon the brow of labor this crown of thorns, you shall not crucify mankind on a cross of gold."

Bryan's populist argument was that the U.S. should have a bimetallic standard, using both silver and gold as backing for money. The reason for using both silver and gold is that it would allow more money to be created, thereby increasing the rate of inflation. Bryan was trying to help farmers and other working people who were large debtors, because they were being hurt by more than two decades of falling prices. If prices were increasing, instead of decreasing, the real burden of their debts would be reduced. On the other hand, Eastern bankers wanted to hold to the gold standard, because, as creditors, they benefited from declining prices and would lose if prices were rising.

That is why Bryan ended his speech with an image of the working people being crucified on a cross of gold. No matter which side you might support in the debate, the fact is that the relationship between money and prices has been understood for a long time.

An interesting idea that has been around for a while is that *The Wizard of Oz* is an allegory based on the populist movement in America; that it is a story that pits the workingman against big bankers and railroads. According to these interpretations, the story is filled with characters and locations and numbers that represent the people, places, and legislation involved in the populist movement. The cowardly lion is William Jennings Bryan. Oz, of course, is the symbol for ounce. In the book, Dorothy's slippers are silver, not ruby red. The yellow brick road represents the gold standard that leads to Oz (Washington DC). And the conclusion, where Dorothy finds out that she had the solution all the time, which is to click her heels together, represents the idea that the solution to the problem of declining prices is to add silver to gold as backing for money, which brings us to the cross of gold speech. The movie loses this idea by changing the slippers from silver to ruby red.

One of the major articles that makes the above argument is "The 'Wizard of Oz' as a Monetary Allegory," by Hugh Rockoff in *The Journal of Political Economy*, volume 98, No. 4 (August 1999) pages 739 – 760.

Someone asked how to explain inflation using the bathtub model.

It is easy to explain inflation using our bathtub model.

When we put the model together, we used a master plumber to represent the fact that someone has to control the money supply in a market economy. As we said, market economies run better and more efficiently when money, rather than barter and trade, is used for transactions. Money is also an efficient store of value, meaning it can be saved easily. And it is an efficient way to assign prices, meaning that it is

Inflation

more efficient to give prices in money terms, rather than trying to list all possible trade combinations, such as how many washing machines, must be traded for a car. And how many vacuum cleaners. And jars of pickles. And so on.

Therefore, we begin by assuming that the master plumber (The Federal Reserve) has just the right amount of money in the system. Too much, and it will cause inflation. Too little, and it can cause a recession.

Now, if the Federal Reserve puts more money into the economy, we can imagine the Fed throwing bags of money into the tub. Each bag raises the water level, but not the real quantity of water. Therefore, the water gauge will not measure the real quantity of water. In order to keep track of the real quantity of water, the water level has to be adjusted to account for the inflationary price increases caused by too much money in the tub.

If the Federal Reserve keeps throwing bags of money into the tub, eventually the tub will overflow, spilling GDP onto the floor. In other words, inflation not only raises prices, it eventually reduces real GDP.

So, once you understand the cause, the cure is simple.

Keep the money supply under control. Do not throw too many bags of money into the tub. And if inflation is a serious problem, take some bags out of the tub.

Recession

24

What about recession?

Recession is defined as an economic slowdown accompanied by unacceptable rates of unemployment, and often by falling wages, profits, and prices. The Great Depression was an extreme recession.

In terms of our model, it means less water in the tub.

In other words, a recession occurs when something reduces the quantity of water in the tub.

It could be any number of things. An increase in oil prices, bad weather (the dust bowl days of the Great Depression), a disruption in investment, a decrease in the money supply, and so on. Some of the causes are beyond our control, such as weather. Some are human error, such as bad management of the money supply.

Although it commonly believed that rising oil prices cause inflation, because higher prices cause increases in the Consumer Price Index and the Producer Price Index, that is not the case. The mistake is to focus on the Consumer Price Index, which tracks the price of a bundle of goods over time, while ignoring the reason for the increase. High oil prices lead to higher production costs and higher prices for consumers. We know that. But, because rising oil process do not increase incomes, the quantity of goods and services purchased declines, which reduces production, employment, wages, and profits, which is a recession, not an inflation. Therefore, whenever the Federal Reserve raises interest rates to stave off an inflation caused by rising energy prices, it is doing the opposite of what it should do, which is to prepare to prevent a recession.

There are a number of examples in U.S. history where a contraction of the money supply caused a recession, the worst being the Great Depression.

That is why it is important to understand what can and cannot be done to increase the level of GDP if it is too low, meaning that there is a recession.

The Business Cycle

25

Someone asked about the business cycle.

A lot of people spend a lot of time trying to explain and predict the business cycle.

There are obvious reasons for wanting to uncover the mystery behind the ups and downs in the economy. One is that anyone who can predict the future can make a lot of money. A more important one, for society, is that if the business cycle can be predicted, then actions can be taken to hopefully prevent bad things from happening to the economy and the people.

Although some business cycle theories look pretty good, such as those that attempt to tie the performance of the economy to a politically motivated presidential cycle, the real evidence supports the argument that there is no natural business cycle, just as there is no natural climate cycle. The evidence for such an argument is simple: Each and every upturn and downturn in the economy can be explained by actions or events that caused it. And, if the causes for upturns and downturns can be explained, there is no such thing as a "natural" business cycle.

The National Debt

26

What about the national debt?

Since the end of World War II, many believed that government debt was not a problem.

Before and during the Great Depression of the 1930s, it was assumed that the federal government had a responsibility to maintain a balanced budget. It was believed that government should be equated to an individual and that an individual in debt was an individual in trouble. The one exception was wartime, when it was acceptable for government to run a deficit as long as it was understood that the necessary borrowing would be repaid when the war was over. But, as the Depression worsened, John Maynard Keynes, whose ideas still guide the teaching of economics at 90 percent of the colleges and universities in America, made the argument that if a nation were stuck in a depression, the government should use deficit spending as a cure. Although most people have heard of Keynes, and many conservatives blame him for the downfall of free-market ideals, few understand that what he offered was an entirely new way of seeing the economic world.

Following Keynes, and using 20/20 hindsight, economists at the end of World war II began to believe that trying to balance the federal budget had made the Depression worse, not better. The argument was simple. If people lost their jobs and their businesses, government lost tax revenues. If government then tried to balance its budget, it would have to reduce it's spending, which would cause more unemployment and further reductions in tax collections. The result is a vicious downward spiral. Fewer jobs mean less tax money. Less tax money means less government spending. And less government spending means fewer jobs. And on and on.

Prior to Keynes, economists assumed that as long as producers produced something, those who sold them the resources needed to make those things, whether it was labor or resources, would then have the money to buy what was produced. According to this view, "supply creates its own demand" and there is no role for the government to play in the economy, other than to keep the markets free. Of course, the notion that production is the key to economic health meant that the depression of the 1930s should not have occurred. But it did.

According to Keynes, the reason for the lengthy depression was that demand, not supply, is the driving force in the economy. And if aggregate demand is not strong enough to pull an economy out of a recession, Keynes argued that it was the government's responsibility to generate a sufficient demand for goods and services by using deficit spending. Then, as with a war, the government debt is to be repaid out of the tax revenues generated by a healthy economy.

It is sometimes believed that President Roosevelt was quick to adopt the Keynesian idea of massive deficit spending as a way to end the depression. But that was not the case. Although there was some social spending, Roosevelt and his advisors clung to the belief in a balanced budget—until the U.S. entered World War II.

It was the deficit spending needed to fight World War II that pulled America out of the Depression. And although there are still people who believe that war is, therefore, good for the economy, it was not war that helped the economy, it was huge deficit spending. If all that money had been spent to recruit people, thereby giving them jobs, and then buying them all sorts of equipment so that they could dig holes in the ground one day and fill them in the next, the economic result would have been about the same.

What changed after World War II?
After World War II, economics entered a new age.

There was, for the first time, a cohesive theory that explained, at least in broad terms, how government could regulate the economy through its impact on total demand.

There was the experience of World War II spending to back up the theory.

And there was a new attitude toward government debt. No longer did everyone believe that government must meet the same budget constraints as individuals. No longer did everyone see government debt as a threat to the economy.

All told, economists believed they had the knowledge and the tools to create an economy that would grow steadily, making everyone wealthier and happier, without suffering the tragic upheavals of either inflation or recession.

To those who continued to complain that debt was bad, no matter who owed the money, economists argued that government debt was very different from private debt. Economists said that government debt, which is the outstanding bonds the government sold to finance its past deficit spending, is "like owing money to yourself." The debt was not supposed to matter because paying it off was "like taking money out of one pocket and putting it in another." When future taxes are used to redeem maturing bonds, the taxes will come from Americans and the payments will go to Americans.

Of course, the theoretical argument did have some detractors. The "Chicago School of Economics," led most recently by Milton Friedman, claimed that in order to have a positive effect on the economy, deficit spending had to be financed with new money creation. A government deficit, whether it is created by increasing spending or cutting taxes, can be financed in only three ways: increasing taxes, selling bonds to the public (debt), or creating new money. According to Friedman, and others, the negative economic impact of the first two choices would essentially wipe out the positive impact of the deficit. Therefore, they said, the only way to increase the level of economic activity is to buy the debt with an increase in the money supply. But if that is the case, then the positive result is due to an increase in the money supply, something that can be done with or without a deficit.

Friedman did not believe in the so called "balanced budget multiplier," the Keynesian idea that the positive impact of an increase in government spending would not be totally offset by an equal increase in taxes.

But, because there have been so few instances of intentionally using deficit spending to spur on the economy, the debate has been mainly a theoretical argument. There was the Kennedy tax cut that seemed to get the economy going. But Friedman always argued that it worked only because it was financed with new money creation. On the other hand Water Heller, who was Chairman of the Council of Economic Advisors at that time, and who helped engineer the tax cut, always claimed it would have worked no matter how it was financed.

There was the Reagan "supply side" tax cut of 1982. But because Reagan was worried that the deficit his tax cut created might bring back inflation, he then raised taxes.

Then there was the George W. Bush 2001 tax cut, which is difficult to judge, because it was accompanied by massive war spending and massive bond purchases by foreigners.

President Reagan's advisors saw Keynes as one of history's worst liberals, and they did not want to promote an economic policy that could be called "Keynesian." So they invented the idea of a tax cut that would encourage business to increase production—a modern version of the old "supply creates its own demand" idea. But the fact is that business cannot increase output unless there is a demand for the extra output.

So, why are there still arguments over whether or not the Reagan tax helped the economy?

Partly because, as Yogi Berra said, we see what we believe.

Partly because it was muddied with tax increases that followed the cuts.

Partly because it is difficult to identify the exact reason for an economic expansion. If the American economy is fundamentally sound, then positive growth is the norm unless some event throws it off course. Therefore, a tax cut that does not help the economy may, years later, when the economy is back on track, be given credit it does not deserve.

The results are also muddied because the Federal Reserve did not want to risk a return to the double-digit inflation rates of the late 1970s by financing what were at the time the largest deficits in American history entirely with money creation. As a result, the Fed did not increase the money supply to buy bonds; instead it let the bonds sink or swim in private markets, which should have led to a large increase in interest rates. But that did not happen. It did not happen because, for the first time in America's history, massive quantities of U.S. bonds were purchased by foreigners, thereby preventing the expected increase in interest rates.

In the end, the Reagan tax cut that created deficits that were financed by selling bonds to foreigners ushered in a major new development in political economics: massive government spending financed by bond sales to foreigners. As a result, we must once again rethink our views of government deficits and of our ability to manage the U.S. economy.

What about the old idea of taking money out of one pocket and putting it in another?

The best explanation is that if large quantities of bonds are sold to foreigners, you can think of it as having a hole in the pocket. The Reagan deficits, and the Bush deficits, forced interest rates higher than they would otherwise have been, and those high rates brought in foreign investors. And the United States benefited by being able to use foreign money to help fund its large deficits without being forced to suffer the negative consequences of higher interest rates.

The downside is that the money has to be repaid, with interest. Now when government taxes Americans to pay the interest on government bonds and to redeem maturing bonds, part of the money goes to foreigners. Now when government pays off government bonds by taking money from one pocket and putting it in another, some of the other pockets are in foreign countries

What new problems does that create?

The large foreign investment in the U.S. creates three new problems.

One: The fact that foreigners hold a large part of our debt means that they have a claim against our present and future wealth. Paying the interest on the debt, which is now the third largest item in the federal budget, sends money abroad. Redeeming bonds does the same. Therefore, when deficit spending is used to promote economic growth that might benefit Americans in the future, some of the future benefits will be owned by foreigners.

Two: The huge federal debt is partly responsible for the growing foreign trade deficit. Massive government bond sales force interest rates higher and attract foreign investors. But in order to invest in the U.S., foreigners have to switch their currencies into dollars. The more money foreigners want to invest in the U.S., the more dollars they need. The more dollars they need, the more they push up the value of the dollar on foreign exchange markets. The stronger dollar makes foreign goods cheaper for Americans to buy and American goods more expensive to foreigners. The result is added pressure on the foreign trade deficit.

Three: The large U.S. debt, coupled with the growth of international investing, may reduce the effectiveness of domestic monetary policy. It is assumed that the Fed has the ability to increase the money supply, lower interest rates, and promote greater capital investment and consumer spending. But, as the foreign-held debt becomes larger and larger, we may reach a point where, if the Fed tries to raise aggregate demand by forcing interest rates lower, foreigners might pull funds out of U.S. bond markets. And as funds are pulled out, interest rates will increase. If that happens, the Fed may lose its ability to juggle interest rates to meet domestic economic needs. As a result, it may become difficult to use expansionary money-supply policies to encourage economic growth without risking inflation.

The National Debt

Is this the end of an era?

From the beginning of the 1950s, we thought we had a handle on the economy. Even the soaring inflation of the 1970s can be traced to understandable policies: We fought two wars, a war on poverty and a war in Vietnam, and financed the efforts with money creation, not increased taxes.

But the policies we believed could be used to "fine tune" the economy—increasing or decreasing government spending, taxes, and the money supply—may now have to be reexamined. We are, very possibly, losing the control we once took for granted.

The United States is now the world's largest debtor nation—measured as the difference between the value of foreign debt owned by Americans and the value of American debt owned by foreigners. And although we understand the dangers of foreign debt in Brazil and Mexico, we do not always recognize that those countries are simply extreme examples of what could happen in the United States.

Whether or not it was ever accurate to say that the national debt does not matter, it certainly matters when a larger and larger portion of it is held by foreigners.

It matters because it means that foreigners have a legitimate claim to a part of our present and future wealth, which will reduce our standard of living in the future.

It also matters because GDP is based in part on our ability to manage our own economy; and our ability to do so may decline as our debt grows and more of it is owned by foreigners.

27

What about economic growth?

We need to grow to prosper as individuals. Equally important, we need to create wealth so that we can try to solve the problems that are not handled very well by private markets.

One of the lengthiest economic debates, it is still going on today, involves the question of the "proper" distribution of income or wealth. The debate has two parts. One is the question of a "fair" distribution of income or wealth among people. Is it best to let the market determine who gets what? Or is it better to redistribute income from the rich to the poor, or from the poor to the rich?

The second question is, how should we distribute the nation's limited wealth between "private" and "public" goods? Private goods are things that are produced because people are willing and able to buy them themselves—houses, cars, toothpaste, clothes, etc. Public goods are things that we do not actually buy—or at least we do not pay the full price for what we use. National defense, education, and medical research are just three examples. The argument is that if government does not step in and use money collected through taxes to provide for such goods, we would not get enough of them and we would, therefore, be worse off as individuals and as a nation.

No one disagrees with the idea that government must play a role in providing public goods. However, there is almost no agreement on just how much of each public good we "need" or on which things are truly public goods.

Some people think we need more defense. Some think we need less. Some think we do not need any. Who makes the final decision? Politicians.

There is no "scientific" way to determine exactly what we "need" to spend on national defense or for medical research. So it is left to politicians and special interest groups to decide how each public good will be treated, as well as to decide which things will be dealt with as public goods.[27]

Why not give each public good all the money it needs or wants? Because, in a world with limited resources, whatever is spent on public goods is not available for private goods. Therefore, one of the most difficult questions to answer will always be: How much should be taken away from private consumption in order to increase the availability of public goods.

---

[27] In some cases, benefit-cost analysis can be used to help make decisions.

We assume, of course, that using our resources for national defense or medical research or education or job training will add to the total happiness or wellbeing of the nation. But, we also assume that reducing the opportunity to buy things in private markets will take away from our happiness.

Therefore, we are faced with a tradeoff. In some cases, government taxes people in order to provide those same people with the benefits of public goods. Why? Because we know that those goods would not be provided in sufficient quantity, if at all, if production decisions are left to private markets. National defense is a common example. As a general rule, individuals cannot arrange for their own defense against foreign threats. Therefore, we can argue that anyone who pays taxes will receive some benefit from that part of their taxes used to provide greater safety and security through a stronger national defense.

In other cases, government taxes some people and uses the funds to help others. This process can result in a direct redistribution of income from taxpayers (the "rich") to welfare recipients (the "poor"). Or, as with some tax cuts, from one class to another. At other times, the redistribution has the sole objective of simply providing more public goods—using money from taxpayers to provide things available to everyone, such as roads and courts.

Given the fact that we "can't get something for nothing," there will always be tradeoffs involved when we do something "good," whether it is to help those who cannot help themselves or trying to solve our own problems.

Therefore, it should be clear that the wealthier the nation is, the more opportunities there are to help those who need help or to provide solutions to problems that can make all of us or some of us better off.

If you asked twenty people to list what they believe are today's ten worst problems, it is almost certain that no two lists would be identical. But there is a good chance that some of the following issues would show up on every list: AIDS, illegal drugs, prescription drugs, the deterioration of the environment, poisons in our food, poverty, homelessness, unfair foreign trade, the spread of nuclear weapons, and the fear of nuclear destruction. Some lists would also include too much government regulation and too much government production.

No one would pretend that all these problems are strictly economic problems. But each and every one is either directly or indirectly related to the performance of the economy.

Each problem could be lessened with greater economic growth, either because the greater wealth would give people more money or more hope, or because the greater wealth would give us more resources that can be devoted to solving our problems.

It is important to recognize, however, that the creation of greater total wealth will not automatically funnel more resources into attempts to solve any of these problems or to increase the incomes of the poor. Also, spending more money on a particular problem does not guarantee a solution, and solving one problem while giving up something else will not necessarily increase the nation's total happiness or wellbeing

But, the wealthier we are as a nation, the better the chances are for dealing with our problems and the better the chances are for having all incomes increase.

Can we intentionally generate economic growth?

In our model, the water in the tub represents GDP for a single year, which means that economic growth is represented by having more water in the tub year after year. Technically, economic growth measures the change in GDP per person, not just in total. And that requires a greater inflow each year, especially when population is increasing.

What causes economic growth?

One of the most important questions in all of economics is: What causes economic growth? The question, which is of crucial importance to both developed and developing nations, is also the least understood in all of economics.

Academic journals and textbooks are filled with all sorts of explanations and theories of economic growth, each of which is of little or no value in the real world.

Does that mean economists do not know anything about economic growth? Especially how to encourage positive growth? The answer is, no. The truth is economists have known for more than two thousand years what the key to economic growth is. But, to be useful, that knowledge must be separated into two somewhat distinct categories—economic growth in underdeveloped (or developing) countries and economic growth in developed countries. The reason for the distinction is that there are important differences between developing and developed countries.

Economic Growth

What causes economic growth in developing nations?

There is a clear list of factors that leads to economic growth in underdeveloped countries.

1) The first factor, which was explained brilliantly by Plato in *The Republic* (360 BCE), is specialization. So far, no one has done a better job than Plato of explaining the incredible benefits of specialization in a pre-industrialized economy. As people move from being self-sufficient individuals or families—meaning that they produce everything they need by themselves—to specialized producers, such as wheat growers, shoe makers, candle makers, or pin makers, a whole market economy develops. Specialization in production lets people produce far more of a single product than they can use themselves, thereby giving them the opportunity to sell some or all of what they make and buy what they need and want. The result is that people and families end up with much more than they could ever produce by themselves. Out of this specialization, markets develop where things are bought and sold—using money, not barter. Then come retailers, wholesalers, and foreign trade. It is all described in *The Republic*. And it is such specialization that is the single most important reason for massive increases in economic growth and the wealth of the nation.

2) The second factor, which was described by Adam Smith in 1776, is specialization in factories. Smith took Plato's description of specialization in a pre-industrialized economy and brought it into an industrialized economy. In Smith's pin factory, workers specialize in making one part of a pin. Instead of Plato's pin makers, who, by specializing in making pins, might make 20 pins a day, each of Smith's pin makers, working in factories, make the equivalent of 200 pins a day. (In Smith's example, ten workers in a pin factory turn out 2,000 pins a day, versus the 20 he assumed each can make on his own.) It is described wonderfully in Smith's *An Inquiry Into The nature And Causes Of The Wealth of Nations*. And it is the single most important reason for the massive increases in economic growth and the wealth of nations that Smith predicted.

3) The third factor is the need for capital to fund the factories that allow the specialization described by Adam Smith. In many developing countries, that capital is difficult or impossible to find. In developed countries, investment in capital goods occurs when some current production is directed toward the creation of productive facilities and infrastructure. In poor nations, there may not be enough current production to meet basic needs—such as food and shelter—which means it is virtually impossible to free up production to build for

the future. In such cases, the needed capital must come from somewhere else. However, it is difficult for benevolent nations to provide capital goods to improve future conditions when millions of people may be starving today.

4) The fourth factor is property rights, because in order for factors one through three to be implemented, it is necessary for people to have property rights to protect what they have. Without property rights, neither Plato's nor Adam Smith's specialization can take place, because without property rights, everything can be taken away from anyone who prospers. And, in both developing and developed countries, if contracts are not enforced and protected, virtually everything is handed over to those with the brute force to take what they want from everyone who is weaker.

5) A fifth factor is stability—a stable government and a stable economy—because without stability, investment cannot take place in either Plato's or Adam Smith's world. Again, in many poor nations, there is no stability. There is, instead, chaos and civil war.

What causes economic growth in developed nations?

The first four factors listed above are already present in developed nations, which is why a reasonable rate of economic growth is the norm.

The fifth factor is also present, but it can vary. Although most developed nations have stable governments, there are times when that is not the case. And although most developed countries have relatively stable economies, that is also not always the case.

Even the most developed countries suffer bouts of inflation and recession, each of which is detrimental to economic growth.

And even the most developed countries experience periods of low saving rates, outside economic disruptions, and bad government policies that can disrupt the normal and expected rate of economic growth.

On the other hand, there are also periods of beneficial change, such as times of significant increases in technology that push economic growth above its expected level.

Therefore, the most important factors for encouraging economic growth in developed countries are economic stability, and wise policies by governments and central banks.

In terms of our model, here is what we know:

Specialization increases the water in the tub.

Avoiding inflation and recession increases the water in the tub.

Correcting market failures and externalities increases the water in the tub.

Education increases the water in the tub.

Property rights increase the water in the tub, because property rights are a necessary part of economic growth, which is why so many underdeveloped countries suffer from limited or no growth.

Too little money in the economy raises interest rates, which decreases the water in the tub.

An increasing foreign trade surplus adds to the water in the tub.

Economic growth requires that some resources that could be used for current consumption be invested, instead, in human and physical capital, thereby increasing the capital base and the productivity of the economy. Because of this, countries that cannot afford to give up any current consumption, because it is needed for survival, cannot grow without outside help.

But, we would like to know more. If there is one question economists would like to have answered, it is: What more can we do to intentionally increase the rate of economic growth in both developed and developing countries?

28

Someone asked about the Japanese economic miracle. The question was: How do you explain the Japanese economic miracle without tying it to the benefits of free trade?

The Japanese economic miracle is an example of the benefits of *controlling* trade, not the benefits of *free* trade. The huge economic expansion in Japan began with the massive decline in world shipping costs that took place during the later half of the twentieth century. But it owed its existence to a policy that promoted exports and restricted imports. While Japanese automobiles and other Japanese products poured into the United States, Japan blocked many imports. Japan's economic miracle occurred while it was protecting and promoting manufacturing at home and running a large foreign-trade surplus. Its economic decline can be traced to the time when its trade surplus began to fall—when Japanese manufacturers began to move production out of Japan and into China, Korea, Indonesia, even the United States.

And you blame that on free trade?

Maybe it was just coincidence. But the decline began at the same time that Japanese companies began moving manufacturing out of Japan. It was then that Japanese workers went from having jobs for life to being unemployed. In historical terms, it was a relatively short miracle. Adding to the problem was a reduction in the exports of manufactured products, caused by the growing weakness in world markets.

The Chinese Economic Miracle

29

Someone asked about the fast rate of economic growth in China.

China, in the twenty-first century, is doing exactly what Japan did in the twentieth century. It encourages exports and limits imports, thereby expanding manufacturing by Chinese companies. A few years ago, it seemed as though every product you picked up said, *Made in Japan*. Today, almost everything you see says, *Made in China*.

What does that have to do with the United States?
The United States is also one history's great economic miracles. For many years, it was supported by the *protectionist* existence of two oceans and high shipping costs. It was an economic miracle with minimal foreign trade that was fueled by vast quantities of valuable natural resources. But it is at risk if its manufacturing base shrinks.

Restricting the supply of imports from other countries hurts consumers, because prices are higher and fewer products are available.

But we cannot sacrifice everything for the chance to spend all our money today on cheap imports. It's like the children's story of the ant and the grasshopper. Whether it's individuals or nations, if we spend everything today, there will be a bleak tomorrow. According to economics, real economic growth takes place only if current consumption is *not* maximized. Some current consumption must be exchanged for the build-up of manufacturing capabilities. That's why we need foreign trade policies that help us prepare for the future, not policies that let us freely spend our way into poverty while increasing the profits of a few.

One way or another, we pay for what we buy today. While the Japanese economy was expanding, the Japanese had a high standard of living; even though Japan, especially Tokyo, was one of the most expensive places in the world to live, high wages made up for the high prices.

You sound like a protectionist.
No, I'm an economist. And economists worry about what things really cost—not what they appear to cost. What is the real cost of imports? It's not just what we pay at the time. It's what we have to give up to buy them. That includes

the price, but it also includes the loss of future wealth if they lead to the loss of manufacturing in America. In economic jargon, it is called opportunity cost. Opportunity cost is defined to be the value to you of what you must give up when you buy or do something. In the case of trade policies that encourage American companies to move manufacturing out of America, the lower prices of imported goods means that we are consuming our wealth. It's like never changing the oil in your car. You save money for a while. Then the car breaks down. We need to keep the car running. That will not happen if we fail to understand the true cost of free-import policies. And it cannot happen without wise government actions aimed at maximizing the wealth of the nation.

A Little More Free Trade Theory

30

Isn't free trade the sacred cow of economics?

Free trade theory *is* the sacred cow of economics—it is an idea that economists are not supposed to question. However, we already know that exports add to GDP and imports subtract from GDP. Therefore, the facts are that a foreign trade surplus increases GDP and a foreign trade deficit decreases GDP.

Given those facts, the question is: What is the purpose of the assumed-to-be-airtight economic theory of free trade that is based on the idea of comparative advantage?

The answer appears to be that its purpose is to support what are called free trade policies or free trade agreements with other countries. In particular, it is claimed that the theory of free trade is all the "proof" we need to argue against any and all restrictions to the free importation of goods and services.

The problem is that the theory is not so good. It is an airtight argument only for one special case—the case where there are two countries, two things to produce, and each country has different relative costs of production. Given those conditions, the theory concludes that both countries will gain if each produces only the thing it is relatively better at producing and then trades some of what it produces for some of what the other country produces. That's great. In that special case, each country gets more stuff than it would get if it produced both things itself and ignored the benefits of trade.

In the real world, where there are countless products, many countries, and where no one trades stuff for stuff—we buy and sell things—the theory means nothing. In the real world, where we buy and sell things, it is possible for one country to produce everything, or almost everything, for a lower cost than anyone else. Even without worrying about that extreme case, the truth is that if the people in one country buy things from other countries, there is no guarantee that anyone in any other country will buy anything at all from that country.

The even larger truth is that all theories based on assumptions apply only to cases where those assumptions are actually true. They do not apply to any other cases or situations.

And, when it comes to foreign trade—which is not trade, but international buying and selling—we have only two hard facts to guide our policies.

One is, as we already know, foreign trade deficits reduce GDP and foreign trade surpluses increase GDP.

The other is that specialization is real. It is not a theory; it is how the world works. As such, specialization is the only logical argument for foreign trade (or commerce). But it is not good enough to let us ignore the importance of trade deficits or surpluses. In other words, specialization is a necessary, but not a sufficient, condition to claim that trade is good.

Just think of what life would be like without specialization: If you couldn't buy anything at all; if you had to be totally self-sufficient; if you were not allowed to use anything you did not make yourself out of resources you own; or if you couldn't buy anything that wasn't made in the state in which you live, using resources only from your state; or if you couldn't buy anything that wasn't made in America, out of totally American resources. Think of what the country would be like if that were the case for everyone.

That is why, instead of living as self-sufficient farmers, people in free societies choose to get jobs, including jobs as specialized farmers, and to have a good life buying stuff from everywhere.

And the better jobs they have, the better off they are. Think of having a job or a business that makes a good profit selling locally. Then think of what you could make if your product is sold statewide. Then nation-wide. Then worldwide. Opening up the world gives you higher wages and greater profits.

That's why free trade is so good.

Not so fast. International commerce is good. But nothing comes without a cost. In the case I just described, you have to ask: What happens to your income or profits if you now have to compete with another local manufacturer? Or with producers from all around your state? Or from all around the nation? Or from all around the world?

Some say, "If you can't compete, get out of the market. The market is not supposed to guarantee anyone anything."

These people also say that the only possible problem with free trade is that some individuals and businesses might suffer in order for the country to benefit; but only temporarily. Even if imports take away jobs, these people say that the increased spending will eventually help everyone, because even those who lose their jobs or businesses will eventually get new jobs and open new businesses, because if consumers can pay lower prices for imported goods, they will have more money to spend on other things—things made in America.

A Little More Free Trade Theory

The problem is that we do not know if the money saved by purchasing cheaper imports will be spent on goods and services produced in the United States. The savings can just as easily be spent on more imports. So, how can we guarantee that jobs and businesses lost to imported goods will be replaced? Or that, if they are replaced, wages and profits will be as high as they were before? We can't.

We know that trade agreements that increase exports can lead to increases in production, employment, and profits at home.

We know that trade agreements that reduce or eliminate restrictions on imports lower prices for consumers. It is pretty simple.

We also know that when we are free to buy and sell things everywhere, individuals and countries gain from specialization.

But these facts do not mean everyone wins.

When exports increase, domestic prices can also increase. That is a big issue whenever U.S. agricultural exports increase dramatically. Farmers like it. Consumers do not, because food prices increase.

And when imports increase, U.S. production can be hurt. Consumers like it, because they get lower prices. Companies that go out of business, and workers who lose their jobs, do not.

In the end, there is one other fact that cannot be ignored. It is: There are no countries with a large and prosperous middle class that do not also have a solid manufacturing base. Countries that earn huge sums of money exporting natural resources, such as oil, have middle class populations only when those in power decide to spread the wealth around, which does happen once in a while. For all other countries, it is necessary to worry about what "free-trade" agreements do to the manufacturing base, as well as to the foreign-trade surplus or deficit.

So, you don't like NAFTA?

NAFTA gave U.S. companies an incentive to move production out of the country. And when U.S. businesses move manufacturing and jobs to other countries, because of low wages and few, if any, environmental regulations, and then ship products back to the United States, the foreign-trade deficit increases. The corporations, and some people, win. The economy may lose.

But won't the extra profits those companies earn trickle down to everyone else?

There are no trickle-down benefits. The only way people become better off is if their wages and profits are pulled higher by a greater demand for what they do. When U.S. companies move manufacturing out of the country, and imports replace domestic manufacturing, the demand for American jobs falls.

So what should we do?

There are no easy answers. Foreign trade is a complex and messy issue that has been made politically divisive because of the easy, but unfounded, claims that free trade is always good or always bad.

The Federal Reserve

31

Is the Federal Reserve really, really smart?

There are times when the Federal Reserve does a good job; there are other times when the Federal Reserve creates absolute disasters.

Everyone thinks the Federal Reserve is good.

It is good, sometimes. Other times, it is not so good. But because fiscal policy is of limited use, manipulating the money supply is the main tool for managing the U.S. economy.

That's exactly what the Federal Reserve does. So what's wrong?

To begin with, although the supply of money, or changes in the rate of growth of the money supply, has a dramatic impact on the economy, it was not until 1980 that the money supply in the United States was truly brought under control. Both before and after 1980, the Federal Reserve was responsible for some of the worst economic times in America.

Is that your opinion?

You decide. The Federal Reserve was created in 1913, with the major objective of protecting banks from failure due to large withdrawals during times of financial panic. It was to be "the lender of last resort" to banks, thereby preventing bank panics. But, its first big test was the 1920s. And it failed; beginning with the fact that The Federal Reserve had a lot to do with the stock market crash of 1929.

How?

The Fed had allowed the speculative run-up of stock prices in the 1920s by letting people legally "invest" in stocks by borrowing almost the entire purchase price. Almost anyone could borrow virtually all the money he or she wanted in order to buy stocks. The part *investors* had to put up is called the *margin* or *margin requirement*. If the margin requirement is very low, you can buy stocks with virtually none of your own money.

Is that bad?

It's might not be so bad if stock prices always increased, and if the increase is due to increases in real corporate profits. But, in the 1920s, prices were rising because of speculative buying, not because of real profits. When it was obvious that the low-margin policy had the stock market running out of control, the Federal Reserve panicked and raised margin requirements. Raising margin requirements gave "investors" two choices: They could give more money to their broker or banker to pay for a larger part of the purchases they had already made, or they could sell their stocks. Those who did not have the money needed to hold their stocks were forced to sell. The sell-off of stocks caused prices to fall, and those who held their stocks now owed their brokers more than their stocks were worth. The result was that people had to sell virtually worthless "investments." And, after they sold, they still owed massive amounts of money. That is why, when the markets crashed, so many individuals and corporations ended up in bankruptcy.

Then what?

Then the Federal Reserve allowed banks to fail and the money supply to shrink, which is what it was supposed to prevent from happening. As a result, the Federal Reserve was partly responsible for the length and depth of the Great Depression, because if the Federal Reserve had protected the money supply, the Depression would not have been as severe, and it would probably have been over before World War II ended it. Many blamed the severity of the Depression on bad fiscal policies—the failure of the federal government to use deficit spending to pull the economy out of trouble. But we now know it was a case of absolutely terrible management of the money supply.

What else did the Fed do wrong?

The Federal Reserve was responsible for the inflation of the 1970s, because it kept increasing the money supply to finance the deficit spending on the Vietnam War. Then, when the resulting inflation caused interest rates to rise, the Federal Reserve increased the money supply even more, forcing interest rates back down. Interest rates have to rise during inflation, because lenders are not willing to make loans at rates that are less than the inflation rate. If they do, when the loans are repaid, the lender receives money that is worth less, in real purchasing power, than the money that was loaned out.

The Federal Reserve

Instead of keeping the money supply under control and letting interest rates rise, which would have choked off the inflation, the Federal Reserve kept increasing the money supply, hoping to keep rates down. But each increase in the money supply added to the rate of inflation. It was a vicious circle that led to the worst modern inflation in the United States.

What else?

The Federal Reserve was partly responsible for the election of Ronald Reagan (which was not a disaster to Republicans), because after deciding to end the inflation of the 1970s by restricting the growth of the money supply, Paul Volcker waited almost a year to act. When he did act, just before the Carter-Reagan election, the unavoidable and predictable explosion of interest rates was blamed on President Carter. And Ronald Reagan was elected president.

What else?

The Federal Reserve was responsible for the stock market crash of 1987, because it raised interest rates to fight what it claimed was the beginning of another inflation. But there was no real threat of inflation, because the only cause of inflation is the Fed itself—when it increases the money supply too fast.

What else?

The Federal Reserve was responsible for keeping economic growth below its true potential during the Clinton presidency, because it kept interest rates high to prevent fast economic growth from causing inflation. But fast economic growth does not cause inflation—not in theory and not at any time in history. It was a bogus argument. The Clinton years gave the U.S its longest economic expansion in U.S. history, but the economy could have grown even faster.

Anything else?

The Federal Reserve was partly responsible for the economic downturn that began in 2001, because it waited too long to lower interest rates. The Fed was concerned with inflation—which was a phony issue—rather than with recession—which was a real concern—given the troubles in the stock market and rising oil prices. By the time the Fed acted, the stock market had crashed, and the economy was in a tailspin.

The same thing happened in the summer of 2008. Once again, the Fed reacted to an increase in oil prices by raising interest rates to fight a non-existent inflation, rather than preparing to fight a possible recession.

The Fed was also in the middle of the economic collapse of 2008-2009, because it did the same thing with margin requirements that it had done in the 1920s, except this time it was with its rules on derivative "investing," which allowed companies to make highly leveraged bets with little or none of their own money.

What do you want to do? Shut down the Fed?
Not at all. The Federal Reserve, which is the main manager of the American economy, may not have the greatest record. But it is frightening to think of what might happen if politicians took control of the money supply and monetary policy. It would be a massive conflict of interest. Politicians could spend whatever they want, knowing they have the power to create money to finance it. Also, those in control would have the opportunity to disrupt or temporarily improve the economy in order to affect elections.

But you are saying the Fed has already done that.
It has. So did the first two central banks in America—the First Bank of the United States and the Second Bank of the United States. Each was shut down after trying to use its power to support a presidential candidate who lost. In each case, the elected president did not renew the bank's charter.

But the Federal Reserve is different. It was created with all sorts of checks and balances. It lets the government control the money supply without having power concentrated in one place.
The government does not manage the money supply. The Federal Reserve does. And the Federal Reserve is not a government agency.

But there are still checks and balances.
That was the idea when Congress created the Federal Reserve System in 1913. The President of the United States was given the power to appoint members to the Federal Reserve Board of Governors. The President was also given the power to appoint the Chairman of the Federal Reserve Board. And the Chairman of the Federal Reserve Board is required to testify in front of Congress about Fed policies. But the Federal Reserve System is an independent

entity. It is really a central bank that, as in other developed nations, manages the money supply.

Why is it called the Federal Reserve System?

On paper, the Federal Reserve is a system, not a single central bank. When Congress created it, it was clear that banks and the money supply had to be managed, especially after the bank panic of 1907 wiped out the savings of so many people. History had shown that banks could not be trusted to regulate themselves. And when banks are out of control, so are the money supply and the economy. But, because of the abuse of power by the two former central banks, many in Congress did not want another central bank. The solution, after years of debate, was to create the Federal Reserve System. Rather than having a single central bank, twelve Federal Reserve Banks were established throughout the country. The idea was to spread the power around.

Has it worked?

It sounded like a good idea in the beginning, but today it is easy to see that a few individuals—often a single individual—have enormous influence over the economy by being able to control the money supply and interest rates.

So, you are saying that the U.S. economy is being managed by a bunch of private bankers? People who weren't even elected?

Not a bunch. A few.

That's pretty scary. But what is the Federal Reserve supposed to do?

In the beginning, it's primary function was to be *a lender of last resort* to banks, meaning it would lend funds to banks that could not meet depositor's demands for withdrawals, which meant it was also looking after the money supply. The Federal Reserve did an adequate job for a few years. But it did a terrible job of protecting banks, deposits, and the money supply during the Great Depression. Even so, its power and influence grew to the point where it is now the main manager of the U.S. economy, and one of the most powerful economic entities in the world. Today, its stated goals are to achieve acceptable economic growth, low unemployment, and steady prices in the U.S. economy. The tools it has at its disposal are its control of the money supply and the authority to set certain interest rates.

The Federal Reserve

The textbooks spend a lot of time showing how a multiple expansion or contraction of the money supply can take place in a fractional-reserve banking system. But I don't understand how it works.

You don't have to understand it. That's not how the money supply works.

What do you mean?

The theory is that when someone makes a deposit in a bank, the bank loans out say 90 percent of the deposit. The loan ends up in another bank that then loans out 90 percent of its deposit. That loan ends up in another bank that then loans out 90 percent of its deposit. And so on. Each deposit and loan in the sequence is smaller, because each is only 90 percent of the previous deposit. And all the loans that end up in checking accounts are counted as money. Therefore, in theory, the whole process leads to an expansion of the money supply that can be as much as ten times the original deposit. The greater the fraction of each deposit that banks can legally loan out, the greater is the increase in the money supply. The percentage of deposits that must be held as legal reserves—and not loaned out—is called the reserve requirement. The Federal Reserve sets the legal reserve requirement, so, in theory, the Fed can increase the money supply by lowering the reserve requirement, thereby allowing banks to make more loans.

But you said it doesn't work.

Not like that. There are too many *leakages* in the process to get a large multiple of the money supply. All the loans do not go into banks or checking accounts. That's why the Federal Reserve's true method for increasing or decreasing the money supply is its Open Market Operations.

So what do I have to know?

All you have to know is that when the Fed wants to increase the money supply, it buys government bonds in the bond market. When the Fed buys bonds, it replaces something that is not money—bonds—with something that is money—Federal Reserve checks. If the Fed wants to decrease the money supply, it sells government securities in the bond market. When the Fed sells bonds, it replaces something that is money—checks drawn against deposits in banks—with something that is not money—bonds. In reality, the increase or decrease in the money supply is equal to the Fed's purchase or sale of bonds.

The Federal Reserve

That's it?

That's it. As simple as the open market process is, it is one of the most powerful tools available for managing modern economies.

Who decides to increase or decrease the money supply, or to change the rate of growth of the money supply?

Technically, the Federal Open Market Committee makes the decision.

What's that?

The Federal Open Market Committee consists of the seven members of the Federal Reserve Board of Governors and five of the twelve Federal Reserve Bank presidents. Four of the five individual bank presidents are selected on a rotating basis. The president of the Federal Reserve Bank of New York is always on the committee, because the Fed's open market operations are conducted through the New York Bank.

What is the Board of Governors?

The Board of Governors is seven people appointed by the President of the United States to staggered 14-year terms that end in January of every even numbered year. The president also appoints the Chairman of the Board of Governors to a four-year term that is staggered with the president's, so that when a president takes office, it is with an existing Chairman. The idea was to prevent any president from easily taking over the Board with his own appointees. The presidents of the twelve regional Federal Reserve Banks are appointed by each bank's nine directors, six of whom are chosen by the member banks in the district.

Pretty complicated.

It is. It was developed by Congress to prevent the concentration of power in one place. But, as I said, today's reality is that power is not only centered in one place, it is centered with one person: the Chairman of the Federal Reserve Board of Governors.

But monetary policy can still be used to regulate or manage the economy?

Within limits. A policy that has the money supply growing too fast causes inflation. And there are questions regarding the ability of monetary policy to pull an economy out of a deep recession. In the 1930s, John Maynard Keynes argued that there was a natural rate of interest—a level below which interest rates would not fall. If true, it meant that monetary policy intended to lower interest rates to encourage spending and business investment was limited. According to Keynes' assumption, once the bottom was reached for interest rates, additional increases in the money supply would do nothing to increase economic activity, because interest rates could not be forced any lower.

Was Keynes right?

No. We know—logically and historically—that interest rates can fall to zero. Adjusted for inflation, the real rate of interest can even be negative.

If that's true, why is monetary policy limited in what it can do?

Because disproving the downward limit on interest rates does not automatically prove the value of monetary policy.

What do you mean?

It is true that as interest rates fall, business and consumer spending increases. The lower the rate of interest, the smaller the payments on loans will be. But there will still be payments, because the loans still have to be paid off. Even if interest rates drop to zero, the money has to be paid back. Zero interest does not mean free money; it means there is no cost to borrow money. And the ability to pay back a loan depends on future income. A business cannot borrow money to fund expenditures it does not expect to recover, even at a zero rate of interest. And an individual will not buy a car, even at a zero rate of interest, without considering the future payments and alternative uses of future income.

That is why pushing interest rates to zero in Japan was not enough to pull the Japanese economy out of a recession. And why everyone does not run out and buy a new car at a zero rate of interest.

The deeper a recession becomes, the less important additional declines in interest rates are to people and businesses making decisions about borrowing money to make purchases or investments, partly because interest rates are already very low. But also because even a zero rate of interest may not be enough to allow firms with poor prospects or individuals without jobs to make purchases on credit.

The Federal Reserve

That is why there are limits to what monetary policy can do?

That's it. However, that does not negate the overall value and importance of monetary policy. What the limitations do is give us one more reason for avoiding the mistakes that cause recessions.

So, what should we do?

We should be more watchful over what the Federal Reserve is doing. If the Federal Reserve is the main manager of the U.S. economy, it should be more answerable for its policies and actions. There should be more debate in Congress about the assumptions the Fed is making about the economy and about what its policies should be.

A good place to begin is to make it clear that the textbooks and the Fed are wrong when they offer two explanations for inflation: demand pull and cost-push. The truth is, there is no such thing as cost-push inflation, which is why it is always wrong to use the term "stagflation" to describe an economy that is both stagnant and suffering from inflation.

To be accurate, there is only one cause of inflation: demand pull, meaning that excessive demand pulls prices higher.

But there are two types of recession: cost push recession and falling demand recession. If everyone understood that an increase in the Consumer Price Index caused by rising oil prices is a signal of a possible recession, not inflation, we, meaning the Fed, would not make so many mistakes.

A Few Conclusions

32

Someone asked if the speaker could offer a few conclusions.

Rising oil prices do not cause inflation. Rising oil prices cause increases in the Consumer Price Index. But believing that all increases in the Consumer Price Index signal inflation is a mistake. Sometimes, the increase signals a recession.

The only cause of inflation is too much money. There are no theoretical arguments and no real-world evidence to support any cause of inflation other than putting too much money into the economy. And it does not have to be too much paper money. When Spain sent ships to the new world, they came back loaded with gold. And that gold, which was money, caused the inflation that helped bring down the Spanish Empire.

Controlling the money supply controls inflation. If the only cause of inflation is too much money in the economy, then the only cure for inflation is to control the money supply.

The Federal Reserve controls the money supply. It does so through its open market operations—buying and selling government bonds in the open market.

There are many possible causes for recession. Some are beyond our control. Some are the result of human error.

There is no natural business cycle. That does not mean people will stop looking for one.

The national debt is a problem in a global economy. National debt in a global economy is different from national debt when the debt is held domestically. If paying interest on and paying off government bonds, which are the national debt, means sending money to foreigners, the negative impact of a large national debt might severely affect the future economy.

A Few Conclusions

Correcting market failure increases GDP. Monopoly tends to reduce economic efficiency and GDP. Policies that correct the inefficiency increase GDP.

Correcting negative externalities increases GDP. Pollution reduces economic efficiency and GDP. Policies that correct the inefficiency increase GDP.

Correcting positive externalities increases GDP. Failing to deal with positive externalities, such as education, reduces economic efficiency and GDP.

Providing public goods increases GDP. Failing to deal correctly with public goods, such as national defense, reduces economic efficiency and GDP.

Managing common property resources increases GDP. Failing to deal correctly with common property resources, such as fish in lakes and oceans, reduces economic efficiency and GDP.

Managing foreign trade increases GDP. Specialization in production, which is the main benefit of foreign trade, adds to GDP. A foreign trade surplus also adds to GDP. But a foreign trade deficit subtracts from GDP. Therefore, in order for "free trade" to increase GDP, trade must be managed so that the benefits from specialization and exports are not more than offset by a foreign trade deficit.

3. Summary

Someone asked the speaker if he could summarize the Rubber Ducky Model. His answer was that he could do better than that. He said he had prepared a short written summary of the main points and that he would now hand it out. He explained that he did not want to hand it out at the beginning of the meeting, because he wanted everyone to listen rather than read.

The Rubber Ducky Model—A Summary

We use the image of a bathtub to represent the economy.

The water in the tub represents Gross Domestic Product.

The water flowing in is:
    consumer spending,
    investment spending,
    government spending, and
    exports.

The water flowing out is:
    imports.

And we need just the right amount of money in the economy.
    Too much money and we get inflation.
    Too little money and we can have a recession.

The actual quantity of water in the tub, after some given time period, depends on how much is coming in and how much is going out.

We decide if the quantity of water in the tub is acceptable by tracking unemployment and growth numbers and the rate of inflation.

Summary

If we do not like the quantity of water in the tub, we can look at ways to change the inflow or the outflow.

There are a number of ways to change the inflow or outflow.

Fiscal policy—meaning changes in taxes or government spending intended to improve the overall economy—may not work; or if it does, it may have a minimal impact, other than an easy-to-see redistribution of income.

Monetary policy—meaning changing the money supply (or the rate of increase of the money supply) to improve the overall economy—may appear to be more effective than fiscal policy, because changing interest rates normally changes consumer spending and investment spending by business. On the other hand, if the Federal Reserve mismanages the money supply, it can cause either inflation or recession. The Federal Reserve can also affect interest rates directly by changing the discount rate, which is the rate of interest the Fed charges banks that borrow money from the Fed to meet the legal reserve requirements set by the Fed. Of course, the expected effectiveness of monetary policy hinges on the assumption that, even in a severe recession, people and businesses will want to borrow money and banks will be willing to make loans in a risky economic environment.

Correcting the misallocation of resources caused by market failures, public goods, positive externalities, negative externalities, and common property resources, increases economic efficiency, which increases real income, consumption, and GDP. Foreign trade agreements that increase exports relative to imports add directly to GDP. In the end, such microeconomic policies may be more effective at increasing GDP than the standard "tools" of macroeconomic policy (government spending and taxes and/or changes in the money supply and interest rates).

I READ THE NEWS TODAY OH BOY

1. What You Now Know About Economics

Here is a short list of what you should now know.

You should have a knowledge of microeconomic theory, whether it is knowing the conditions for perfect competition or how events, such as a freeze that damages the orange crop, affects the prices of oranges and apples, and of how economic efficiency is upset by market failure and externalities.

You should have a knowledge of macroeconomic theory, whether it is the determination of Gross Domestic Product and employment, or how intentional actions by government or the Federal Reserve will or will not improve incomes, employment, and GDP.

You should have a knowledge of environmental economics, which focuses on externality problems. Environmental economics relies on the same logic used in the field of Law and Economics.

You should have a knowledge of monetary theory and policy, which means knowing who and what the Federal Reserve is, what its function is, how it can protect banks and manage the money supply, how it changes the money supply, why it changes the money supply, and how it has been both successful and unsuccessful.

You should have a knowledge of how economics developed over time.

You should have a knowledge of the interaction of economics and politics.

You should have a knowledge of how economics interacts with science.

2. What You Now Know About Politics & Economics

You should now be a good judge or critic of political rhetoric and politically motivated policies. For example:

Tax cuts are good.
Of course, they are—for those who get a tax break. They are not so good for the economy as a whole.

Government can fix all our problems.
No it can't.

A small government is better.
Why is it better? What do we want to give up in order to have a small government? Public goods, like national defense? Government regulations that correct market failures and externalities? Government regulations that protect markets from excessive speculation?

Communism helps the people.
Not exactly. Communism is pretty much a dictatorship. And, like all dictatorships, those in power often help a few at the expense of the many; pretty much the opposite of what Karl Marx hoped for.

Government regulations disrupt the free market.
They can. But if regulations are used to correct market failures and the misallocation of resources caused by externalities, public goods, and common property resources, then government regulations do what the private market cannot do—they create what a free market would do if a free market existed.

Protecting the environment is bad for the economy.
No, it's not. Correcting negative externalities and managing common property resources increases Gross Domestic Product.

Free trade is good.

Yes, it is. But there are no theories that truly support the free trade policies or agreements made by politicians. There is the reality of the gains from specialization, from Plato to today, which is why trade is good. But trade deficits are not so good, and massive exports can raise domestic prices.

People can spend their money better than government can.

Reread the Richard Green story and everything on public goods, common property resources, and externalities.

There is a lot of government waste.

This issue is not discussed in this book, but it is true. It is also true that most government waste is the result of bad deals with "friends" that allow corporations to overcharge government and you—the taxpayer. The government cannot buy a $600 hammer from no one.

3. I Read the News Today Oh Boy

You can now read the news, or watch it on television, and listen to political discussions and think about who and what does and does not make sense.

You can judge solutions to problems, or create your own, based on rational thought and reason, without being misled by political ideology. Or not. You can, if you choose, leave it all up to others.

Here are a few current issues, along with the economic principles used to address them.

Health care.
A public good, an externality problem, an exclusion problem, an economic efficiency issue, or a case of civilized compassion.

Global warming.
A negative externality, a public good, the interaction of science and economics, possibly a life and death struggle.

Pollution.
A negative externality. Can also be a life or death issue.

Education.
A positive externality or a public good.

Managing natural resources.
A common property resource issue or a negative externality.

Free trade policies.
Specialization, competition, and economic efficiency.

There are many more. All you have to do is open a newspaper.

A time to read and write.

The point of this book is not to tell anyone how to think, but to help you know how economists think, so that when you read or watch the news, or follow political dialogues and debates, you will be an informed and, possibly, an interactive citizen living in and contributing to a great nation.

This is not a normal text, based on lengthy theoretical discussions. Instead, it follows Alfred North Whitehead's definition of education, which is that "Education is the acquisition of the art of the utilization of knowledge."

Hopefully, it will help everyone learn the art of using economic knowledge.

Referring to Whitehead once again, one of his major arguments is that it makes no sense to learn principles without learning—at the same time—how to use them. He argued against the educational philosophy that says it makes sense to teach students principles without applications, based on the assumption that they will, sometime in the future, learn how to apply them.

Therefore, to complete a semester that follows Whitehead's advice, it is now time to read about, write about, and discuss as many additional issues as there is time to cover.

One final note about examining issues:

The point is to both understand the political arguments behind each issue, and to then get past political dogma by using what you have learned.

For example, if someone brings up the issue of universal health care or national health care, someone else is certain to complain that he or she is not interested in liberal or socialist schemes that get the government involved in private markets. But health care is not a liberal or conservative issue. If you look at the above list, it is a problem that can be "solved" only by understanding public goods, externalities, exclusion, economic efficiency, and civilized compassion. In fact, the greatest supporters of a national health care system might be corporate America. Most analysts believe it was a mistake to have ever made corporations responsible for their employees' health insurance. Aside from technical or fairness issues, many corporations are being hurt by the high costs of medical insurance, especially when trying to compete with foreign manufacturers who do not have to pay.

Therefore, once it is understood that health care is a truly important economic issue, it is possible to look at what the real options are. That means looking at European and Asian systems that combine free medical care provided by government with private care for whoever is willing and able to pay for it; like the Post Office and FedEx, or education. It also means not accepting the argument that the Canadian system is not so good, without even knowing how it works. No matter which side you think you are on, the truth is that we already know there are better health-care systems elsewhere, meaning that they cost less adn provide better results.

In many cases, the importance of using the economics in this book is not to come up with a solution to a particular problem, but to use economics to dismiss political rhetoric and dogma that get in the way of searching for real solutions. Once that is accomplished, then "everything is on the table," as they say. And that is how it should be. If there are problems, there should be no predetermined exclusion of solutions based on political dogma, or prejudice, or laziness.

Then we can all think for ourselves.

APPENDIX

1. Commonly Used Terms

Cartel: An organization of producers that colludes in order to control a market. OPEC is an example. It is a reason for market failure that can lead to a restriction of output and an increase in prices.

Common Property Resources: Resources not owned by anyone until someone takes them. It is a cause of market failure that destroys economic efficiency. It can be corrected only by government actions.

Consumer Price Index: The Consumer Price Index calculates the cost of a given "basket" of goods for different time periods. The measure assigns weights to items based on the percentage of total expenditures they accounted for during a base period.

Debt, Federal Government: Outstanding bonds sold by the government to cover past annual deficits.

Deficit: An annual shortfall between government revenues and expenditures. Can be financed by selling bonds, raising taxes, or by cutting government spending.

Demand, market: The maximum quantity of a good or service buyers are willing and able to buy during a given time period at various prices.

Discount Rate: The rate of interest The Federal Reserve charges banks that borrow money from the Fed to meet legal reserve requirements. This is one of the interest rates the media likes to watch, because when the Fed changes the discount rate, other interest rates tend to follow.

Efficiency: Economic efficiency means resources are used in ways that maximize the satisfaction of society.

Equilibrium: A market equilibrium occurs when there is a price such that the quantity buyers are willing and able to buy is equal to the quantity sellers are willing and able to sell at that price.

Federal Funds Rate: The rate of interest banks charge each other when they borrow money from each other to meet the legal reserve requirements set by the Federal Reserve.

Federal Reserve: The central bank of the U.S. It regulates commercial banks, controls the money supply, and conducts monetary policy to alter economic performance.

Fiscal Policy: Changing taxes and/or government spending to improve the economy. It does not work very well, unless the Federal Reserve pays for the deficit by creating money.

Imperfect Competition: A market where a buyer or seller affects price. Includes monopoly and monopolistic competition. It is an example of market failure.

Inflation: Constantly rising prices over time. It means the purchasing power of money is declining. It is caused when too much money is put into the economy.

Interest Rates: A general equilibrium variable that is the cost of borrowing money. The Federal Reserve can control interest rates by controlling the supply of money and by setting some interest rates.

Market Failure: A technical term meaning that prices do not allocate resources efficiently. Can be caused by imperfect competition, such as monopoly, or externalities.

Monetary Policy: Changing the money supply to affect interest rates and the economy. It is the most effective tool for managing the economy.

Money supply: The most used designations are M1 and M2. M1 is defined as coins and currency in circulation plus deposits in checking accounts. M2 is M1 plus savings accounts, money market accounts, and CDs of less than $100,000. Coins are produced by the U.S. Mint. Paper money is printed for the Federal Reserve by the Bureau of Printing & Engraving.

Monopolistic Competition: An industry with a small number of large firms, where each producer has an identifiable product, most often with a brand name. It is the most common cause of market failure in America, and the main form of business in America.

Monopoly: Market failure that occurs when a single firm controls an industry.

Negative externalities: Negative byproducts of production or consumption that are external to the producer or consumer, such as pollution. A cause of market failure that reduces economic efficiency.

Oligopoly: A market with a small number of producers. It is one type of imperfect competition that causes market failure.

Perfect Competition: A theoretical concept. A market where no firm or individual is large enough to affect price. It assumes that the products of each producer in a market are identical, and that competition is the result of producers trying to produce at the lowest cost.

Positive externalities: A positive byproduct of production or consumption that is external to the producer or consumer. Education is an example. Without government help, the free market will not provide a sufficient quantity of goods with positive externalities to maximize the wealth of the nation.

Producer Price Index: The PPI, from the Bureau of Labor Statistics, is used to measure average price changes received by domestic producers. Began in 1891 when the U.S. Senate authorized the Senate Committee on Finance to estimate the impact of tariffs on exports and imports, growth, and prices in both agriculture and manufacturing. Was called the Wholesale Price Index until 1978.

Public goods: Goods and services whose benefits cannot be excluded from those who do not pay for them. In almost all cases, such goods can be provided only by government.

Recession: An economic slowdown with rising unemployment and little or no economic growth. A depression is a severe recession.

Reserve Requirements: The percentage of deposits banks are required to hold as reserves against potential withdrawals. Set by The Fed.

Supply, market: The maximum quantity of a good or service sellers are willing and able to sell during a given time period at various prices.

Wealth: The nation's *real* wealth takes account not only of money or financial wealth, but also the environment and things such as economic stability, crime, and health, that add to or take away from the wellbeing of society and individuals.

2. A Market Model

1. Economics is the study of decision-making.

Economics is the study of how individuals, firms, and governments make decisions concerning the production, selling, and buying of things, and of how those decisions affect changes in important variables.

Microeconomics uses an understanding of how decisions made by households, firms, and government affect individual markets and the allocation of resources. Its emphasis is on how prices are determined in markets, how prices are affected by market imperfections or government actions and policies, and how resources are allocated among alternative uses. Because of its focus on prices, microeconomics is often called "price theory."

Macroeconomics uses an understanding of how decisions made by households (individuals), firms, and government determine the values of aggregate variables, such as total production, employment, national income, economic growth, and the overall price level. Because of its emphasis on the interaction of the private market and government, economics was, for many years, called "political economy."

In the study of both microeconomics and macroeconomics, the values of variables are normally assumed to be equilibrium values, because it is difficult or impossible to make meaningful statements about any variable that is in a disequilibrium situation.

The standard economic approach to a problem is to explain or predict the values of variables in equilibrium; to explain how a change affects the initial equilibrium; and to explain or predict the new values of the variable or variables under consideration. When the analysis sticks strictly to explaining and predicting the values of variables and the allocation of resources, it is called **positive economics**. When value judgments or personal opinion are used to judge an equilibrium, it is called **normative economics**. Explaining the results of an agricultural price support policy on the incomes of farmers and taxpayers is positive economics. Saying it is good to help farmers because farmers are nice is normative economics.

One of the most important functions of positive economics is to understand market failure. Examples of market failures that will, without question, reduce the nation's wealth include the misallocation of resources caused by letting unregulated markets deal with: 1) negative externalities, such as pollution, 2) positive externalities, such as education, 3) public goods, such as national defense, 4) common property resources, such as a fish population, and 5) monopolies and other factors that eliminate or restrict competition.

Virtually all economic questions and answers relating to individual markets are based on understanding how to use the principles of supply and demand.

Demand is defined as the maximum quantity of something that buyers are willing and able to purchase during a given time period at various prices, all other things held constant.

Supply is defined as the maximum quantity of something that producers are willing and able to sell during a given time period at various prices, all other things held constant.

Supply and demand are concepts that apply to the buying and selling of goods, services, and resources that are traded in a market. The concepts also apply to resources that are not traded in a market. There is a price and quantity of apples in the market for apples, and for oranges in the market for oranges, and for any other item produced and sold in a market. There is also a supply and demand for air quality and water quality, although such things may not be traded in a market.

Why do supply and demand exist? They exist as a result of decisions and actions made by households and firms trying to reach goals, given the existence of constraints and choices.

Economists often divide the economy into three sectors: households, firms, and government. Each sector buys and sells things in the market. Each makes decisions as to what, when, and how much to buy and sell.

2. Making decisions.

Decision-making is always a "constrained maximization" problem. It means having a goal, constraints, and choices. Without a goal, such as maximizing profits, there is no real decision to make, because it does not matter what choice is made; one is as good as another. Without constraints, such as prices or income, there is no decision to make because it is possible to have or do everything. Without choices, such as alternative things to do, there is no decision to make, because the only possibility is to take or do whatever exists.

Therefore, a constrained maximization problem means choosing to do something that attempts to maximize a stated goal, given more than one alternative to pick from, and given constraints that make it impossible to have or do everything. It is an attempt to maximize something within given limits, where some of the limits or constraints are beyond the individual's or firm's control.

3. Decisions and opportunity cost.

The word decision is from the Latin "from" and "to cut." It means that choosing (deciding) to do one thing requires being cut off from being able to do other things.

In the language of economics, the value of the best option that is cut off is called **opportunity cost**.

Opportunity cost, which has been called the most important contribution of economic thought, is the foundation of most economic principles.

At its core, opportunity cost is nothing more than common sense. It is impossible not to understand that when we choose to do one thing we must give up the benefits we could have received from buying or doing something else. A child at a candy counter, trying to decide how to spend a dollar, understands the concept completely. The dollar buys only so much candy, so the child takes all the time necessary (or allowed) to make sure that what is bought is more "valuable" than what must be left behind. The expected happiness from each item is weighed against the happiness of all the other options before deciding what to buy.

Over the years, economists have attempted to define or explain what economics *is* by relying on the combined ideas of scarcity and human wants.

In the 1950s, the standard definition of economics or **the economic problem** was "the allocation of scarce resources among competing ends." That definition requires both scarce resources and competing ends. If resources are not scarce, then everyone can have all he or she wants at a zero price and there is no economic problem. If there are no competing ends, meaning there is only one thing to do with a resource, then there is no economic problem because there is no choice as to how to use the resource.

By the 1990s, the definition had changed. The economic problem became "the allocation of scarce resources among *unlimited* human wants."

The definition from the 1950s is not very good. It limits the usefulness of economics to situations that are difficult to understand. The definition from the 1990s, using "unlimited wants," is ridiculous. It is a definition of a non-functional discipline based on absurd assumptions.

The truth is: Scarcity is always a fact. Scarcity is not something that exists here and there. It is always a part of the decision-making process. Even in a world with sufficient resources so that everything is "free," the fact is: nothing is free.

The same economists who use the above definitions also want to make it clear that, "There is no such thing as a free lunch." Why not? Because if someone accepts an invitation to a "free lunch," he or she must give up the opportunity to do something else. He or she could be working, sleeping, going for a walk, meeting with friends, reading a book, or whatever. According to the principle of opportunity cost, the real cost of the free lunch is the value to the person who attends it of what he or she must give up to be there.

Therefore, the best way to understand "the economic problem" is to understand that, because of opportunity cost, nothing is free. *Everything* has a cost, measured by the value of the best alternative. As a result, every decision must consider which option adds the most to the stated goal. The idea of scarce resources and competing ends is nothing more than a curious and useless footnote to the simple statement that every decision involves opportunity cost and that it is necessary to understand such costs in order to make the "best" choices.

In the end, it is the decision-making process of households and firms that leads to the existence of supply and demand functions; and it is supply and demand that determine prices and the allocation of resources in markets, which are sometimes affected by government actions, policies, programs, or laws. As with all decisions, the decision-making process of households and firms is a problem of constrained maximization that involves goals, constraints, and choices.

4. The purpose and objective of economics.

The purpose of economics is to help make the world a better place.

The objective of microeconomics is to explain, predict, and judge what happened, is happening, or is expected to happen in individual markets.

The objective of macroeconomics is to explain, predict, and judge what happened, is happening, or is expected to happen in the economy as a whole.

If what is happening or is expected to happen is not "good," economic analysis offers possible actions to "fix what is wrong."

The analysis is almost always based on the use of "comparative statics." Comparative statics is an analytical approach that compares one equilibrium (one static position) with another equilibrium (another static position). It is normally difficult to say anything meaningful about the impact of a change if the beginning or ending situation is not assumed to be an equilibrium.

Economic explanations and predictions deal with the results of changes that are beyond our control, such as weather; outside our control, such as increases in the price of imported oil; or intentional, such as actions by firms or government that impact a market or the overall economy. Government spends money and collects taxes; firms may act to encourage or limit competition.

A market equilibrium, or existing situation, is sometimes judged according to the concept of "perfect competition," which, among other things, assumes that each producer and consumer is responsible for all costs of producing or consuming goods and services and that each producer and consumer receives all the benefits of its production or consumption. The conditions of perfect competition and "economic efficiency" are often used to explain why a "free" market is good—because it will maximize the wealth of the nation—and why markets sometimes do an unacceptable job of allocating the use of resources, thereby causing a decrease in the nation's wealth.

5. Explaining and predicting.

Economic analysis is somewhat abstract, because economists use arguments and models that ignore large parts of the world in order to make explanations and predictions about variables that affect our lives. Such abstractions are necessary if economics is to be useful. Attempting to use "everything that is known" about the world in order to explain something or to make a prediction is a useless task. It is useless either because it can never be completed or, if it were completed, because the explanation or prediction would depend upon so many variables it could not serve any functional purpose. It would be impossible to use.

The strength of economics is that it can use a small amount of information to make rational and accurate explanations and predictions quickly enough to be useful. Spending more time and money to make what might be more accurate estimates could delay answers until they are no longer needed.

6. Judging.

Although the focus of economic analysis is on explaining and predicting, an underlying concern is with the wellbeing or happiness of society. Unfortunately, no one has yet determined how to actually define or measure wellbeing or happiness. Psychologists or sociologists may try to help the individuals they deal with become "happier." But happiness cannot be defined the same for each individual. And wellbeing cannot be measured simply by money income.

Even in the simplest possible cases, there are differences among individuals. Some people look for the chance to work overtime so they can add to their money incomes. Others look for every possible opportunity to skip out early and head for the beach. To make the problem even more complicated, individual "needs" and interests are constantly changing. This week or this year, someone may want to buy *things*, which means he or she may be willing to work more or harder. Next week or next year, that same person may prefer more free time to more stuff.

Therefore, how well someone does cannot be measured strictly in dollar terms. If it could, then it might be possible to make everyone "better off" by sacrificing everything else on the altar of greed. Make everyone do whatever is necessary to increase his or her money income. Pull people away from family and friends and move them to better-paying jobs. Make people live in terrible places if that is where the best jobs are. Force people to work 16 to 18 hours a day, seven days a week, to maximize their money incomes. Do not let anyone choose his or her own profession. And so on. Few people would choose such a world, because, for most people, happiness or wellbeing is affected by many factors, not just money. Some of those factors are under an individual's control. Others are not.

The problem is: If no one can define exactly what it takes to make an individual happy, how can any discipline be used to help make an entire society as happy as possible?

A quick answer might be to give everyone the greatest number of choices, with the greatest possible freedom to choose. That would not work, of course. Too many children would drop out of school before they understand the long-term importance of education. And some people would add to their happiness by taking things away from others. That is why societies have laws and rules to stop people from hurting either themselves or others.

A second problem facing anyone who hopes to make the world a better place is: How can we judge a change that helps some while hurting others?

If a proposed change is expected to help 1,000 people at the expense of one, is it a good plan? If you happen to be one of the 1,000 winners, chances are it will sound okay. On the other hand, if you are the one being sacrificed for the good of the many, it may not sound as good.

But what if you are neither? What if you are an outside policy maker trying to do your best? How would you judge such a policy? Would you say that the total gains to 1,000 people would obviously be greater than the loss suffered by one? Or would you recognize that if the objective is to maximize society's total happiness or wellbeing that is possible for one person's loss to be greater than the happiness gained by 1,000? If you could actually measure happiness, and if maximizing total happiness were your goal, then you could make a rational decision, even though it would mean having winners and losers. But if you admit that it is impossible to make such a measurement and also that it is possible for one person's loss to outweigh the gains of many, then you are faced with an unanswerable question.

Economists devised two ways to avoid being trapped by that unanswerable question.

One, invented by Vilfredo Pareto in the mid 1800s, is to say that a policy or change is good if it helps at least one person without making anyone else worse off. It is a good idea, in theory, but it has little use in the real world.

An alternative solution is to avoid the question altogether. Instead of making an unsupportable decision or recommendation, the economist explains who the winners and losers will be and leaves it up to someone else to decide what to do. Someone else being society.

Such a solution accepts the reality that once a problem has been analyzed and the potential winners and losers identified, economics may not be able to say any more. If it cannot, then the next step—deciding whether or not to implement the change or policy—is not an economic decision. It is a decision based upon social and personal values.

As individuals, economists have opinions. But when those opinions cannot be supported with economic logic, then it must be made clear that the economist is talking as an individual and not offering an economic solution. It is important to understand the distinction between an economist as an "economist" and an economist as a "person" in order to understand the limits of economic analysis.

It is also important to understand the difference between a pure democracy and a republic in order to understand the limits of social decisions. In a pure democracy, fifty percent plus one of the people can vote to do whatever they want, including taking away the life, liberty, and pursuit of happiness of the other fifty percent minus one of the population. In a republic, the minority has rights that cannot be voted on.

The United States is not a pure democracy. It is a republic. And, like any society that chooses to bestow unalienable rights on its citizens—rights that are not subject to a democratic vote—it must constantly question its actions. Actions aimed at improving the wellbeing of an individual or a group, including the majority, must be weighed against the possible harm to the wellbeing of others.

7. Market supply and demand.

Demand is the relationship between two variables: the price of something and the maximum quantity of that something that buyers are willing and able to purchase during a given time period, all other things constant.

Supply is also the relationship between two variables: the price of something and the maximum quantity of that something that sellers are willing and able to offer for sale during a given time period, all other things constant.

Each statement is an absolute truth, in the sense that such relationships do exist. To be useful, however, a little more must be known. Are the relationships positive or negative? Are they stable?

8. The simple logic of supply and demand.

The "theories" of demand and supply that take up a lot of space in most textbooks may be interesting (to economists), but they do not "prove" anything about the relationship between price and quantity for either supply or demand. The truth is that such theories belong more to an understanding of the history of economic thought than to an understanding of functional economics.

On the other hand, simple logic using the concept of opportunity cost tells us that, in the short run, market demand curves will have negative slopes and market supply curves will normally have positive slopes.

All such statements describing supply and demand must be accompanied by the condition, "all other things constant" because if, when the price of apples increases, incomes are also increasing and the prices of oranges and all other things are also changing, there is no way of predicting what will happen to the quantity of apples bought or offered for sale. Even so, it is still possible to isolate the impact of the price of apples on the quantity of apples demanded or supplied.

SUPPLY AND DEMAND

Demand. As the price of something (such as apples) increases, with everything else held constant, buyers of apples must give up more of other things to purchase the same quantity of apples. Therefore, the higher the price of apples, the greater is the opportunity cost of buying apples. As a result, the higher the price of apples, the fewer apples consumers are willing and able to purchase.

Therefore, a market demand curve based on the logic of opportunity cost is negatively sloped. At an arbitrarily chosen price, consumers are willing and able to buy a given quantity during a given time period, all other things constant. At a higher price, consumers are willing and able to buy less. At a lower price, consumers are willing and able to buy more.

Figure A.1 shows a market demand curve based on the logic of opportunity cost. It is negatively sloped. At price p_1, consumers are willing and able to buy q_1 units of q during a given time period, all other things constant. At a price higher than p_1, consumers are willing and able to buy less than q_1; at a price lower than p_1, consumers are willing and able to buy more than q_1.

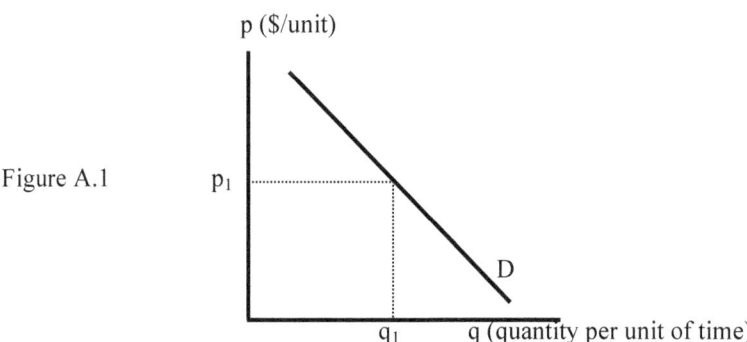

Figure A.1

Supply. As the price of something increases, all other things held constant, the opportunity cost to producers of not selling more of that thing and less of other things increases. Therefore, the higher the price of something is, the greater the quantity of that thing that will be offered for sale during a given time period.

Therefore, a market supply curve based on the logic of opportunity cost is positively sloped. At an arbitrarily chosen price, sellers are willing and able to sell a given quantity during a given time period, all other things constant. At a higher price, sellers are willing and able to sell more. At a lower price, sellers are willing and able to sell less.

Figure A.2 shows a market supply curve based on the logic of opportunity cost. It is positively sloped. At price p_1, sellers are willing and able to sell q_2 units of q during a given time period, all other things constant. At a price higher than p_1, sellers are willing and able to sell more than q_2; at a price lower than p_1, sellers are willing and able to sell less than q_2.

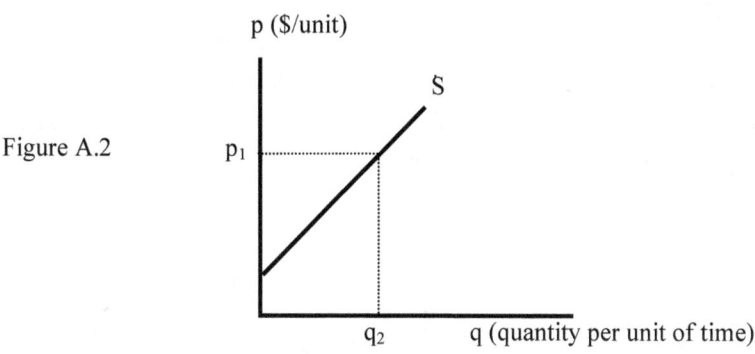

Figure A.2

In the real world, most market problems can be solved by using demand and supply curves that look like those in Figures A.1 and A.2.

SUPPLY AND DEMAND

9. Other possibilities for supply and demand.

To be complete, the logic of supply and demand should be aware of all legitimate possibilities, even if most market problems are solved using a negatively sloped demand curve and a positively sloped supply curve.

Demand.

A "life-and-death" product (or possibly an addictive drug) could yield a demand curve that is a vertical line at the quantity "needed," such as D_1 in Figure A.3. Such a demand curve means that consumers are willing and able to pay any price to obtain the quantity q_1.

Figure A.3

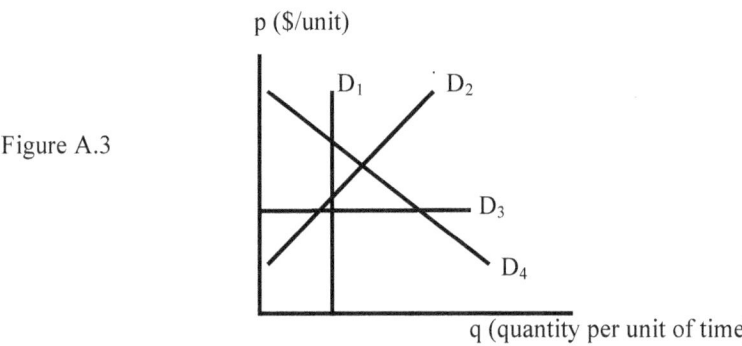

A single seller of an undifferentiated product (the idea of pure or perfect competition) is assumed to be able to sell as much as he or she can produce at the existing market price; and nothing if the price is set above the market price. Such a demand curve would be a horizontal line at the market price, which is determined by market supply and demand. D_3 in Figure A.3, which is horizontal at the market price, represents a demand curve faced by a perfectly competitive firm.

Every so often someone tries to uncover an exception to the downward sloping demand curve by finding a good or service where a greater quantity is bought at a higher price, such as D_2 in Figure A.3. So far, no one has succeeded.

Goods that might be bought in greater quantities at higher prices are often called "Giffen goods," named after the man who spent considerable time trying to find an exception to the rule. Giffen focused on items he thought were purchased as a show of wealth, such as fur coats. His argument was that if the price of fur coats fell, people would not be able to "show off" their wealth by wearing them and would, therefore, buy fewer of them.

Giffen may have been correct in assuming that a decline in the price of a "conspicuous consumption" item would lead some to buy less. But a decrease in "conspicuous consumption" is more than offset by increased purchases by those who could not formerly "afford" the good or service. Therefore:

> *The "law of demand" is that as the price of something declines, consumers are willing and able to buy a greater quantity of that commodity or service during a given time period, all other things held constant; a smaller quantity at a higher price.*

D_4 in Figure A.3 above is the normal short-run demand curve discussed above and described by the "law of demand."

Supply. Figure A.4 shows a number of possibilities for market supply curves.

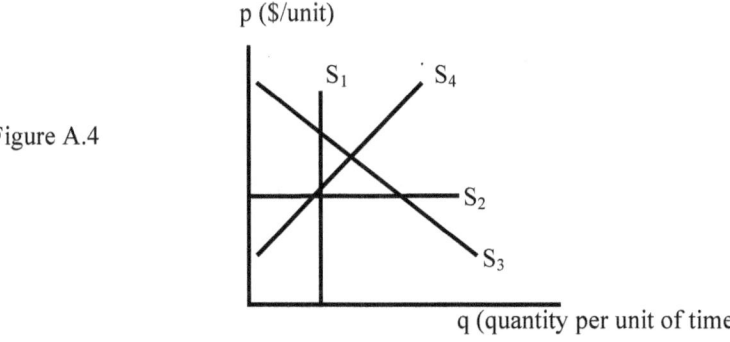

Figure A.4

S_1 represents the supply of something that is put on the market and that sellers are willing and able to sell for whatever price they receive. It is a vertical line at the quantity offered for sale. An example is a commercial fisherman's daily catch. If it is not sold on the day it is caught, it will be worth nothing the next day.

S_2 represents the supply curve facing a single consumer. It says that the consumer can purchase as much or as little as he or she wants at the existing market price. If the consumer offers a price that is below the market price, nothing can be purchased. Horizontal supply curves can also represent government imposed price floors (such as rent control) or price ceilings (such as agricultural price supports).

S_3 represents the idea that, in the long run, as the quantity produced increases, economies of scale can lead to falling costs of production. In such cases, as the quantity increases, the price at which sellers are willing and able to sell each quantity declines.

S_4 is the normal short-run supply curve discussed above. It is positively sloped.

10. Reading supply and demand curves.

If you are not used to dealing with such diagrams, they look more complicated than they are. To read a demand curve, choose any point on the vertical price axis, such as p_1 in Figure A.1. From p_1, draw a straight, horizontal line to the demand curve. When you reach the demand curve, draw a straight, vertical line down to the horizontal quantity axis. The point where the vertical line from the demand curve touches the quantity axis shows the maximum quantity of the item that buyers are willing and able to buy at the price p_1. In Figure A.1 above, that quantity is q_1.

Using p_1 and q_1 is an abstraction. Some find it easier to see what is happening if numbers are used. For example, instead of p_1, choose a price, such as $4; and instead of q_1, choose a quantity, such as 45 units.

In either case, if you now choose a price higher than p_1 (higher than $4) and draw a horizontal line from that point on the price axis to the demand curve, and then down to the quantity axis, the vertical line from the demand curve will reach the quantity axis at a quantity less than q_1 (less than 45 units).

If you choose a price lower than p_1 (lower than $4) and draw a line from that point on the price axis to the demand curve and then down to the quantity axis, the line from the demand curve will reach the quantity axis at a quantity greater than q_1 (greater than 45 units).

In other words, a negatively sloped demand curve shows that the higher the price of something, the lower the quantity of that thing buyers are willing and able to buy during a given time period, all other things held constant.

Reading a supply curve is the same as reading a demand curve. Choose a point on the vertical price axis, such as p_1 in Figure A.2. From p_1, draw a straight, horizontal line that reaches the supply curve. When the line reaches the supply curve, draw a straight, vertical line down to the horizontal quantity axis. The point where the vertical line from S touches the quantity axis shows the maximum quantity of the item that sellers are willing and able to sell at the price p_1. In Figure A.2, it is q_2 units.

If you now choose a price higher than p_1 and draw a line from that point on the price axis to the supply curve, S, and then down to the quantity axis, the line from S will reach the quantity axis at a quantity greater than q_2. If you choose a price lower than p_1 and draw a line from that point on the price axis to S and then down to the quantity axis, the line from S will reach the quantity axis at a quantity less than q_2. Therefore, for a normal, short-run supply curve, the higher the price, the greater the quantity sellers are willing and able to sell during a given time period, all other things held constant.

Therefore, logic concludes that:

1) Figure A.1 is a picture of what a normal market demand curve looks like.

It is a negative relationship that applies to any market, whether it is a market for goods and services, resources, inputs to production, or investments. It is necessary to be careful when labeling each axis so that each is an accurate representation of what is being studied.

2) Figure A.2 is a picture of a normal, short run market supply curve.

It is a positive relationship that is expected to exist in markets where the quantity studied varies with its price.

11. A "normal" individual market.

Given the above discussion, Figure A.5 is a picture of an individual market. In certain situations, however, the demand curve can be either horizontal or vertical; and the supply curve can be horizontal, vertical, or negatively sloped. Therefore, each such possibility for supply and demand should be considered when solving economic problems.

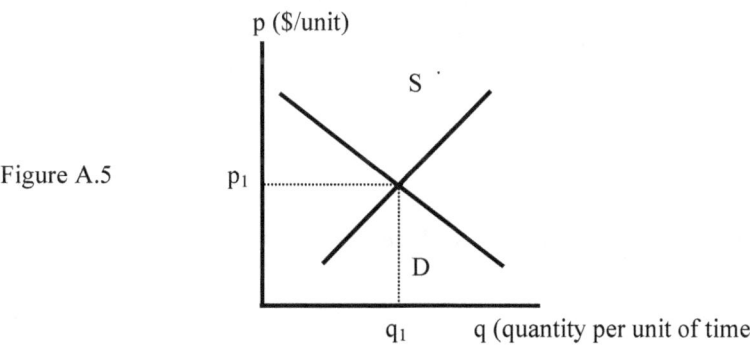

Figure A.5

12. A change in supply and demand versus a change in the quantity supplied or the quantity demanded.

The economic meanings of demand and supply are precise. But they are often confused. The term "demand" or "demand curve" refers to a schedule or function representing the maximum quantities of a good or service people are willing and able to buy at different prices during a specific time period. The phrase "quantity demanded" refers to how much will be bought at a particular price during a specific time period. The *quantity demanded* is one point on a given demand curve or schedule. The term "supply" or "supply curve" refers to a schedule or function representing the maximum quantities of a good or service sellers are willing and able to sell at different prices during a specific time period. The phrase "quantity supplied" refers to how much will be offered for sale at a particular price during a given time period. The *quantity supplied* is one point on a given supply curve or schedule.

A change in the "quantity of grapefruit demanded" or the "quantity of grapefruit supplied" occurs when the price of grapefruit changes.

A change in the "demand for grapefruit" occurs when the price of oranges or apples changes, when incomes change, or when medical researchers announce that "grapefruit is good for you."

A change in the "supply of grapefruit" occurs when the weather changes, a freeze affects the crop, or new techniques for growing grapefruit are developed.

To discuss the demand for grapefruit, even as an abstract concept, it is necessary to understand that incomes, personal likes and dislikes, and the prices of other goods and services all affect how much grapefruit people are willing and able to buy at various prices. If incomes increase, consumers are likely to buy more of everything they like (all normal goods). And because everyone loves grapefruit, an increase in incomes means that the demand for grapefruit would increase. At any given price, people would be willing and able to buy more grapefruit than they did before. If the prices of related goods and services change, the impact on the demand for grapefruit is less certain.

A similar understanding of how various things affect the supply of grapefruit is also needed.

13. Most microeconomic problems are solved using market supply and demand.

Most economic problems—*in the real world*—are market problems. The reason textbooks devote so much time and effort to the study of how individuals and individual firms act and react is mainly to explain as much as possible about what is behind the market demand and supply curves they create.

It is normally assumed that each individual firm wants to maximize its profits. Therefore, an analysis of the effects of tighter air pollution standards for automobiles begins with the assumption that the existing supply of automobiles is determined by all manufacturers currently selling automobiles in the U.S. and that each one—GM, Ford, Chrysler, Toyota, VW, etc.—is currently acting to maximize profits.

It is also assumed that each manufacturer will react rationally to the new legislation, meaning that each will continue its attempt to maximize profits, even though there is a new law to deal with.

Of course, profits are normally a long-term objective, not a one-shot goal, for a large corporation. But if each firm is trying to maximize its profits over time, then it is correct to assume that if it is more expensive to produce automobiles that cause less air pollution, manufacturers will be willing to sell fewer automobiles at each price than they were previously willing to sell. On a graph, the supply of automobiles decreases—moves to the left or upward.

As with demand, a change in any variable other than the price of the product under examination can cause a change in supply.

Any change that makes it more expensive to produce automobiles means fewer automobiles offered for sale at each price. Alternatively, it can be said that the minimum price at which each quantity of automobiles is offered increases. Therefore, the supply curve of automobiles moves to the left or upward.

Any change that makes it less costly to produce automobiles—for example, a decrease in the price of steel—means that more automobiles will be offered for sale at each price, or that the minimum price at which each quantity is offered decreases. The result is an increase in supply—the supply curve moves to the right or downward.

A leftward or upward move of a supply curve looks the same on a graph, but it is less confusing to think of a decrease in supply as a leftward move because it can seem odd to show a decrease in supply by an upward move of a supply curve.

A rightward or downward move of a supply curve looks the same on a graph, but it is less confusing to think of an increase in supply as a rightward move because it can seem odd to show an increase in supply by a downward move of a supply curve.

---

14. Equilibrium.

An equilibrium exists in a market at the price where the quantity buyers are willing and able to buy equals the quantity sellers are willing and able to sell.

On a graph representing a market, equilibrium exists where the demand and supply curves intersect. It is possible to imagine a market where supply slopes upward but is above demand at any given quantity.

SUPPLY AND DEMAND

In such a market, the equilibrium output is zero; there is no price at which the quantity buyers are willing and able to buy equals the quantity sellers are willing and able to sell. It can be assumed that a market in which things are actually being bought and sold has an equilibrium.

In Figure A.6, there is an equilibrium at p_1 and q_1. At a price of p_1, the quantity buyers are willing and able to buy is equal to the quantity sellers are willing and able to sell: q_1.

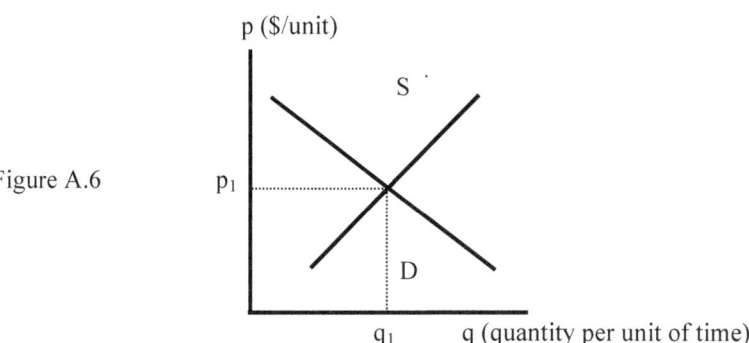

Figure A.6

15. Is the equilibrium stable or unstable?

Economists are careful to identify the conditions necessary for a stable equilibrium. The reason for the concern is obvious: An unstable equilibrium, meaning that if something causes a movement away from equilibrium, the market will not return to a position of equilibrium, would be very disruptive.

Fortunately, unstable markets are uncommon in the real world. Even without knowing the specific details of every possible market, an unstable market would be relatively easy to notice.

The conditions necessary for a stable equilibrium are:
1) If the market price is pushed above the equilibrium price, supply *must be* greater than demand. If it is, then the **excess supply**—sellers trying to sell more than buyers are willing and able to buy at the higher price—causes sellers to lower prices and bring the market back to equilibrium.
2) If the market price is pushed below the equilibrium price, demand must be greater than supply. If it is, then the **excess demand**—buyers trying to buy more than sellers are willing to sell at the lower price—causes buyers to bid up the price and bring the market back to equilibrium.

SUPPLY AND DEMAND

As long as demand is negatively sloped (buyers are willing and able to buy more at lower prices) and supply is positively sloped (sellers are willing and able to sell more only at higher prices), the market has a stable equilibrium at the price and quantity where supply equals demand.

If supply is vertical (suppliers are willing to sell "everything" at whatever price they can receive) the equilibrium is stable.

If supply slopes downward, the market equilibrium will be stable as long as supply intersects demand from above. If supply intersects demand from above, then at any price above the equilibrium price, there will be an excess supply that pushes the price back to equilibrium; at any price below equilibrium, there will be an excess demand that pushes the price back to the equilibrium price.

A vertical supply curve exists when a given quantity of some commodity, normally a perishable resource, is offered for whatever price it can receive.

A horizontal supply curve, describing, for example, a labor union that sets a "take-it-or-leave-it" wage rate, and a downward sloping demand curve is also a stable equilibrium.

In Figure A.7, the initial equilibrium is at p_1 and q_1.

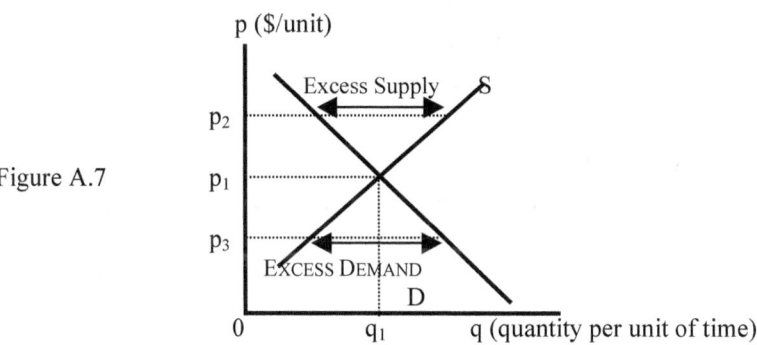

Figure A.7

If the price rises above p_1, to p_2, for example, an excess supply is created because, at the price p_2, sellers want to sell more than buyers are willing and able to buy. As a result, the price will fall, and it will continue to decline until the excess supply is eliminated, which is when the price returns to p_1.

If the price falls below p_1, to p_3 for example, an excess demand is created because at the price p_3, buyers want to buy more than sellers are willing and able to sell. The excess demand will cause the price to increase, and it will continue to rise until the excess demand is eliminated, which is when price returns to p_1.

> An unstable equilibrium exists if supply slopes downward and intersects demand from below. In such a case, if the price is pushed above the equilibrium level, an excess demand is created that pulls prices higher and higher. If the price is pushed below equilibrium, an excess supply is created that causes prices to fall lower and lower, farther and farther away from equilibrium.

16. How to solve economic problems.

Economic problem solving almost always relies on the logic of "comparative statics," an analytical approach that compares one equilibrium (one static position) with another equilibrium (another static position). It is normally difficult to say anything meaningful about the impact of a change if the beginning and ending markets are not assumed to be in equilibrium. It is also normally difficult to say much that is meaningful about the dynamics of the change—of exactly how the move from one equilibrium to a new equilibrium takes place.

1. Begin with the question.

The analysis always begins with a question. After being given a problem, make certain that you can state the question.

The question is important; it is what sets up the problem. Without a specific question, there is no problem to solve.

What information is being asked for? State exactly what is to be explained or predicted. Is it a change in market price? Or equilibrium quantity? Or profits? Or the wellbeing of an individual? Be precise. In most cases, it will take only one or two sentences. Be clear about what is being studied. Which variables are being explained or predicted?

It is also necessary to be clear about the change that led to the question? The change may be an outside effect or it may be the desire to achieve a different equilibrium.

In either case, the change is likely to affect many things. If the change is increased competition from foreign producers, an announcement from the medical community that some product is good or bad for people's health, or a government program intended to help an identifiable group, you must be clear about what is happening, or happened, or is expected to happen.

2. The three steps of comparative statics.

Given a question, which is often triggered by a change in something that was assumed to be held constant, or a need to explain what happened or is happening, the steps to follow are: (1) describe the initial equilibrium; (2) explain how the change affects supply and/or demand; (3) describe the new equilibrium and compare the old and new equilibrium values.

(1) Describe the initial equilibrium.

Draw a market diagram using supply and demand curves.

The question or problem determines exactly what must be described in the diagram. It may be a situation that existed in the past, that exists in the present, or that can exist in the future. Describe the equilibrium that existed or exists before the change. It is almost always assumed that the beginning position is an equilibrium situation. If not, it may be impossible to say anything about what happened or is expected to happen.

Describe the beginning situation of the firm, market, individual, or overall economy by sketching a simple supply and demand diagram.

In the initial equilibrium, there is an equilibrium price and an equilibrium quantity, both for the market and for individual buyers and sellers.

Label each axis with the "loose" designations p and q. Label the supply and demand functions S_1 and D_1. Label the initial equilibrium values p_1 and q_1.

In most cases, there is no reason to worry about precise values. Simply sketch in the functions. But be careful to label each axis and each curve. When a question asks for an explanation of how a market or the overall economy works, rather than asking for a prediction of how a change will impact particular variables, the analysis is centered on explaining what is behind the functions in the model.

(2) Explain, and show on the diagram, how the change causes an increase or decrease in S and/or D.

Explain how or why the change (and ONLY that change) affects or is expected to affect supply or demand or both in the market or markets being studied. If more than one change is introduced, it is likely that nothing meaningful can be said. It is almost always necessary to isolate individual changes in order to understand the impact of each.

How will the function or functions change? Will they increase or decrease? Will one or both remain constant? For example, increased competition from foreign producers of television sets increases the supply curve of television sets on the market. The change does not, however, affect the demand for television sets.

Show the change on the diagram. An increase in demand or supply means there will be a new curve to the right of the original curve, because buyers are willing and able to buy more at any given price and sellers are willing and able to sell more at any given price. A decrease in D or S means there will be a new curve to the left of the original curve. Sketch in the new supply and/or demand curves and label them S_2 and D_2.

> Note:
> An increase in demand is shown as a new demand curve either to the right of or above the original demand curve.
> An increase in supply is shown as a new supply curve either to the right of or below the original supply curve. Because it is sometimes confusing to think of an increase in supply as a new supply curve below the original supply curve, it is normally easier to show a change in supply by drawing a new curve either to the left or right of the original curve.

(3) Describe the new equilibrium and explain what happens to the equilibrium values of the variables under consideration.

The new equilibrium is determined by the supply and demand functions that exist after the change has worked its way through the system. Label the new equilibrium quantity q_2 and the new equilibrium price p_2.

How do the new price and quantity compare to the original price and quantity? In other words, what happened or will happen to what is being studied?

For example, it might be concluded that: "The equilibrium price increased from p_1 to p_2 and the equilibrium quantity decreased from q_1 to q_2." When describing the new equilibrium, it is normally not necessary to be any more specific than to describe the direction of change of equilibrium price and quantity, and, in some cases, profits. In the case of an increase in the quantity of imported television sets, the equilibrium market price falls, equilibrium quantity increases, profits of domestic producers fall.

Conclusion

Most problems end with a conclusion that describes the new equilibrium and summarizes what happened. It might restate the problem, describe the expected change or changes in supply and/or demand, and state the change in the variable or variables being examined. It should also specify the assumptions that were made to reach the given conclusion. Some questions or problems focus mainly on the initial equilibrium. For example, questions about market failure (such as externalities, common property resources, or public goods) are normally concerned with explaining the reason for the failure and the resulting misallocation of resources, and *then* with finding a solution to the problem: How can the misallocation of society's resources be corrected?

After solving a number of problems, it will be seen that the same logical framework is used over and over again. New problems do not require "new" procedures, new ways of thinking, or new theories.

The world is logical. Knowledgeable individuals know things that can help explain and predict what is happening or is expected to happen as the result of changes.

But all opinions are not of equal value. Individuals with greater knowledge about certain things have opinions about those things that should be more valuable than the opinions of less knowledgeable observers. It is easy to say that an increase in the demand for apples will cause the price of apples to increase. It is better to be able to explain—step by step—why that is the correct answer, even though the answer appears obvious.

It is sometimes possible to determine if a change makes an individual or a nation better or worse off, but not always. Economics is seldom able to *judge* an equilibrium position in a market, other than to point out the possible winners and losers. The exception is when it can be concluded that the change has a positive or negative impact on economic efficiency. Economic efficiency is a term used to describe a situation where resources are used in a way that maximizes the satisfaction of society.

On a larger level, it is often impossible, in a world of scarce resources, to make one person better off without making someone else worse off. And because economics cannot make interpersonal comparisons, economists may be limited to identifying the winners and losers, and not claiming that the change is "good" or "bad."

17. Rules of action.

In general, economic theory is concerned either with understanding how decisions are made or with understanding how to make decisions that will maximize the welfare or wellbeing of individuals, individual firms, or the nation as a whole.

The following concepts form the foundation of the economic approach to problem solving. They are not definitions. They are not digested versions of textbook discussions. They are *rules of action* that will become second nature by the end of this text, although some might not be totally understood at this point.

1. Solve economic problems by comparing one equilibrium with another.

The typical economic problem is solved by comparing one equilibrium with another. It is a logical procedure called "**comparative statics**." It means to compare one "static" position with another.

There is an initial equilibrium (one static position).

A change is introduced.

The impact of the change is explained.

A new equilibrium is described (a new static position).

The values of the variables in the "old" and "new" equilibrium situations are compared.

2. Solve economic problems one step at a time.

Economic problems are solved by completing a step-by-step explanation of how one thing is affected, then another, and another, until the answer is determined. The analysis begins with a described equilibrium, or with a reason for no existing equilibrium. The equilibrium may be that of an individual, an individual firm, a particular market, or the economy as a whole.

Skipping steps or "jumping to conclusions" about a new equilibrium can lead to unacceptable answers or major errors.

3. The existence of an equilibrium does not mean that the value of any variable is "justified."

Solving economic problems means explaining or predicting the past, present, or future. However, the "answer" is almost never a justification of what happened, is happening, or is expected to happen.

4. Most economic problems are answered by explaining or predicting the direction of change of the values of one or more variables.

Few economic questions are given with enough information, time, or money to allow "exact" estimates of future values.

5. Problems with insufficient information to explain or predict the direction of change of a variable's value are often answered by stating the conditions that would cause the variable's value to increase, decrease, or remain unchanged.

Sometimes there is not enough information to determine even the expected direction of change of a variable's value. It is, however, almost always possible to state the conditions that *would* cause a particular variable's value to change in a given direction.

6. State the assumptions behind answers.

Economic explanations and predictions are conditional; they depend upon the assumptions made while solving the problem.

All explanations and predictions depend upon assumptions made about many things. It is impossible to list the assumptions regarding everything in the world that could affect the answer. Therefore, it is normally stated that all things, other than those discussed while solving the problem, are assumed to remain unchanged. When specific or unusual assumptions are made, they should be clearly stated.

7. Unless there is a reason not to, begin the solution to economic problems by assuming a normal equilibrium with normal functions.

Unless the problem states otherwise, or there is information to the contrary, assume that a market problem begins with normal supply and demand functions and a stable equilibrium; and that macroeconomic problems begin with normal aggregate supply and aggregate demand functions.

8. Use all available information and knowledge to describe the initial equilibrium.

A question or problem may require the description of an initial equilibrium based upon a demand function that is vertical (a product that is an absolute necessity) or horizontal (the demand facing an individual firm in a perfectly competitive market) or a supply function that does not slope upward to the right.

9. Do not assume that "everyone" has the same response to a change.

Economic analysis works on the margin. Changes almost never lead to "all-or-none" effects. An increase in the price of oranges means that consumers, as a whole, are willing and able to buy fewer oranges. More precisely, it means that, as the price inches upward, some consumers will buy fewer oranges.

A higher price does not, however, mean that EVERYONE will buy fewer oranges. Some will buy the same quantity of oranges and less of something else. (Unless their incomes are rising or the prices of other things they buy are also changing.)

10. Hold all things, but one, constant while explaining or predicting the results of a change.

The reason for "holding all other things constant," meaning that nothing else changes unless it is a change caused by whatever set off the problem, is to explain the consequences of a single action.

If the price of apples declines, will consumers buy more apples? The answer is: Yes. No. Maybe. If nothing else changes while the price of apples falls, consumers will buy more apples per time period. It is a simple move along the demand curve for apples.

If the prices of oranges, grapefruit, bananas, all other fruit, and all other food items, decline at the same time the price of apples is falling, fewer apples *may* be bought. As other prices fall, the demand curve for apples changes. If it decreases, fewer apples may be bought at any given price. Therefore, the new equilibrium, determined by the new supply and demand curves for apples, can be at a higher, lower, or unchanged quantity and price of apples.

The more things are changing, the less can be said about what happens in the market for apples. That is why, in all cases, a clear statement can be made only by assuming that nothing else is changing while explaining or predicting the impact of a particular change. If tastes and preferences change, consumers may be willing and able to buy fewer apples even if the price falls. Or more if the price rises. Because a change in tastes and preferences can cause the demand for apples to change. A change in income can also cause a change in the demand for apples, and in the demand for everything else.

It is only by being able to use a logical process that permits analyzing one change while holding everything else constant that the impact of any particular change can be understood.

A second reason for explaining one change at a time is that once the analysis is complete, it is then possible to explain and predict the consequences of changes in all the things that were initially assumed to be held constant.

11. A problem is "solved" when something can be said about the variable or variables asked about in the question.

In the "real world," any change that occurs leads to changes in an "infinite" number of variables. Therefore, the impact of each and every change can be discussed "forever." To be useful, an answer must be delivered while it still has value. That means knowing when to stop. In every discipline or activity, one of the keys to success is "knowing when to stop." An artist must know when to stop working on a painting or sculpture. A writer must know when to stop writing or editing a book or article. Nothing is ever "finished." It is only brought to a conclusion that is believed to be the best under the circumstances, and given the constraints that exist at the time.

SUPPLY AND DEMAND

18. A problem with apples.

A simple example of a market, or microeconomic, problem is: What happens to the equilibrium price and quantity of apples in the United States if blight destroys the apple crop in the state of Washington?

The question.

If blight destroys the apple harvest in the state of Washington, what happens to the equilibrium price and quantity of apples in the United States?

(1) The initial equilibrium.

The initial equilibrium is shown by the normal supply and demand curves, S_1 and D_1, in Figure A.8.

No information is given that would lead to the assumption of non-normal supply and demand functions.

The initial equilibrium price is p_1.

The initial equilibrium quantity is q_1.

There is no market failure to explain.

Figure A.8

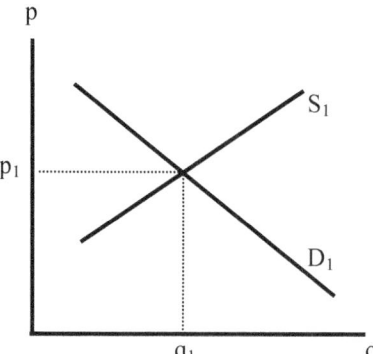

(2) The change.

In the case of blight, the supply curve will change.

A decrease in supply means there will be a new supply curve to the left of (or above) the original supply curve.

The new supply curve in Figure A.9 is S_2.

The demand curve remains at D_1.

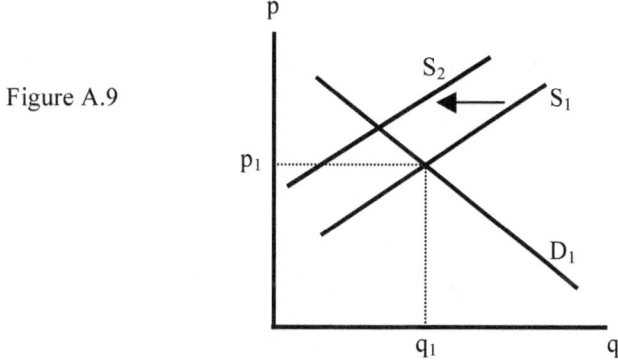

Figure A.9

Blight is an example of an "exogenous" change. It is a change in something that was assumed to be held constant when deriving the original supply function—the conditions for growing apples.

There is no reason to assume that something that affects the growing of apples will have any effect on the demand for apples—the maximum quantity of apples that buyers are willing and able to purchase at various prices.

The blight causes the market supply of apples to decrease. At any given price, sellers (nationwide) are now willing and able to offer fewer apples for sale, or, for any given quantity of apples, the minimum price at which that quantity will be offered for sale is higher.

Demand is unchanged.

(3) *The new equilibrium*.

Assuming there is nothing to prevent the new equilibrium from being achieved in the market, the new equilibrium will occur where the new supply curve and the original demand curve intersect. The new equilibrium, determined by the new supply curve S_2 and the original demand curve D_1, is at the new equilibrium price, p_2, and the new equilibrium quantity, q_2. It is important to note that the change that initiated the problem did not affect the market demand for apples. It affected the market supply of apples only. The change in supply resulted in a move along the original demand curve—a change in the quantity demanded—not a change in demand.

Figure A.10

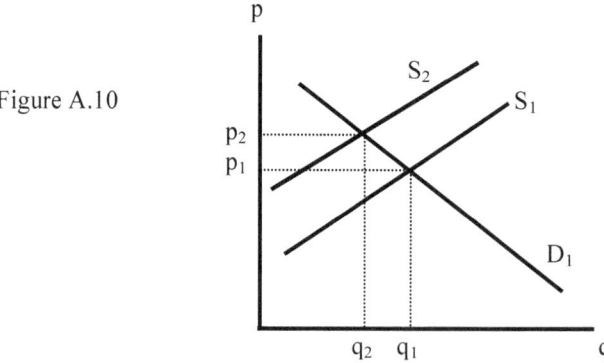

Conclusion:

The conclusion is that something that reduces the apple harvest in the state of Washington results in a decrease in the supply of apples, leading to an increase in the equilibrium price and a decrease in the equilibrium quantity of apples, assuming that all other things remain constant.

Are there winners or losers? In this case, it can be concluded that the profits of apple producers whose crops were not affected by the blight would increase, as long as nothing else changes, because their costs have not changed, but the price at which they can sell apples has increased. Other possible winners and losers, aside from consumers who lose by paying higher prices for fewer apples, are the producers and sellers of substitute and complimentary products.

Suppliers of complimentary products, products used in combination with apples, lose. The demands for complimentary products fall, because, with fewer

The suppliers of substitute products can either win or lose as the higher price of apples causes consumers to consider substitute products.

How to Solve Microeconomic Problems—A Worksheet
(Virtually any market issue can be explained by completing this worksheet.)

The question: *What is being asked for? It is often to explain or predict how a change will affect the value of a particular variable.*

(1) The initial equilibrium: *Describe the initial equilibrium.*
Draw a market diagram using supply and demand curves.
Is there a reason to assume non-normal curves?

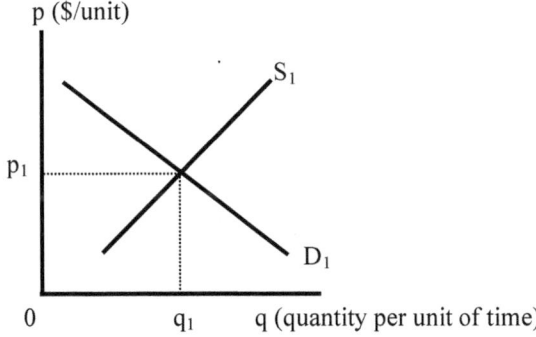

(2) The change: *Explain, and then show on the diagram, how the change causes an increase or decrease in S and/or D.*

(3) The new equilibrium: *Describe the new equilibrium and explain what happens to the equilibrium values of the variables under consideration.*

Summary or conclusion:

www.ingramcontent.com/pod-product-compliance
Lightning Source LLC
Chambersburg PA
CBHW082317230426
43664CB00035B/2812